Philip Perring

Hard Knots in Shakespeare

Philip Perring

Hard Knots in Shakespeare

ISBN/EAN: 9783337063825

Printed in Europe, USA, Canada, Australia, Japan

Cover: Foto ©Thomas Meinert / pixelio.de

More available books at **www.hansebooks.com**

HARD KNOTS

IN

SHAKESPEARE

BY

SIR PHILIP PERRING, BART.,

FORMERLY SCHOLAR OF TRINITY COLLEGE, CAMBRIDGE.

All difficulties are but easy, when they are known.
'Measure For Measure,' Act IV. 2. 221.

LONDON:
LONGMANS, GREEN & CO.
1885.

PREFACE.

This little work, which I have ventured to commit to the press, treats of a very small portion of a very large subject. It cannot pretend to be much more than a supplement, or appendix, to the numerous publications which have been issued from time to time on the text, the sense, the language, the style, the spirit, the whole life and character of Shakespeare.

My object has been not to do over again work which has already been sufficiently well done, but to endeavour to throw new light on what I conceive to have been misunderstood by previous expositors, and to explain, or emend, certain passages, where, according to the Cambridge editors, 'the original text had been corrupted in such a way as to affect the sense, no admissible emendation having been proposed,' or where 'a lacuna occurs too great to be filled up with any approach to certainty.'

Whether I have succeeded in reclaiming any of these waste patches, abandoned by others as uncultivable, can only be ascertained by ocular observation. It is true that I have not examined a single impression of either Folio or Quarto, but I have followed the trustworthy guidance of the editors of the 'Cambridge Shakespeare,' in the footnotes of which the various readings of the original copies are set down with conscientious accuracy. To this extent, then, I have been a borrower; but I have not borrowed my ideas, my interpretations, my arguments, my matter generally. If, as has sometimes happened, I have occupied ground which some one else had occupied before me, I can truly say that, at the time that I appropriated it, I was not aware that another possessed it. Even my quotations and references I have not fetched from a Concordance, but have myself culled them after carefully considering them. The 'Globe' Shakespeare has been my text-book, partly because, coming from Cambridge, it would seem to carry with it a Collegiate, not to say, a University recommendation, partly because it was convenient for reference, the lines in it being numbered.

I have taken, as I was bound to do, the utmost pains with every one of my papers, caring less for form than for substance, and aiming not so much at fine writing, as at fair argument and the discovery of the truth—not but that I have endeavoured, where I could, and as far as I could, to give some sort of shape and polish to my rough and unattractive materials.

I have been encouraged and assisted in my labours by two of my friends, who have taken an interest in the progress of my work, and to whom I now record my heart-felt thanks; they must not be held responsible for any of my opinions, yet their sound judgment and kind counsel have saved me from many doubtful, and from some dangerous positions.
P. P.

EXMOUTH,
    March, 1885.

CONTENTS.

	PAGE.
1. *THE TEMPEST*	1—21.
Act I. Sc. 1. 66-68 ; Sc. 2. 26-32, 53, 172-74, 306-307, 376-386, 486-491.	
Act II. Sc. 1. 130-131 ; Sc. 2. 15-16.	
Act III. Sc. 1. 15 ; Sc. 3. 49-51.	
Act IV. Sc. 1. 61, 164.	
2. *THE TWO GENTLEMEN OF VERONA*	22—35.
Act II. Sc. 5. 2.	
Act III. Sc. 1. 81.	
Act V. Sc. 4. 82-83, 129.	
3. *MEASURE FOR MEASURE*	36—52.
Act I. Sc. 1. 8-9 ; Sc. 2. 125 ; Sc. 3. 20, 42-43 ; Sc. 4. 30.	
Act II. Sc. 1. 37-40.	
Act III. Sc. 1. 126-128 ; Sc. 2. 275-96.	
4. *THE COMEDY OF ERRORS*	53—66.
Act I. Sc. 1. 37-39 ; Sc. 2. 35-38.	
Act II. Sc. 1. 103-115.	
Act IV. Sc. 1. 98 ; Sc. 8. 12-20.	
Act V. Sc. 1. 405-407.	
5. *A MIDSUMMER-NIGHT'S DREAM*	67—76.
Act II. Sc. 1. 54.	
Act III. Sc. 2. 14.	
Act IV. Sc. 1. 150-163.	
Act V. Sc. 1. 56-60, 92.	
6. *THE MERCHANT OF VENICE*	77—88.
Act I. Sc. 1. 35.	
Act II. Sc. 7. 69.	
Act III. Sc. 2. 97-99, 160-167 ; Sc. 3. 26-29 ; Sc. 5. 78-83.	
Act IV. Sc. 1. 50, 379.	

CONTENTS.

		PAGE.
7.	*AS YOU LIKE IT*	89—98.

Act I. Sc. 1. 1-5.
Act II. Sc. 4. 1 ; Sc. 7. 53-57, 71-74.
Act III. Sc. 2. 206-207 ; Sc. 5. 7, 23.
Act V. Sc. 4. 4.

8. *THE TAMING OF THE SHREW* ... ... 99—106.

Induction. Sc. 1. 17, 64.
Act I. Sc. 2. 6-7, 28-31.
Act III. Sc. 2. 16.
Act IV. Sc. 2. 59-62.

9. *ALL'S WELL THAT ENDS WELL* ... ... 107—124.

Act I. Sc. 1. 179, 237-241 ; Sc. 2. 31-45 ; Sc. 3. 141.
Act II. Sc. 1. 3, 27, 175-177 ; Sc. 5. 52.
Act IV. Sc. 1. 17-21 ; Sc. 2. 38 ; Sc. 4. 30-33.
Act V. Sc. 3. 6, 66, 216.

10. *TWELFTH NIGHT: OR WHAT YOU WILL* ... 125—130.

Act II. Sc. 5. 71.
Act III. Sc. 3. 13-16 ; Sc. 4. 86-91.
Act IV. Sc. 1. 14-15.

11. *THE WINTER'S TALE* ... ... 131—142.

Act I. Sc. 2. 273-276, 324, 457-460.
Act II. Sc. 1. 133-136, 143,
Act III. Sc. 2. 60-62
Act IV. Sc. 3. 98 ; Sc. 4. 250, 590-592, 760.
Act V. Sc. 1. 55-60.

12. *KING JOHN* ... ... 145—153.

Act II. Sc. 1. 183-190.
Act III. Sc. 1. 259, 263-297 ; Sc. 3. 39.
Act IV. Sc. 2. 40-43.
Act V. Sc. 6. 12 ; Sc. 7. 15-17.

13. *KING RICHARD II* ... ... 154—160.

Act I. Sc. 2. 67-70 ; Sc. 3. 127-128.
Act II. Sc. 1. 246-248 ; Sc. 2. 39-40, 108-114.
Act III. Sc. 2. 175-177.
Act V. Sc. 1. 25.

CONTENTS. vii

| | PAGE. |

14. **KING HENRY IV** ... ... 161—175.
   FIRST PART.
   Act I. Sc. 1, 5-6
   Act IV. Sc. 1, 31.
   Act V. Sc. 2, 8, 77-79.

   SECOND PART.
   Act I. Sc. 3, 36-37.
   Act IV. Sc. 1, 50, 88-96.

15. **KING HENRY V** ... ... 176—187.
   Act I. Sc. 2, 91-95, 125-127, 273-275.
   Act II. Sc. 2, 138-140.
   Act III. Sc. 3, 35.
   Act IV. Sc. 1, 262.

16. **KING HENRY VI** ... ... 188—200.
   FIRST PART.
   Act I. Sc. 1, 56, 62.
   Act IV. Sc. 6, 42-47.
   Act V. Sc. 3, 70-71, 193 ; Sc. 5, 64.

   SECOND PART.
   Act I. Sc. 3, 153.
   Act II. Sc. 1, 26.
   Act IV. Sc. 10, 56.

   THIRD PART.
   Act 1. Sc. 4, 152-153.

17. **KING RICHARD III** ... ... 201—207.
   Act I. Sc. 2, 64, 101-103 ; Sc. 3, 62-69, 113, 188.
   Act III. Sc. 3, 23.
   Act V. Sc. 3, 173 ; Sc. 5, 23-31.

18. **KING HENRY VIII** ... ... 208—218.
   Act 1. Sc. 1, 63, 75-80, 204-207, 222-226.
   Act II. Sc. 2, 92-98 ; Sc. 3, 46.
   Act III. Sc. 2, 62-71, 190-192, 383.
   Act V. Sc. 3, 1-2, 10-12, 108, 130.

		PAGE.

19. *CORIOLANUS* ... ... 219—247.

   Act I. Sc. 1. 195-198, 262 ; Sc. 3. 46 ; Sc. 4. 31 ;
   Sc. 6. 76, 80-85 ; Sc. 9. 41-46.
   Act III. Sc. 1. 131, 189-191 ; Sc. 2. 29, 52-80, 123-128 ;
   Sc. 3. 130.
   Act IV. Sc. 3. 9 ; Sc. 6. 2-3 ; Sc. 7. 28-57.
   Act V. Sc. 1. 15-17, 65-73 ; Sc. 2. 17.

20. *TITUS ANDRONICUS* .. .. 248—255.

   Act II. Sc. 3. 126.
   Act III. Sc. 1. 170, 282.
   Act IV. Sc. 1. 129 ; Sc. 2. 152, 177-178.
   Act V. Sc. 1. 132 ; Sc. 3. 124.

21. *TIMON OF ATHENS* ... ... 256—272.

   Act I. Sc. 1. 235-241 ; Sec. 2. 73.
   Act III. Sc. 2. 43 ; Sc. 6. 89.
   Act IV. Sc. 3. 133-134, 223.
   Act V. Sc. 2. 6-9 ; Sc. 3. 1-10 ; Sc. 4. 62.

22. *JULIUS CÆSAR* ... ... 273—286.

   Act I. Sc. 2. 155 ; Sc. 3. 62-65, 129.
   Act III. Sc. 1. 174, 206, 262.
   Act IV. Sc. 1. 36-39 ; Sc. 2. 49-52.
   Act V. Sc. 1. 35.

23. *MACBETH* ... ... 287—308.

   Act I. Sc. 2. 14, 16-23, 49, 58 ; Sc. 3. 95-98 ; Sc. 5.
   23-26.
   Act II. Sc. 1. 25, 55.
   Act III. Sc. 1. 130 ; Sc. 4. 32, 105, 132.
   Act IV. Sc. 2. 18-22 ; Sc. 3. 15, 136-137.
   Act V. Sc. 3. 21 ; Sc. 4. 11.

24. *HAMLET* ... ... 309—321.

   Act I. Sc. 1. 113-125 ; Sc. 3. 73-74 ; Sc. 4. 36-38.
   Act III. Sc. 4. 169.
   Act V. Sc. 1. 68 ; Sc. 2. 39-42, 118.

CONTENTS. ix

		PAGE.
25. *KING LEAR*	... ...	322—336.

Act I. Sc. 2. 17-22 ; Sc. 3. 18-20.
Act II. Sc. 2. 175-177 ; Sc. 4. 165, 273-274.
Act IV. Sc. 1. 71 ; Sc. 2. 57 ; Sc. 3. 20-21, 33.
Act V. Sc. 3. 129-130, 204-207.

26. *ANTONY AND CLEOPATRA* ... ... 337—345.
Act I. Sc. 5. 28, 48.
Act II. Sc. 2. 53.
Act III. Sc. 11. 47 ; Sc. 13. 10.
Act V. Sc. 1. 15 ; Sc. 2. 355.

27. *CYMBELINE* ... ... 346—355.
Act III. Sc. 3. 23 ; Sc. 4. 51-52, 135, 150.
Act IV. Sc. 2. 7-9, 16-17.
Act V. Sc. 1. 14-15 ; Sc. 5. 95.

28. *PERICLES* ... ... 356—370.
Act 1. Sc. 1. 17 ; Sc. 2. 1-5, 74 ; Sc. 3. 28.
Act II. Sc. 1. 56-60.
Act III. Sc. 1. 53 ; Sc. 2. 55.
Act IV. Sc. 1. 11.
Act V. Prologue. 23 ; Sc. 1. 174, 209.

INDEX ... ... 371—374.

THE TEMPEST.

"THE TEMPEST" was printed for the first time in the Folio of 1623. There is no earlier edition of it extant in Quarto, as is the case in more than one half of the thirty-six plays. What does this mean? It means that, if there should happen to be any errors in the text of the play, as it has been set down in the Folio, made I will not suppose by the author, but by the author's friends, or by those who were employed by them to copy and print his works, we have no means of correcting those errors, or of recovering the true original reading, because we have no second independent authority to fall back upon; no well-authenticated reserve testimony to appeal to; the staff upon which we leaned fails us; the candle which lighted us leaves us in the dark. There is no help for it but to acquiesce in the irremediable, and register in each successive edition the blunders of the Folio. To be sure there are the various conjectural emendations of learned men, but of these, though some are plausible and clever, and even more or less probable, by far the larger number are wild and extravagant, almost *all* are precarious and uncertain.

It would seem, then, as if the critic might throw aside his pen for all the good that he would be likely to do. Such, however, is very far from being the case. In almost every play of Shakespeare there are a number of passages, where, either because a word occurs which is unexampled in its use or strange and singular in its meaning, or because a sentence is interrupted and apparently unfinished, or because the sense is not easily discernible and perhaps differs from what might have been expected, or because the versification seems irregular or inharmonious, or because there is a possibility, so tempting to the brilliant critic, of some other word having been used in the original, for which the one that has been set down in the copy might easily have been mistaken, the purity of the text is arraigned, and emendations are started, and sometimes introduced; yet in most cases I think it will be found that objections have been raised by an over-hasty criticism on wholly insufficient grounds, and that they crumble away and come to nothing, when all the circumstances are considered that should be considered—the extraordinary variety of idiom that pervades the English language, the peculiar character of pieces intended for theatrical representation; the informality, elasticity, and frequent ellipses of common conversation; the licence which the poet's age allowed him, the licence which the poet—a master linguist, an Englishman to the core—allowed himself, to say nothing of the special circumstances of particular passages, so that, even though we should not care to do as others do, and take a shot now and then at a venture, we shall have enough to occupy us, while we strive to defend Shakespeare's text from faulty emendation or fallacious interpretation.

I could not, if I wished it, give a more striking example of the narrow boundary which sometimes separates the true and the false, and of the difficulty at times of coming to a decision, than is afforded by a passage in the 'Tempest' at the very end of the first scene—Act I, 1, 68-70—where Gonzalo, in imminent peril of momentary shipwreck, cries

> Now would I give a thousand furlongs of sea for an acre of barren ground, long heath, brown furze, anything.

This Hanmer by a masterly stroke of critical cunning converted to '*ling*, heath, *broom*, furze, anything,' and the Cambridge editor has signified his approval of the change by introducing it into the 'Clarendon Press Series' edition, no doubt considering the Folio reading poor and unnatural. Yet it is not impossible that those common epithets, which Mr. Knight held to be 'quite intelligible, and much more natural than an enumeration of various wild plants'—the epithet 'long' applied to the heath (and there is, I believe, a kind of long-growing heath in that part of the world to which Gonzalo's thoughts would naturally revert), and the epithet 'brown' applied to the furze (and there are times when the furze looks poor and shabby), were intended to keep up the idea of the barrenness of the acre which Gonzalo coveted, lest, associating with the heath its beautiful delicate purple hue, and with the gorse its rich golden glory, we should have presented to our eye a picture not of a bare uninteresting spot, but of a landscape full of beauty and bloom. The Folio reading best describes the *poverty of the ground*, and on that account best represents Gonzalo's *pauper cravings*.

But whatever view we may be disposed to take of this passage, after we have heard what the naturalist, the traveller, the critic, have to say on the subject, there ought not to be a shadow of doubt that the reading of the Folio is not only right, but cannot be bettered, in Act I, 2, 26-32, where Prospero, addressing Miranda, says

> The direful spectacle of the wreck, which touch'd
> The very virtue of compassion in thee,
> I have with such provision in mine art
> So safely ordered that there is no soul—
> No, not so much perdition as an hair
> Betid to any creature in the vessel
> Which thou heard'st cry, which thou saw'st sink;

yet Mr. Aldis Wright, who, we freely acknowledge, has done good service as a Shakespearian commentator, here tells us that there is 'some imperfection in the text,' and that Rowe would read, 'no soul lost,' and that others would change 'soul' to 'loss,' or 'soil,' or 'foil.' I feel sure that the learned expositor cannot really approve of these miserable emendations; I almost wonder that he should have thought it worth while to mention them at all. There is no imperfection whatever; there is merely a change of construction, and *that* not accidental, but deliberate and purposed. The ordinary construction would have been, 'There is no soul, no, not so much as a hair of any of them lost'; but Prospero, wishing to give full prominence to the marvel, that there had been not only no loss of *life*, but no loss of *any kind* whatsoever, breaks off after the words 'There is no soul,' as if, in saying no more than that, he had not said enough, and, after a moment's pause, as if deliberating how best to unfold the full extent of the wonder, he recommences with quite a new order of words, and a more emphatic assurance, thus producing an effect far surpassing any which a more rigid adherence to grammatical accuracy could have produced. An irregularity like this—for an imperfection, I repeat, it is not—may displease those who look a little too much at the frame and mounting of the picture, and not sufficiently at the picture itself, but it is a delightful surprise to those who contemplate the work as a whole, and study the general effect; it is instinct with animation and life; it is *dramatically perfect*; we admire in it the marvellous power of Shakespeare, thus to make Prospero command not only the elements, but also......the *grammar*.

I have no wish to attempt to write a dissertation on the prosody of Shakespeare—a subject intolerable to all but a few of the most insatiable thirsters after knowledge—but, when we are told *ex cathedra* that a line must be scanned in one particular way, which quite consistently with Shakespearian usage *admits* of being scanned in no less than four different ways, I may be pardoned, if I digress for a moment to say just a passing word on such a dry subject as metre. I declare, then, that the 53rd line of Act I, Sc. 2, may be scanned in the following fourfold fashion— either thus,

Twelve ye | ar since, | Miranda, | twelve ye | ar since,

where 'year,' each time that it occurs, is tantamount to a dissyllable; or thus,

Twelve ye | ar since, | Miran | da, twelve | year since,

where on one occasion only 'year' is used dissyllabically; or thus,

Twelve | year since, | Miran | da, twelve | year since,

where in the first instance only 'twelve' is a dissyllable—either actually so, the letter *w* being of the nature of a vowel, or virtually so, because of the length of time, which it is necessary to pause upon the word, in order to give it its full and proper emphasis; or lastly thus,

Twelve | year since, | Miranda, | twelve | year since,

where in both instances 'twelve' has a dissyllabic

value. Seeing then that we have a right of way by four different roads, I protest against any attempt to interfere with or infringe this our fourfold liberty.

From a question of prosody I pass to one of accidence in the same Act and Scene, lines 172-174, where in the 'Globe' Shakespeare we find

> Have I, thy schoolmaster, made thee more profit
> Than other princesses can that have more time
> For vainer hours and tutors not so careful.

But '*princesse*,' or '*princess*' is the word of the Folios; why, then, change to 'princesses'? A plural noun, it will be said, is required; but, according to Sydney Walker's rule, "the plural of substantives ending in *se, ss, ce*, are found without the usual addition of *s* or *es*, in pronunciation at least, although in many instances the plural suffix is added in printing, where the metre shows it is not to be pronounced." But here the plural suffix is *not* added, yet they add it; the metre, so far from requiring it, rejects it, yet notwithstanding they add it. He who in 'King Henry V,' Act V, 2, 28, did not scruple to write,

> Your *mightiness* on both parts best can witness,

where 'mightinesses' would have been as ill-sounding as it would have been inconvenient, was content, I cannot doubt, to write 'princess' here, where the plural termination is certainly not a metrical necessity. For my own part, I have a strong suspicion that there are more lines than this in Shakespeare, where the plural ending has been tacked on by the copyist, to the lengthening of the metre unnecessarily.

In Act I, 2, 306-307, we have an instance of what I cannot but call injudicious annotation; the Folio has
>   the strangeness of your story put
> Heaviness in me.

Yet the Cambridge editors would like to read '*strange* heaviness in me'! Surely these learned men must have been drowsing. The accommodation of sound to sense, as it is generally called, is a literary artifice perfectly familiar to all the great poets both of ancient and modern times. It would have been strange if Shakespeare had not occasionally availed himself of it in a species of composition in which of all others it is strikingly telling. He who admirably adapts both words and matter to the various characters whom he introduces, making a king speak like a king, a priest like a priest, a clown like a clown, sometimes also makes the words themselves more expressive by the manner in which he arranges them—by the metrical value which he attaches to them: thus in the line in 'King Richard III,' Act III, 7, 240,

> Long live Richard, England's royal king,

as we pause upon 'long,' we observe the length that the acclaimers affected to wish for Richard's reign, and at the same time we satisfy the metre; again in the line in 'King Richard II,' Act I, 3, 118,

> Stay, the king hath thrown his warder down,

as we linger on the first word, we make the stay

that the king commanded ; and so in the line which
commences with that drowsy word, '*Heaviness* in
me,' the poet admirably expresses the comatose
feeling that had crept over Miranda under Prospero's
magic charms, so that, even after the mighty wizard
had bid her wake, we seem still to hear the
magnetized maiden's sleepy tone. The rhythm here
echoes the sense.

I have hitherto in every instance without exception
stuck fast to the reading of the Folio, but I am now
going to propose an alteration not indeed in the
words, but in the arrangement of the words, in
Ariel's song, Act I, 2, 376-86, for which I must
own I have neither Folio warrant, nor commentators'
authority, yet still, I fancy, sense and reason and
probability in my favour. The song is thus set
down in the 'Globe' Shakespeare :

ARIEL'S *Song.*
Come unto these yellow sands,
 And then take hands :
Courtsied when you have and kiss'd
 The wild waves whist,
Foot it featly here and there ;
 And, sweet sprites, the burthen bear.

Burthen. [*dispersedly.*] Hark, hark !
Bow-wow.
The watch-dogs bark :
Bow-wow.

Ari. Hark, hark ! I hear
The strain of strutting chanticleer
Cry, Cock-a-diddle-dow.

Now was this the song as the author originally constructed and eventually left it? Was this his arrangement, this his termination of it? Is it possible that the last line formed any part of it at all? Has it not rather been tacked on by some transcriber or typographer, who either did not think, or did not know, what he was doing? For my own part, I am not so surprised that it should have crept into the text, as that it should have been permitted so long to continue there; that it should not have been challenged, should not even have been suspected by a single one of the numerous critics, whose names figure in the footnotes of the Cambridge Shakespeare, and who have not been backward with their offers of emendation in other parts of Shakespeare. Yet the oracles are dumb; the vigilance of Theobald is eluded for once. For it is surely neither modern English, nor Shakespearian English, nor English at all—it exceeds even the large licence of poetry—to say, 'I hear the *strain* of chanticleer *cry*'! '*Strain* of chanticleer' is enough in all conscience; '*cry*' added is needlessly—I had almost said, is nonsensically added. It needs not, however, be obliterated; it has a place proper to it, but not in the song; it was in all probability a stage-direction; had it been inclosed by brackets, the confusion would not have happened. 'Cock-a-diddle-dow' is the cry of the fowl, not the spirit's imitation of it.

If it be objected that the bark of the watch-dogs is a part of the song, and that it is but reasonable that the crowing of the cock should be so too, I reply that the *latratus canum*, both in the first and in the second instance, is as distinctly extra-metric, as is the cry of chanticleer. And, as touching the rhyme, are we to suppose that the second 'Bow-wow' rhymes to the first, and 'Cock-a-diddle-dow' to both? The couplet

Hark, hark!
The watch-dogs bark,

is complete in itself; to add 'Bow-wow' to each line is to disarrange both. Observe the latter part of the song;

Full fathom five thy father lies;
Of his bones are coral made;
Those are pearls that were his eyes:
Nothing of him that doth fade
But doth suffer a sea-change
Into something rich and strange.
Sea-nymphs hourly ring his knell:

Burthen. Ding-dong.

Ari.   Hark! now I hear them,—Ding-dong, bell.

Here it is manifest that 'Ding-dong, bell' rhymes to 'knell.' The intermediate 'Ding-dong' has nothing whatever to rhyme to it. It is clearly *extra metrum*. Well then, this intermediate 'Ding-dong,' so distinctly extra-metric, justifies me in treating 'Bow-wow' in a precisely similar manner. Grant this, and we *have* nothing for 'Cock-a-diddle-dow' to rhyme to, and, I may add, we *want* nothing, if we arrange the passage thus:

>Come unto these yellow sands,
> And then take hands;
>Courtsied when you have and kiss'd
> The wild waves whist,
>Foot it featly here and there,
>And, sweet sprites, the burthen bear:

Burthen. [*dispersedly.*]　Hark, hark!
　　　　　　　　　　　[Bow-wow.
　　　　　　　　The watch-dogs bark:
　　　　　　　　　　　[Bow-wow.
Ariel.　　　　　Hark, hark! I hear
　　　　　　　　The strain of strutting chanticleer.
　　　　　　　　　　[Cry. 'Cock-a-diddle-dow.'

I shall in all probability be asked, whether I can produce a single parallel from any other portion of Shakespeare's works of such an extraordinary blunder having been committed. A second example, though it would not conclusively prove the correctness of my surmise, might at least show that it was not impossible, and perhaps in the eyes of some might even give it an air of probability. One such example then I am prepared to produce; those who are better acquainted with the Folios and Quartos than I can pretend to be will be able to supply other illustrations. Long after I had written my thoughts on the passage, my attention was drawn to a note in the 'Cambridge Shakespeare,' which informs us that in the Forester's song in 'As You Like It,' Act IV, 2, 11,—which, as it is printed in the Globe edition, commences thus,

> What shall he have that killed the deer?
> His leather skin and horns to wear.
> Then sing him home;
> [*The rest shall bear this burden—*

the words 'Then sing him home, the rest shall bear this burthen' are printed in the Folios as part of the song. Theobald first gave 'The rest shall bear this burden' as a stage-direction, whereas Knight, Collier, Dyce, take the whole to be a stage-direction. So then the mishap which I contend has befallen Ariel's song is neither without parallel nor destitute of credibility.

I proceed to dilate on another passage at the very end of Act I, Sc. 2, lines 486-491, which is by no means unencumbered with difficulty. Ferdinand thus speaks,

> My father's loss, the weakness which I feel,
> The wreck of all my friends, nor this man's threats
> To whom I am subdued, are but light to me,
> Might I but through my prison once a day
> Behold this maid.

We seem here to be listening to a man who knows what he wants to say, but has a difficulty in saying it. His affirmations and his negations are at cross purposes; he contradicts himself, and confuses us. May not the poet have intended the confusion, in order to mark the change which all of a sudden had come over Ferdinand? The magician had motioned with his wand, and the prince confesses that he is reduced to impotence.

> My spirits, as in a dream, are all bound up.

What wonder, if, thus spell-bound, his ideas, though upon the whole intelligible, are a little incoherently expressed; his language lacks its usual grammatical precision. His speech bewrays him; he is not the man that he was. The poet violates the law of grammar for the higher law of his art. From a man confused what can we expect but confused utterances? This is quite as fair a way of dealing with the complication, as to say, as some do, that 'nor is' a misprint for 'and' or for 'or,' or that Shakespeare forgat himself, and, after beginning to express himself in one way, ended by expressing himself in a totally different way.

There is another solution, however, possible, and some may think more probable. In most languages, the English language among others, it occasionally happens that, where the conjunctional expression 'neither .. nor' has place, the first negative is omitted, and has to be mentally supplied by the reader. Thus we have in 1 Henry VI, Act I, 2, 142-43,

> Helen, the mother of great Constantine,
> *Nor* yet St. Philip's daughters, were like thee;

and in 'Cymbeline,' Act V, 1, 28,

> And thus, unknown,
> Pitied *nor* hated, to the face of peril
> Myself I'll dedicate.

Sometimes, though more rarely, but one negative is expressed, where ordinarily we should have three, as in 'A Lover's Complaint,' 264,

> Vow, bond, nor space,
> In thee hath neither sting, knot, nor confine;

Daniel, as quoted in Dr. Johnson's Dictionary,

> Power, disgrace, *nor* death could aught avail
> This glorious tongue thus to reveal thy heart.

Now let us suppose that in this passage in the 'Tempest' we have an instance—a bold instance, if you like—of this undoubted English idiom. Whereas a prose-writer would have said, '*neither* my father's loss, *nor* the weakness which I feel, *nor* the wreck of all my friends, nor this man's threats are but light'—that is, are otherwise than light—'to me,' the poet, availing himself of a known idiom, obscure enough to indicate that the person represented had lost his self-possession, but not so obscure as to leave the hearer in the dark as to the meaning intended to be conveyed, omits all but the *last* negative, the presence of which idiomatically excuses the absence of the rest. Seeing that Shakespeare frequently accumulates negatives where we should only allow one, it would not be surprising if he occasionally reverted to the opposite idiom, and were sometimes as parsimonious, as he is at other times profuse.

There is a hitch too, through the unexpected intervention of the preposition 'at,' in some lines **spoken by Sebastian in Act II, 1, 130-31,**

> You were kneel'd to and importuned otherwise
> By all of us, and the fair soul herself
> Weigh'd between loathness and obedience, *at*
> Which end of the beam should bow.

What would be more easy than to cut down this troublesome little word, which stands in our way? And this is exactly what some would do. But the fair and upright critic will refuse to resort to such a murderous proceeding, until at any rate he has assured himself that he has reason and justice on his side. In days gone by prepositions were frequently used, where now we should not think of using them; and those were selected for use, which nowadays would not be selected. Such lines as

> I envy at their liberty,
> 'King John' Act III, 4, 73;

> To have a godly peace concluded of,
> '1 Henry VI,' Act V, 1, 5;

> Let your highness
> Command upon me,
> 'Macbeth' Act III, 1, 17;

> To whose sound chaste winds obey,
> 'The Phœnix and The Turtle;'

would be rejected now as out of date and barbarous. And so in the 'Tempest' a modern poet would have written, 'To weigh which end of the beam should bow,' but Shakespeare's age tolerated the interpolation of the preposition 'at,' upon which the noun-sentence, 'which end o' the beam should bow,' depends. Thus the subject of the verb 'should bow' is plainly 'which end o' the beam,' and we must not be snared to understand 'she' with Malone, or 'it' with Mr. Aldis Wright, much less listen to the more violent proposals of less discreet critics. Every lout in the theatre in Shakespeare's day would have swallowed as a gnat, what all the literati of later days have strained at as a camel.

Illiterate and brutal as Caliban was, I cannot think that there is much amiss with the language used by him in Act II, 2, 15, 16,

> Here comes a spirit of his, *and* to torment me
> For bringing wood in slowly,

where the Cambridge editors would substitute 'sent' for 'and.' But the conjunction 'and' has a great variety of uses in the plays of Shakespeare— in the English language. Witness such passages as Act II, 1, 252, of this play,

> She that from whom
> We all were sea-swallow'd, though some cast again,
> *And* by that destiny to perform an act
> Whereof what's past is prologue;

where, by the way, Mr. Spedding, unable to tolerate the loose and inartistic but by no means impossible expression, 'she that from whom,' had recourse to a change of punctuation, which, though it has been accepted by some editors, seems to me to be neither urgently needed, nor likely to be correct; also Act III, 3, 56,

> the never-surfeited sea
> Hath caus'd to belch up you, *and* on this island;

'Merry Wives of Windsor,' Act III, 5, 72-78,

> Master Brook......comes......and at his heels a rabble...*and*, forsooth, to search his house for his wife's love.

'Midsummer Night's Dream,' Act II, 1, 192,

> And here am I, *and* wode within this wood.

Caliban's 'and' may very well be let alone.

As touching Act III, 1, 15, where the first Folio reads

> Most busy lest, when I doe it,

the other Folios having 'least' for 'lest,' the Cambridge editors tell us that, as none of the proposed emendations can be regarded as certain, they have left the reading of F_1, though it is manifestly corrupt. The spelling 'doe,' they add, makes Mr. Spedding's conjecture 'idlest' for 'I doe it' more probable.

For my part, I do not like Mr. Spedding's conjecture at all. If the text has not been imperfectly executed, the only meaning that the words will bear as we have them—and it is a meaning that it seems to me just possible that they may bear—is that Ferdinand represents himself as at once most busy, and least busy—a comma will have to be placed after 'busy,' and 'busy' will have to be understood after 'least'—most busy, because of the quantity of logs which he has to pile; least busy, because, when he does it, he is revived by the thought of Miranda on whose account he undergoes the task-work. In 'Midsummer Night's Dream,'

Act V, 1, 105, the superlatives are similarly opposed, and in similar juxtaposition ;

> In least speak most to my capacity.

I at one time thought that 'busiliest' had originally stood, where 'busy lest' now stands — a mode of solving the problem, which I find has occurred to others before me; but this uncouth superlative, which might be placed in the same category as 'proudlier' in 'Coriolanus,' and 'easiliest' in 'Cymbeline,' I cannot now regard with any favour. I am disposed to deal more summarily with the text. I am confident that the copyist wrote 'most busy' by *mistake*, and, becoming conscious of it, too late added 'lest'—which the other Folios show was intended for 'least'—in its *wrong* place after 'busy,' and then omitted to erase 'most,' so that we have both the wrong word and the right word in the text—the right word unfortunately in the wrong place—'most busy least,' when we should have

> Least busy, when I do it,

Ferdinand saying that, when actually engaged in his log-piling work, he is least busy, because of the love-thoughts which that work suggested.

Such then is my ultimatum, and such also I find was Pope's conclusion, though, by what process of reasoning he arrived at it, I have not been able to ascertain.

Is it a mere accident that by a slightly different arrangement in Act III, 3, 49-51, we can secure a rhyming couplet? *

> I will stand to and feed, although my last:
> No matter, since I feel the best is past.
> Brother, my lord the Duke, stand to, and do as we.

But we need not be punctilious about what is rather a question of form than of matter.

Before I leave the troubled waters of the 'Tempest,' I will just let down the sounding line at Act IV, 1, 61, where two epithets have caused no little agitation: but may not

> Thy banks with *pioned* and *twilled* brims

be the poet's way of describing a neat and well made hedge? If, as Henley thought, 'pioned' refers to the digging and facing—and the opinion should not have been received with such scorn by some—'twilled' may well refer to the ordering and interlacing the branches along the hedge. The reverse of the picture we have in King Henry V, Act V, 2, 42-44,

> her hedges even-pleach'd,
> Like prisoners wildly overgrown with hair,
> Put forth disorder'd twigs.

A comparison between the two passages, presented in parallel columns, if it does not confirm, will not invalidate the interpretation which I have suggested.

---

* Note: I find that this has been already noticed by Mason.

'THE TEMPEST.'	'KING HENRY V.'
1. *rich leas*	1. *vineyards*
2. turfy mountains	2. *hedges even-pleach'd*
3. *flat meads*	3. *fallow leas*
4. banks with *pioned and twilled* brims	4. *even meads*
5. broom-groves	
6. *pole-clipt vineyards*	
7. sea-marge	

In the 164th line of this same scene Theobald was in all probability right, when he proposed to read

> Come with a thought. I thank you :—Ariel, come.

Even if we do not change 'thee' into 'you,' as he did, we should certainly punctuate, as he did, in which case 'thee' must be taken as referring to Ferdinand only.

THE TWO GENTLEMEN OF VERONA.

The difficulties which confront us in 'The Two Gentlemen Of Verona' are for the most part of a geographical character, and they are of such exceptional magnitude, that they have baffled every effort which has been made hitherto to bring them into harmony with the rest of the play. Having recently made a fresh attempt to explore them, I propose to state as succinctly as I can the results of my observations, and I shall leave it to those who are competent judges to say, how far I have succeeded in breaking the ice, and opening a track which may be safely followed by future investigators.

There are three well-known passages, where the obstacles to progress are seemingly insurmountable.

In Act II, 5, 2, Speed welcomes Launce to *Padua*, when there is not a doubt that they were both in *Milan*.

In Act III, 1, 81, the Duke of *Milan*, while conversing with Valentine in *Milan*, speaks of a lady in '*Verona here.*'

In Act V, 4, 129, Valentine declares to Thurio, who was a citizen of *Milan*, that, if once again he laid claim to Silvia, *Verona* should not hold him, whereas it is thought that he should have said that *Milan* should not.

What are we to make of these seeming contradictions? Are we to say that they are errors? and, if errors, errors of the copyist, or errors of the author? or, if not errors, how are we to explain them? Choose which line of defence we will, we shall have enough to do to make good our position.

Let us suppose that a transcriber made the first-mentioned blunder—that he set down *Padua*, when *Milan* was black as ink before his face: is it likely that he would have made two more Geographical blunders in a play, in the rest of which he has done his work upon the whole so exceedingly well, that he has left the critics hardly any thing to fight about? We should have expected either more accuracy in the topography, or less accuracy in the other matter. We will suppose, however, that geography was a weak point of his; the worst part of the tangle yet remains; he could not have made the second and the third errors without deliberately tampering with the text, Milan and Verona not being metrically interchangeable. Now to alter a line, or to make a fresh one, is not a thing to be done offhand; at any rate, it is not exactly the task that we should imagine that a copyist would without any apparent object set himself. And yet in this case we are asked to believe that in two separate instances he has either altered the original line, or composed a fresh one, and that he has done it so capitally, that, but for the bad geography, we should not have known that the lines were not Shakespeare's own. I cannot believe that a copyist would have attempted any such thing, or that, if he attempted it, he would so well have executed it. A simpleton would not have left us such good lines; a prudent and careful copyist should not have left such bad geography. Patchwork is usually easily discoverable. It is not easy to detect it here. I reject, therefore, the theory, that the mistakes, if mistakes they are, were made, at least *all* of them, in the copying or the printing.

Were they, then, made by the author? This seems to me to be even more improbable. It is true that Shakespeare has not been always accurate in his geography, but he has not been inconsistent in his inaccuracy; he has not in one and the same play contradicted himself; he has not, for example, in one Act made Bohemia an inland, in another Act a maritime, country. This I contend that a dramatist of Shakespeare's brilliant genius, comprehensive knowledge, marvellous general accuracy, and uncommon power could not have done. To geographical accuracy a dramatist is not bound; to geographical consistency he is. This distinction it is essential to bear in mind. If, then, the names of places set down in the passages I have indicated in the 3rd and in the 5th Acts of ' The Two Gentlemen Of Verona ' were set down by Shakespeare, depend upon it, they admit of being explained. We will suppose, however, that Shakespeare set them down, and set them down by mistake—that he overlooked two glaring contradictions in the composition, in the transcription, in the rehearsals, in the representation of the play. He lived in an age, which, so to speak, was dramatically educated. Among his audience were many who were intelligent, many who were able to criticize—some who were disposed to be captious and censorious. Were there none among the actors, were there not many among the playgoers, sharp enough to detect at once such palpable incongruities? Say they passed one night; could they have passed night after night? Would not some friend have whispered them? some enemy have noised them abroad? Shakespeare corrected, revised, recast many of his plays; would he have left blots such as these, if he had made them? Where else in any single play of his can we find such dramatic impossibilities? These are egregious errors: err Shakespeare might, but not to the extent that these errors would imply. And if the play had been a very complicated one, if there had been a constant shifting of the scene to a number of different places, we might have allowed for a slight lapse or two, though hardly then for three serious blunders; but, when the play is so extremely simple, and the scenes are laid, if we exclude the forest scene, in two places, and two places only, namely

Milan and Verona, no one who was not either very stupid, or habitually careless, could have gone so far out of the way. In every other portion of the play the topography is just as it should be: where Milan should be, there we have Milan; where Verona, there Verona. The author's general geographical accuracy forbids us to believe that he faltered in these three particular instances. A skilful composer could not leave in a piece of music three discordant notes.

Is it possible, then, that these so-called blunders may not, save perhaps one of them, be blunders at all, but correct copies from the author's correct MS? For to this corner we are now driven, and it would seem to be our last and only standing-ground.

I acknowledge that I am not prepared to defend the *first* geographical inaccuracy. If Speed's 'Welcome to Padua' were executed by Shakespeare, I am positive that it would admit of being explained somehow; but the only explanation that I can conceive possible is that, the moment Speed saw Launce, he began to play the fool, shouting out the name of a city in the very opposite direction to that to which they had come, viz. *Padua*, which lay to the *East*, rather than *Milan*, which lay to the *West* of Verona; to which Launce paid no manner of heed, being too much taken up with a thought of a visit to the tavern at Speed's expense. It is even just possible that Padua was lugged in for the sake of an

execrable pun on the word, to which Launce
promptly responded, when he claimed that 'certain
shot should be *paid*.' I do not, however, really
believe that Padua ever blotted the author's MS; I
believe it to have been an after-insertion by another
hand; I pronounce it a gross blunder. It may be
accounted for in this way. Launce no sooner heard
the word 'Welcome' drop from Speed's lips, than
without giving him time to utter a syllable more, if
at least he intended to utter more, he took him up
smartly, cavilling at a word, which had no meaning to *him*, unless it were accompanied with the
rattle of ale-glasses. The passage, then, I take it,
originally stood thus, 'Launce, by mine honesty!
welcome,' or, 'welcome to—.' The name of the
place was purposely omitted; but those who took
upon them to revise Shakespeare's plays could not
understand the reason of the omission; they filled
up the void, but filled it up badly, inserting *Padua*,
when they should have inserted *Milan*. Why they
should have inserted Padua, which is not so much
as once mentioned in the play, we can only
conjecture. Perhaps the learned dons had in their
minds the famous university of Padua, whither they
fancied at the moment that the young Italians had
come to pursue their studies; perhaps Verona and
Padua were so intimately associated in their minds
from their occurring repeatedly in 'The Taming Of
The Shrew,' that they made Valentine here, as

Petrucchio there, come from Verona to *Padua*, rather than, as they should have done, from Verona to *Milan*; perhaps it was a mere fit of mental absence, for which, however, we must not hold either the transcriber or the printer, much less the author, responsible.

Having thus obliterated the first of the topographical difficulties, I proceed to an examination of the second, which is much more pronounced and enigmatical; for it is interwoven with the metre; it holds its place easily, and as it were by right. Yet how is it possible that it can be right? The Duke of *Milan*, speaking to Valentine, evidently in *Milan*, says—

> There is a lady in *Verona here!*

Did the Duke mean that there was a Veronese lady sojourning in Milan? or that the lady dwelt in a Veronese quarter of the city? But neither of these explanations will be accepted as satisfactory. Did he, then, lest haply he should arouse too early Valentine's suspicion, and so defeat his own object, which was first to blind, and then to trap him, *put the case hypothetically, so far as the place was concerned*; just as sometimes we, not caring to particularize the place which we have in our minds, substitute for it for the nonce some other place—'let us call it,' we say, 'Paris, or Berlin, or Vienna, any place you like'—and so the Duke, affecting to ask Valentine's advice in his imaginary love-fix, put the case hypothetically—if it were Verona, what would Valentine do? There might have been deep and crafty policy in laying the scene at Verona; for, if Valentine had scented danger, he might have pleaded inability to give an opinion as to what had best be done in a city in which he was a comparative stranger; his own native place being chosen, he had no alternative but to walk straight to the pit into which he fell. In a got-up story, in which, so far as the Duke was concerned, there was not an atom of truth from beginning to end, and the object of which was, at any rate in the first instance, to throw dust into the eyes of Valentine, some allowance may be made for a certain amount of unreality—of mystification.

But I have yet another, and, if am not mistaken, a stronger string to my bow. At any rate the view of the matter which I am now about to put forward is entitled to consideration.

Just after the Duke had been informed by Proteus of Valentine's intended elopement, he espied Valentine hurrying away as fast as he could; on his asking him the object of his haste, Valentine replied that he merely wanted to despatch a letter of no great importance to his friends in Verona. A letter he had in his possession sure enough, and anxious enough he was that it should be safely delivered; *but his Verona was situated near the very spot that he was then treading with his feet; it was in the Duke's palace in Milan;* it was (to use now the Duke's own words) '*in Verona here*'; and the friend, to whom the letter was addressed, was a lady in that same Pseudo-Verona; it was no other than Silvia, the Duke's own daughter. The Duke was perfectly aware of all this: when, then, Valentine, in the most innocent manner in the world asked,

> What would your Grace have me to do in this,

and the Duke answered,

> There is a lady in Verona *here*,

he sounded the very depths of Valentine's deceit; he answered Valentine according to Valentine's own geography, he echoed back to him his lie—*Verona*—with a flash of truth in it—*here*. If Valentine did not at once perceive that mischief was brewing, it was not long ere he discovered it; meanwhile the Duke's eye, the Duke's tone, the Duke's manner, as he named a geographical impossibility, a geographical absurdity, fairly shook the house with laughter. When at last the letter dropped from the cloak, and the Duke read it aloud, and it became manifest that Valentine's Verona was in *Milan*, and the *friend* he was corresponding with was a lady *there*, then was felt the full force and fun of that mysterious announcement, that extraordinary piece of Cloud-cuckooism to fall from the lips of a Duke of Milan in Milan, proved, however, to be strictly and strikingly true—'*Verona here.*' To find the place, we must not look into Keith Johnson's Atlas, but into *Valentine's love-map.* It may serve as some little confirmation of this view of the question, that in no other part of this Act is there the slightest confusion between the two places, but only where the Duke is engaged in unearthing Valentine's secret.

I now come to the last, I had almost said the least, of the three geographical puzzles, where Valentine, indignant that Thurio should lay claim to Silvia, tells him that, if he did it again, 'Verona should not hold him.' It is assumed that Shakespeare meant Valentine to say, that Thurio should never see his own city alive again; and, if such had been the poet's intention, undoubtedly we should have expected some such words as Theobald has proposed, 'Milan shall not behold thee.' But there is no occasion for such licentious emendation; we have merely to re-arrange the stops—to substitute a semi-colon or a comma for the present full stop after 'Verona shall not hold thee,' in order to show how closely that sentence is bound up with the words that follow, and then it becomes merely a question of what meaning should be given to the verb 'hold.'

'Verona shall not hold thee' may mean 'Verona shall not receive you within the circuit of its walls,' or 'Verona shall not be a stronghold to thee,' or 'Verona shall not keep thee in check.' Take the last meaning first, which is possibly the least likely. 'Hold' would be used in the sense of 'withhold,' 'restrain,' 'check' — the simple verb for the compound, *more Shakespeariano*. 'Do not fancy,' Valentine would say, 'that I shall look to the fortifications of Verona to keep thee at a distance from me; lo! I, I, Valentine, alone and undefended, pit myself against thee, and here, yes, here, and not in Verona, aye, and at this very instant, I challenge thee to the combat.'

Or, if the meaning rather be, 'Verona shall not serve as a stronghold to thee,' Valentine supposes that Thurio might flee to that, the nearest inhabited and fortified city, in the hope of finding there a refuge and hiding-place.

Or it may be simply, 'Verona shall not receive you within its compass; I shall not wait for you to follow me *thither* to prosecute your claim, or to repeat your insulting interference; it is not *there*, it is *here* that the matter shall be be decided';

here she stands;
I dare thee but to breathe upon my love.

I suggest these various modes of solving the problem, without selecting any particular one of them; it is sufficient if they are possible; the critics must choose which is the most probable. Perhaps there was a purposed vagueness in the threat, just as we hear angry people sometimes cry out, 'Let me catch you there, that's all'—indicating the spot where they themselves are usually to be found. This last difficulty, then, I consider a mere bogey conjured up by the commentators; we are scared to no purpose. It is true that we may not perceive the exact shade of meaning which the author intended should be given to the words, but we may be certain that he, who, before he wrote this play, had carefully and successfully adapted several, and was already beginning to be favourably known as an original playwright, to whom it was a matter of precious reputation, as well as of pecuniary interest (to say nothing of his innate love for literary excellence *per se*), to observe all the dramatic proprieties—we may be certain, I say, that he would not have written carelessly and at random, much less have left a grave error that a novice could hardly have been guilty of.

There is a difficulty of a totally different kind in Act V, 4, 82-83, which has given a deal of trouble to commentators.

When Proteus found himself face to face with Valentine whom he had deceived and betrayed, and could no longer conceal his base unnatural conduct, overwhelmed with shame and remorse, he confessed his guilt, and implored forgiveness. Valentine, feeling that such an abandoned transgressor needed something more than the ordinary 'I forgive you,' wishing to make him feel that he was forgiven without stint or grudging, addressed to him, by way of encouragement, this remarkable assurance,

> And that my love may appear plain and free,
> All that was mine in Silvia I give thee.

These words, which have quite dumbfoundered the expositors, seem to me to express not so much the quantity, as the quality of the love, which Valentine promised. Proteus well knew, how deep, how full, how true, how stedfast had been Valentine's love for Silvia. Such then was the *kind* of love which Valentine assured Proteus he might count on.

In thus giving to Proteus, was he taking from Silvia? In restoring him, was he renouncing her? Was he shaking *his* hand, and wringing *her* heart? Impossible: he was merely giving his penitent friend the strongest pledge that it was possible for him to give that bygones should be bygones. But even supposing that quantity rather than quality of love were here indicated—no matter. Give as much as Valentine might to Proteus, he would have no lack of love for Silvia. There is no bankruptcy in love. It is inexhaustible as the sea, infinite as eternity. The more it spreads, the more intense and immense are its fires. To borrow an illustration *suggested by the context,* the eternal Father, in restoring to his bosom the returned prodigal, does not reject from it the unfallen child; *he guarantees to the former all the love that had been his in the latter, without detracting aught from the latter.* The multiplication of objects loved is a manifestation and magnification of love. It may be objected, that Julia, who swooned immediately she heard the words, understood them otherwise. Possibly so;

but that would not prove that Valentine otherwise intended them. Here, as elsewhere, *e.g.*, in 'Romeo and Juliet,' Act III, 5, 95, the poet uses words that are capable of being understood two ways; the ambiguity was perhaps necessary at a critical juncture; matters as between Valentine and Proteus had come to a head, causing immense sensation. There was need of some startling incident to sustain the interest, to divert and arrest the attention. The fainting fit of Julia is a sort of '*Deus ex machina*'— a special interposition. The ruse succeeds. We turn without an effort, nay, with eager interest and curiosity, from Valentine and Proteus to Proteus and Julia. Thus are the threads of the piece all taken up, and woven together so as to form one beautiful whole of elaborate and exquisite workmanship.

MEASURE FOR MEASURE.

We have hardly read half a dozen lines in 'Measure for Measure,' before we come, at any rate in the 'Globe' Shakespeare, to a breach in the text, the vacant space being filled with a number of dots, the miserable substitutes of not less than two half lines which are supposed to have been lost. It is true that there are no dots in the Folios, nor any traces of any interruption; but the want of a finite verb, the prolongation of the metre, and a supposed harshness of rhythm, have led editors to conclude with Theobald—an excellent, but not an infallible judge—that the metrical chain has been broken: accordingly the Duke's opening address is thus presented to us:

> Of government the properties to unfold,
> Would seem in me to affect speech and discourse ;
> Since I am put to know that your own science
> Exceeds, in that, the lists of all advice
> My strength can give you : then no more remains
> But that to your sufficiency ....
> .... as your worth is able.

Most readers will acquiesce in this arrangement, without stopping to consider whether it is right or not. But the critic may not be so compliant. It is his business to strike out the conjectural dots, and try how the two fragmentary halves will read, as they appear in the Folios, *as a whole*. And this is what first strikes us, that the line of the Folios will scan; the rhythm may be a little harsh and jumping, but not more so than in a number of other lines, which are found in Shakespeare, the soundness of which has never been contested. As for the line being an Alexandrine, *that* can be no solid ground for rejecting it, Alexandrines being a recognized portion of Shakespearian versification. If, however, we are pressed to assign a reason for one being introduced here, we might plead that it conveys with more than ordinary solemnity and emphasis the Duke's estimate of Escalus' high character. Undoubtedly there is a verb wanting for the clause, 'but that to your sufficiency,' but verbal ellipses are common both in the dialogue and in the drama, and if the present instance may not be catalogued with such examples as

> I'll to this gear,
> Let him to field,
> Come answer not, but to it presently,
> I to this fortune that you see me in,
>
> 'Comedy of Errors,' Act V, 1, 355,
>
> Come, Friar Francis, be brief; only to the plain form of marriage,
> 'Much Ado About Nothing,' Act IV, 1, 1,

—the last but one being particularly noticeable for

its close and striking resemblance—we may remark that it is quite in Shakespeare's style to use at times a common idiom in a slightly uncommon way; a subtle critic might even argue that there is a special fitness in the verb being suppressed here; the Duke on the eve of a hurried departure has no time for superfluous diction or regular formal grammatical instructions; his words are brief, or at least as brief as ducal dignity and the gravity of the occasion allow. He exhorts Escalus to *have recourse to*—some such phrase has to be supplied—his sufficiency, to the utmost ability of his worth. By 'sufficiency' is meant intellectual capability, by 'worth' high character, the two capital qualifications of a civil governour. To be sure, the adjective 'sufficient' is used more frequently in this sense than the noun, yet in 'Winter's Tale,' Cleomenes and Dion are said to be of 'stuffed sufficiency,' and compare 'Othello,' Act I, 3, 224. There is no need, then, to split the line of the Folios into two separate halves; still less to discredit the phrase (as has been done very lately) 'I am put to know'—a rare bit of good old English, which should on no account be disturbed. Perhaps we are more familiar with the phrase, 'I am *given* to know'; yet we still speak of 'putting a person up to a thing,' and in 'Othello,' Act III, 4, 29, Desdemona says that her loss of the handkerchief, which Othello had given her,

were enough
To put him to ill thinking.

In spite, then, of the pages which have been written on this passage, to which I am adding one page more, I see no sufficient reason for distrusting here the chart of the Folios; but I am not prepared to go by the Folios' chart, as I presume that the 'Globe' editors do, when in Act I, 2, **125**, they make Claudio say,

> Thus can the demigod Authority
> Make us pay down for our offence by weight
> The words of heaven ; on whom it will, it will ;
> On whom it will not, so ; yet still 'tis just.

The punctuation here seems to me to be faulty. 'The words of heaven' should not be connected grammatically with the preceding line; it should stand independently; any roughness of construction is amply compensated for by raciness of expression. Such exclamatory moralizings are conversational—are dramatic; there is an ease and offhandedness about them which is natural. Somewhat in the same strain are those words in 'The Comedy of Errors,' Act IV, 4, 45,—these resemblances are worth observing—

> The prophecy like the parrot, 'beware the rope's-end.'

A colon, then, should be placed after 'weight,' and after 'The words of heaven,' a comma, or else a hyphen should stand.

Nor can there be a question that editors are right, when they refuse to believe that Shakespeare, notwithstanding a habit he has of occasionally mixing together different metaphors, could possibly have written 'curbs to headstrong weeds,' in the 20th line of the 3rd Scene.

> We have strict statutes and most biting laws,
> The needful bits and curbs to headstrong weeds,
> Which for this nineteen years we have let slip.

Theobald, I believe, was the first to suggest 'steeds,' —an obvious and by no means impossible correction, which has been endorsed by many editors; no one has whispered the simpler word 'deeds'; yet, when I come across such passages as

> The reverence of your highness *curbs* me from giving *reins* and *spurs* to my free *speech*.

and in 'The Taming of the Shrew,'

> I'll *curb* her mad and headstrong *humour*,

I cannot but think that the metaphor, which is dropt in 'speech' and in 'humour,' may have been dropt also in 'deeds,' which, and not 'steeds,' I reckon that Shakespeare wrote. The insertion of a wrong letter, *w* for *d*, is, I need scarcely sa common printer's error. Here too is a line w the critics may ponder, *where the very wo¹ I favour is found after exactly the same metaphor*,

> A *spur* to valiant and magnanimous *deeds*.
> 'Troilus and Cressida,' Act II, 2, ?.

Further down in the 3rd Scene, the 42nd and 43rd lines have given a lot of trouble to commentators;

> I have on Angelo imposed the office;
> Who may, in the ambush of my name, strike home,
> And yet my nature never in the fight
> To do in slander.

The Duke's *name* and the Duke's *nature* are evidently here placed in contradistinction to each other, his 'name representing his magisterial and judicial authority which was a terror to evil doers, his 'nature' a byword for kindness and indulgence which had been too ready to overlook offences. Things had come to such a pass that a change of policy was absolutely necessary. The 'name' of terror must occupy the foreground; the good easy 'nature' must stand back. The Duke had arranged that the two should be separated; his 'name' he would leave behind him; his 'nature' he would carry with him far from the scene of contention. Angelo was in ambush in his 'name,' authorized to act, willing to strike. Had the *Duke* remained, and taken an *active* part in the prosecution of offenders; had he shown that he could not not only pass laws, put them in force—that he could dare to strike, execute, to kill—in a word (and it is the word ich I believe Shakespeare puts into the mouth of the Duke here, a mild little word, if you like, as the nature of the Duke was mild, but the significance and comprehensiveness of which cannot be mistaken) '*to do*,' he could not have escaped malignant misrepresentation for having so long permitted what now he punished. By absenting himself and empowering Angelo to act in his name, the blow would be struck, the deed *done*, yet the slander avoided. Such I conceive to be the gist of the passage. With regard to the meaning which I have given to '*do*,' we may call to mind such phrases as 'to do him dead' (3 Henry VI), 'do execution on the watch' (1 Henry VI), and that mysterious threatening of the witch in 'Macbeth,'

> I'll do, I'll do, and I'll do;

and 2 King Henry VI, Act III, 1, 195-96,

> My lords, what to your wisdoms seemeth best,
> Do or undo, as if ourself were here;

and yet again 3 King Henry VI, Act II, 6, 105,

> Warwick, as ourself,
> Shall do and undo as him pleaseth best.

There are various degrees of punishment, and various modes of dealing with offenders. *To do* is a dark word which sums up all. After 'my nature' the verb 'may be' must be supplied. Upon the whole, then, I consider that the difficulty of this passage has been exaggerated. It stands now as it stood ever. As the actor intelligently repeated it, giving each word its proper emphasis, an Elizabethan audience would 'take the meaning' at once. Was there any imperfection? Well then, the poet left it to them 'to piece it out with their thoughts.'

In the next Scene,—Act I, 4, 30—many have stumbled over the half line,

> Sir, make me not your story,

and, failing to understand it, would fain have altered it. But Isabella does not say, 'make me not the subject of your story,' but 'none of your story-telling, I pray,' or 'none of your story-telling to me,' as is evident from Lucio's replying, ''Tis true,' as though, in what she had said to him, she had expressed a doubt of his veracity. 'Me' is not an objective case after a factitive verb, but a dative. We may compare it with such expressions as

>Come me to what was done to her;
>Leave me your snatches;
>Villain, I say, knock me here soundly.

'To make a story' is a phrase which needs neither explanation nor illustration.

Having removed this stumbling block, I pass to a passage in Act II, 1, 39, where the question is not as to the meaning, but as to the exact words in which that meaning was intended to be conveyed. 'Brakes of ice' is the phrase of the Folios; 'brakes of vice,' has been suggested as more appropriate and probable: the change is a small one, involving the addition of but a single letter, and that letter the letter of all others most likely to have fallen out after an f: moreover it supplies an excellent antithesis—

>Well, heaven forgive him! and forgive us all!
>Some rise by sin, and some by virtue fall:
>Some run from brakes of ice, and answer none,
>And some condemned for a fault alone.

A miscarriage in the administration of justice is the theme descanted on. The lucky undeserved escape of some is contrasted with the luckless hardly deserved capture of others; the latter for a mere slip of the foot, a stumble, a fall—'a fault alone,' as the text has it—are pounced upon, arrested, arraigned, condemned, punished; the former run from 'brakes of'—what? Whatever the word be, it is evident that it should indicate some great and grievous transgression, some heinous sin, the very opposite of 'a fault alone.' Let us remember that it is poetry, and not prose that we are reading. Why not then 'brakes of ice?'' 'Breaks of ice'—I adopt the modern spelling—brings before us a vast frozen expanse, with a number of rifts and chasms, traps of death, pools of destruction, where we should expect not one fall only, but a succession of them—a drenching at the very least, if not a drowning—yet there are some who get off without any such disastrous consequences—without a scar, a bruise—get off at a run. Miraculous escape, indeed! Now if physical occurrences may be used to picture moral haps, how could we have more vividly represented to us vast mischief done, vast risks undergone, ruin wrought for many, with, strange to say! safety to self? This is what the context demands, and this 'brakes of *ice*' supplies. By all means retain it, therefore, neither obliterating it, nor adding a letter.

I shall next take notice of a passage in Act III, 1, 126-128, where the question is not merely one of dry grammar, but involves also physiological, not to say spiritualistic, considerations. In those magnificent lines, where Claudio, imagining that he had come to the very confines of the grave, shrinks from the dark outlook, and sums the dreadful possibilities of future existence, he supposes the following horror,

> to be worse than worst
> Of those that lawless and incertain thought
> Imagine howling.

What part of speech is 'thought,' and what is its relation to the rest of the sentence? Is it a participle, or is it a noun? Who are they that imagine howling? The spirits of the damned? or others who imagine they hear *them* howling? The latter, I take it, in both cases. 'Thought' is a singular noun in the nominative case, which by a Shakespearian licence, of which we are not without examples, is the subject of the plural verb 'imagine,' unless it be allowed that the continual recurrence of the thought gives to a singular noun a plural signification, or, as a last resort, it be surmised that the plural termination has been accidently omitted by the copyist. Anyhow, explain it as you will, 'thought' is the subject of the verb 'imagine.' 'Lawless and incertain thought' is a periphrasis expressive of the mental idiosyncracy of lunatics. It is they who fancy they hear the damned ones howl. This connexion between the maniac and the demon—a subtle theological mystery! a dreadful physiological problem!—is often touched by Shakespeare in those of his plays, in which maniacs, or would-be maniacs figure,—comically in the 'Comedy of Errors,' tragically in 'King

Lear'; but, not to take too wide a range at present, the passage, to which I wish to draw particular attention, as bearing more immediately on that which is now being considered, is in 'Troilus and Cressida,' Act V, 10, 29,

> I'll haunt thee like a wicked conscience still,
> That *mouldeth goblins swift as frenzy's thoughts.*

Here, if I am right in thinking that 'mould goblins' should be supplied after 'frenzy's thoughts,' we have a striking parallel to Claudio's words, and one which illustrates the interpretation which I have given of them.

At the end of the third Act there are a score or so of octosyllabic lines, within the short space of which we are asked to believe that no less than three passages are hopelessly corrupt. This is such an unusual number of errors at such short intervals, that we are strongly inclined to suspect the judgment of the critics rather than the accuracy of the copyists. It is the practice of expositors to tell us, when they are puzzled for a meaning, that some lines have been lost. This plea cannot be urged here; the lines rhyme, and neither the rhyme, nor the rhythm can reasonably be objected to. Nor can there be any doubt as to the general drift of the passage:

> He who the sword of heaven will bear
> Should be as holy as severe,
> Pattern in himself to know,
> Grace to stand, and virtue go,

can only mean that Heaven's sword-bearer should

have a pattern within himself of what is right, in order that he may know what he ought to do; should have grace in order that he may be able to stand; should have virtue, in order that he may make progress, or, in a word, 'go.' What then is objected to? I suppose it is the insufficiency of the words to convey that meaning, the baldness of the syntax, in fact, the extreme brevity. But this is hardly a fault at all; and Shakespeare sometimes, for force and vigour's sake, hesitates not to carry terseness even to the verge of obscurity. Nor is it to be wondered, if, where the metre is so short, the diction should be a little scanted; the exigency of the rhyme must be taken into account; in octosyllabics there is positively not room for a host of monosyllables; if there is to be much expression, there must be some ellipse. Provided the sense is clear, what matters it if the syntax is a little indistinct? The licence of omission here is not nearly as bold as it is in lines of the same length in 'Pericles.' Whether, then, we consider Shakespeare's general style, or the metrical necessity of this particular passage, we see no sufficient reason for fault-finding here. But a little further on, where we come to the lines,

> O, what may man within him hide,
> Though angel on the outward side!
> How may likeness made in crimes,
> Making practice on the times,
> To draw with idle spiders' strings
> Most ponderous and substantial things!

there does seem something out of joint; we catch
the sense, but we miss the sequence; a finite verb
is wanting. Our first impulse is to look at the
sentence immediately preceding, and borrow, if we
can, a verb for the occasion; but 'hide'—the only
verb available—though it just serves, hardly suits.
What then? Admitting this, have we exhausted
every available resource? Not so: it is a well-
known fact that one verb is sometimes made to serve
for two clauses, which in its strict acceptation
applies only to one of them. The usual plan is to
take out of the verb which is expressed the idea
which is required. We may do so here. 'Dissemble,'
suggested by the verb 'hide,' will answer our
purpose. This is not a Shakespearian peculiarity;
it is not even a poetical license; it is a perfectly
legitimate literary artifice. So then it was not for
the printer, nor for the transcriber, nor even for the
author, unless he chose to do so, to supply a verb—
it is for the good sense of the reader to borrow one.
Nor is this the only way of getting out of the
difficulty; there is another equally possible, if not
equally probable; for do but interpose a hyphen
between the preposition 'to' and the verb 'draw,'
and the infinitive is an infinitive no longer; it
becomes a finite verb; the stone of stumbling is a
stepping stone of progress; examples of such verbs
abound in Chaucer—in Spenser; the reader will
insist on my showing that Shakespeare was not

averse to the use of them; here then are two instances, one of them at any rate uncontroverted and uncontrovertible: 'Merry Wives of Windsor,' Act IV, 4, 57,

> Then let them all encircle him about
> And, fairy-like, to-pinch the unclean knight.

'Pericles,' Act IV, 6, 23,

> Now, the gods to-bless your honour!

If the last-mentioned mode of explaining the passage involves the acceptance of an old fashioned and now disused compound, it must be remembered that archaisms are of more frequent occurrence in the octosyllabic, than they are in the ordinary decasyllabic lines.

But I think I hear the critics say, 'It will not do; it is too far-fetched, too strained, too antiquated.' Well then, if they will yet bear with me a little, I will start one theory more, which shall be simple, easy, unobjectionable, and thoroughly Shakespearian, and one by which I for my part shall be quite willing that the passage shall stand or fall.

Although it is the custom nowadays to omit the preposition 'to' before the infinitive after what are called the auxiliary verbs, such as 'may,' 'can,' 'will,' and the like, yet in the 'antiquary times' this omission was by no means invariable; as a matter of fact, the sign of the infinitive was very frequently inserted. Now Shakespeare, who stands intermediately between the ancients and the moderns, although in this particular he is fortunately more frequently at one with *us*, yet occasionally sides with *them*. This will be found to be mostly the case, where the infinitive precedes the auxiliary, or where it is separated from it by a parenthesis, or by a subordinate clause, or by a succession of subordinate clauses; where, therefore, it was deemed advisable, for clearness' sake, to mark the infinitive by its proper sign. The following passages will strikingly and sufficiently illustrate what I have said: 'Tempest,' Act III, 1, 61-63,

> I would, not so!—and *would* no more *endure*
> This wooden slavery than *to suffer*
> The flesh-fly blow my mouth.

'Comedy of Errors,' Act V, 1, 14-16,

> I wonder much
> That you *would put* me to this shame and trouble,
> And, not without some scandal to yourself,
> With circumstance and oaths so *to deny*
> This chain which now you wear so openly.

'All's Well That Ends Well,' Act II, 5, 52,

I have spoken better of you than you have or *will to deserve* at my hand.

'2 Henry VI,' Act II, 1, 127-28,

If thou hadst been born blind, thou *mightst* as well *have known* all our names as thus *to name* the several colours we do wear.

'2 Henry IV, Act I, 2, 213,

> To approve my youth further, *I will not.*

'Troilus and Cressida,' Act V, 1, 104,

> I *will rather leave* to see Hector, than not *to dog* him.

'Othello,' Act I, 3, 191,

> I *had rather to adopt* a child than *get* it.

Pericles, Act II, 5, 16, 17,

> *She'll wed* the stranger knight,
> Or never more *to view* nor day nor light.

These quotations—and more might be added—may be compared to so many scattered rays, which, when taken one by one, throw but a pale and doubtful light over the obscurity of our way, but, when concentrated, they supply a powerful illuminating body, which shows up every part clearly and distinctly. With a change of times forms of speech have changed; and what the most sagacious critics have toiled in vain to discover was apprehended readily and at once in Shakespeare's time by every blockhead, who could pay his shilling to secure a seat in the theatre. Nor should *we* have remained so long in the darkness of ignorance, had half as much time been spent in mastering Shakespeare's style, and marking his phraseology, as in presupposing corruption, and busying ourselves in either pulling down, or building up, each according to the fashion of his own fancy. The distance of the infinitive from the auxiliary, on which it depends, explains and excuses the interposition of 'to' between 'may' and 'draw.' The passage is sound sans crack or flaw.

The Act closes with

> So disguise may, by the disguised,
> Pay with falsehood false exacting,
> And perform an old contracting.

'Disguised' has been suspected, because 'disguise' immediately precedes. The suspicion is unreasonable. *The repetition is in harmony with the character of the piece.* The play is full of disguises. Isabella disguised her real intentions, and promised to meet Angelo, though she never had any intention of meeting him; Mariana disguised herself, and personated Isabella; in *this* word the former, in *that* the latter is probably alluded to. I am fully aware, however, that the *Duke* was the disguised figure *par excellence* of the play; it was *he* who moved behind the scenes, and took his full share in the development of the plot; *he* trapped, caught, and convicted the hypocrite; through *him* the old contract was consummated. If any, therefore, choose to insist that 'the disguised' points rather to the *Duke* than to Mariana, though I do not myself prefer that view, I will not take upon myself to say that it is impossible.

THE COMEDY OF ERRORS.

In 'The Comedy of Errors' I should not think it necessary to say a word on Act I, 1, 37-39,

> In Syracusa was I born, and wed
> Unto a woman, happy but for me,
> And by me, had not our hap been bad,

if the writer of the second Folio had not, by interpolating 'too' after 'by me' in the last line, sown a suspicion, which has since taken root and grown, that the metre is defective. But, if defect there were, it would not be set right by a miserable expletive. As a matter of fact, there is no defect; the line may be scanned as an Iambic Dimeter, or 'our' may pass, as it does sometimes, as a dissyllable, and then we have a line of the ordinary length.

Nor in Act I, 2, 35-38, where we read

> I to the world am like a drop of water
> That in the ocean seeks another drop,
> Who, falling there to find his fellow forth,
> Unseen, inquisitive, confounds himself,

is there any need to disturb the text, although Mr. Spedding has actually been commended for proposing to put 'in search' in the place of 'unseen;' Mr. Staunton would change the punctuation to 'Unseen inquisitive!' while another ingenious critic cuts 'forth' in half, and, leaving the preposition 'for' at the end of the line, tacks on the definite article to the beginning of the next. Strange hallucination! 'Unseen' is a participial adjective, used absolutely, and refers not to the drop that seeks, but to the fellow drop that is sought; 'his fellow having been unseen by him,' or, to put it more colloquially, 'without having seen his fellow, in his inquisitiveness, he confounds himself.' A person, not intimately acquainted with Shakespeare's style, will hesitate to believe that a participle can stand thus abrupt and isolated, without any thing for it to refer to, save what the wit of the reader can supply from the context; I can only refer him at present to King Richard II, Act III, 2, 168, where 'humour'd' stands in the same bare fashion; but I promise him, that, as I proceed with my examination of the several plays, I will point out, and comment on, not one instance only, but several most remarkable ones, which will satisfy him that the way, in which I propose to construe 'unseen' here, is neither unprecedented nor impossible.

Having disposed of these two small outlying questions, I will proceed to grapple with a real difficulty in Adriana's speech in Act II, 1, 103-115, in the latter part of which it is certain that some explanation, some think that some emendation is absolutely required.

I will leave it to others to estimate the worth of Pope's extraordinary version, which is chiefly remarkable for its bold violation of the text of the original copies; it will be sufficient to ponder the more modest proposals of soberer emendators, who for the most part confine themselves to the single alteration of 'where' 'to wear' in the 112th line; though Theobald in the same line, to make the sense clear, and the metre complete, after 'and' introduced 'so.' The whole passage is thus set down in the 'Globe' Shakespeare:

> Unfeeling fools can with such wrongs dispense.
> · I know his eye doth homage otherwhere:
> Or else what lets it but he would be here?
> Sister, you know he promised me a chain;
> Would that alone, alone he would detain,
> So he would keep fair quarter with his bed!
> I see the jewel best enamelled
> Will lose his beauty; yet the gold bides still,
> That others touch, and often touching will
> † Wear* gold: and no man that hath a name,
> By falsehood and corruption doth it shame.
> Since that my beauty cannot please his eye,
> I'll weep what's left away, and weeping die.

· Now here there are three distinct questions which present themselves for consideration. In the first place, is any addition to the line necessary for the metre's sake—in other words, has a monosyllable fallen out which originally stood there? Secondly,

---

* will, Where Ff.

should 'wear' of the emendators supersede 'where' of the Folios? Thirdly, what is it that Adriana under the veil of metaphor really says?

The first question I answer in the negative; nothing has been omitted; nothing needs be added; the line may remain precisely as we find it, and yet be pronounced metrically complete. How can this be? I answer that 'gold' may be ranked among that numerous class of words, which, either from the length of time that it takes to pronounce them, or from a dissyllabic sound, which they seem to have, when distinctly pronounced, or from the emphasis which properly belongs to them in the position in which they stand, are *permitted* to have, so far as the metre is concerned, a dissyllabic value; this is known to be the case with such words as 'fire,' 'hour,' 'sour,' 'year,' 'near,' 'aches.' I think I shall be able to show that the same privilege is enjoyed by 'cold,' and if by 'cold,' why not by 'gold' also?

Now it is not a little singular that there are no less than four lines in Shakespeare, having 'cold' in them, which lack their full quantum of syllables, and on that account have been sought to be corrected by emendators, or have been stigmatized by them as incorrigible. Take for example the following lines from 'All's Well That Ends Well, Act I, 1, 115,

>   Virtue's steely bones
> Look bleak i' the cold wind; withal, full oft we see
> Cold wisdom waiting on superfluous folly.

Here the second line is too short to be an Alexandrine, too long to be a line of the ordinary measure; but let 'cold' be tantamount to a dissyllable, and we have a capital Alexandrine, which, so far as poetic expression is concerned, cannot be surpassed. It may be objected that 'cold' on its second occurrence is used strictly as a monosyllable, but the objection will not hold; for Shakespeare does not scruple to use the same word in two different ways even in the same line.

Consider next the following line from I Henry IV, Act IV, 3, 7,

> You speak it out of fear and cold heart.

Here again we have the word 'cold,' and significantly enough, along with it, a seeming defect of metre. This instance is in some respects remarkable; for it might easily be supposed—nay, it has actually been conjectured—that the indefinite article has been accidentally omitted before 'cold'; but against this theory it may be urged that in another part of the play, where the same phrase occurs—this time, however, in prose, not in verse—where, therefore, the presence or absence of the article can be of no metrical moment, and where perhaps we should rather have expected it than otherwise, the article does not appear; the words are in all respects just as they are here. I refer to that part of Hotspur's soliloquy, where he says, 'in very sincerity of fear and cold heart.' I think it probable, therefore, that we should in this, as in the former instance, lengthen the metre not by introducing the article, but by treating 'cold' as virtually a dissyllable. At the same time I am aware that it would be possible to find the needful extra syllable in 'fear' rather than in 'cold;' but I do not rest my case on a single line, but on a succession of lines, so that, should one fail me, I have others to prop me up.

My third instance I fetch from 3 Henry VI, Act IV, 3, 14,

> While he himself keeps in the cold field.

An additional syllable is plainly wanted here. At one time I was tempted to think that 'cold' must be a noun substantive, and that 'a-field' must have been the word that originally followed it; but I now look to the adjective 'cold' for a solution of the difficulty.

Lastly, there is the witch's line in 'Macbeth,' Act IV, 1, 6, which almost every critic is shocked at, but not one is venturesome enough to meddle with,

> Toad that under cold stone.

Here, then, are four lines out of four different plays, where, the same word recurring, the same peculiarity also recurs. What shall we say? Can the apparent metrical deficiency be imputed in every one of these instances to chance?—to inaccuracy on the part of the transcriber? Would it not with much more probability be ascribed to a license known to exist in

Shakespeare's versification, whereby a monosyllable is sometimes treated as a dissyllable, a dissyllable as a trisyllable, and even a trisyllable as a quadrisyllable? There is no question that such a licence exists; the only question is whether 'cold' is a word which has it; if so, 'gold,' which, barring a letter, is a facsimile of it, may have it also. It is better in my opinion to explain the difficulty so than to import an adventitious word into the text.

With respect to the second question, which I proposed for consideration, whether 'where' or 'wear' be the true reading, it will not be necessary for me to enter upon any lengthy inquiry, nor even to come to any definite decision, as the explanation which I shall give will *admit* equally of either, though there will be some little difference in the meaning, according as we prefer this word or that. If with the Folios we read 'where,' 'touching' will have to be taken not as a verbal noun, but as a participle used absolutely, in which case the sense will be, 'though people often touch, gold will bide, where it is gold, and not adulterate metal,' and the stops will have to be shifted thus,

> That others touch, and, often touching, will,
> Where gold.

Having now cleared away, as I believe, all obstructions in respect of the metre, and in respect of the reading, I will address myself to the more important, and not less arduous task of explaining the drift of Adriana's parabolic utterances. Under the figure of a jewel best enamelled losing its beauty I think she refers to her own precious person of matchless workmanship,. which, partly through the touch of time, but principally through the lapse of her husband's regard, no longer retained the delicacy of outline and consummate beauty which it once possessed; and this view of the passage agrees with what she presently says in no ambiguous language,

> Since that *my beauty cannot please his eye*,
> I'll weep *what's left* away, and weeping die.

Further, under the figure of gold biding still, she signifies that, though her fair enamel was no longer what it had been, the material on which it had been wrought had not deteriorated; the underlying golden metal still remained; her fine moral and mental faculties had lost none of their pristine excellence; the wear of time, the rough dirty fingers of the world, had had no power over *them*; inwardly, if not outwardly, she retained all her original charms— the essence of true beauty: and here let the reader choose, whether 'wear' shall have the ascendancy, in which case Adriana would hint that that precious part of her, which had not been impaired, might not for ever be proof against the rough collisions of the world; or whether 'where' should be allowed to remain fixed, in which case she would protest, that the fine gold of her inner self, come what might, would bide still, undimmed, undiminished. Turning then from reference to herself to reference to her husband, she says that, even if he did not respect his wife's golden qualities, he should have some regard to his own good name, and not suffer it to be tarnished by corruption and falsehood, which no man of respectability would voluntarily endure.

Such I conceive to be the most probable interpretation of the passage; but there is just a possibility that, after alluding to *herself* under the figure of a *jewel* best enamelled, which she perceives may lose its beauty, as in her husband's eye she seemed to have lost hers, under the figure of *gold* she may refer to her *husband*, who, although owing to the robustness of his constitution he showed as yet no signs of wear,—and now I cheerfully accept the word of the emendators—yet would, she intimates, in spite of the natural hardness of his metal, most certainly become depreciated, if he persisted in his adulterous connections, albeit regard for his fair fame should of *itself* be sufficient to keep him from the ways of corruption and falsehood.

We may now read on without let or hindrance, till we come to Act IV, 1, 96, where, Antipholus of Ephesus and Dromio of Syracuse stumbling against each other, everything as usual goes wrong.

    Ant. E. Thou drunken slave, I sent thee for a rope
             And told thee to what purpose and what end.
    Dro. S. You sent me for a rope's end as soon:
             You sent me to the bay, sir, for a bark.

The first line of Dromio's reply lacks the usual number of feet, but I do not say that it cannot stand for all that; yet it is possible that it may have met with an accident; and it is certain that Dromio's retort would not have been less spirited and effective, if he had said,

> You sent me for a rope! rope's end as soon!

But to import a word into the line, and to alter the punctuation, without a single copy of the Folio on my side, and with, in all probability, a whole army of critics arrayed against me, is more than I can hope to carry; without, therefore, insisting on this change, I will advocate another, for which I expect to secure the suffrages of at any rate a very respectable minority.

In Act IV, 3, 12-20, we find the following dialogue between the Syracusan Antipholus and the Syracusan Dromio:

Dro. S. Master, here's the gold you sent me for. What! have you got the picture of old Adam new-apparelled?

Ant. S. What gold is this? What Adam dost thou mean?

Dro. S. Not that Adam that kept the Paradise, but that Adam that keeps the prison: he that goes in the calf-skin that was killed for the Prodigal; he that came behind you, sir, like an evil angel, and bid you forsake your liberty.

What are we to make of Dromio's question, 'Have you got the picture of old Adam, new-apparelled?' Theobald, who was usually as sharp in detecting error, as he was shrewd in emending it, took the bull by the horns, and boldly stuffed in two new words, 'Have you got *rid of* the picture of old Adam, &c. ?' There is little doubt that there is something wrong. The vicious word, the impostor of the text, is, I believe, 'picture,' which has been suffered to creep in, and filch the place of some other word, similar to it in form, but vastly different from it in meaning. What can that word be? Change the labial *p* into the labial *v*, and, as it were by magic, 'picture' is metamorphosed to 'victure.' Now, precisely as 'augury'—this we have on incontestable authority—was sometimes written 'augure,' so I have little doubt that 'victory' was set down in this passage in what to us would be the strange guise of 'victure.' Hence arose the mistake. 'Picture' is a blunder for 'victory," which may have been so pronounced as to be heard as, or (which is perhaps more likely) so misformed as to be mistaken by the reader for 'picture.' Dromio, on his return, finding the officer no longer with Antipholus, asks him whether he had got the victory of this old Adam in new apparel. 'Victory' is the word that exactly suits the passage, and 'victory,' I am pretty sure, was the word that was set down in the author's original MS. Should we not now restore it to its rightful place?

There is one more passage which I have to notice before I have done with 'The Comedy of Errors.' In

Act V, 1, 400-406, the Abbess is represented as saying,

> Thirty-three years have I but gone in travail
> Of you, my sons; and till this present hour
> My heavy burthen ne'er delivered.
> The Duke, my husband, and my children both,
> And you the calendars of their nativity,
> Go to a gossips' feast, and go with me,
> After so long grief, such nativity.

It has been thought highly improbable, that Shakespeare, after commencing a line with 'Go to a gossips' feast,' should have ended it with 'and go with me.' Hence various emendations have sprung up, amongst which Dr. Johnson's 'and gaud with me' is most conspicuous. But a little consideration, I think, will satisfy us that the words are not the poor weak repetition that some fancy.

Here was a woman, who for many a long year had lived a conventual life, devoting herself to prayers and charitable deeds; all of a sudden a discovery is made, which restores to her her husband, her sons, and, we may almost say, herself to herself. [The cause of her seclusion has ceased to exist; the time of her joy has come; not only does she encourage others to go to a feast, but *she herself now will go with them*—'Go with me'—she cries—'with me, with me, the Abbess! for I also will go,'

> After so long grief, such nativity!

I have struck out the semicolon which I have found after 'and go with me,' and substituted for it a comma; I have restored the Folios' word 'nativity,' which had been forced to give way to Dr. Johnson's conjecture 'festivity.' An indigenous flower had been eradicated, a sickly exotic planted in its stead. On what ground is 'nativity' objected to? Is it because it is found twice in the short compass of three lines? But this is not sufficient reason for even suspecting it. Such repetitions are occasionally found in the works of all great writers, and of Shakespeare among the rest, of which we could furnish abundant proof; they are not uncommon in familiar conversation, and in dramatic composition, in both of which the language is more or less of an autoschediastic character. With as much reason might 'festivity' be objected to, because in three consecutive lines we should have 'feast,' 'festivity,' 'feast.' 'Nativity' is the dominant idea of the passage. The repetition of the word emphasizes the *double event*. There were two nativities; the one literal, and the other metaphorical. The Abbess, who had not inaptly compared the reappearance of her long lost sons to a regeneration, or second birth of them, repeats more than once, what more than once had happened—more than once she pondered. 'Nativity' was her word—a cry of triumph after her groans of travail—a not unnatural iteration. But let all this go for naught, and still I hold that 'nativity' is not only the right word, but the only word that the context admits of.

The Abbess distinctly indicates (400-402) two operations, which in the course of nature succeed each other—first, the *parturition*,

> Thirty-three years have I but gone in travail
> Of you my sons;

secondly, *the bringing to the birth*,

> and till this present hour
> My heavy burthen ne'er delivered.

When, then, in the lines that follow, she invites the several parties to the feast that was usually celebrated on such occasions, she distinctly intimates, as the reason of their rejoicing, the auspicious termination of those two operations; only what in that place she had called 'thirty-three years of travail,' in this place she calls 'long grief;' what *there* was 'delivery,' *here* is 'nativity.' The two pairs exactly correspond to each other. To put some other word in the place of 'nativity' is to destroy that correspondence: 'such' briefly summarizes the many peculiar circumstances of the delivery, or birth, its long postponement, its extraordinary nature, its providential unexpected jubilant character. This is Shakespeare's meat, and it is infinitely to be preferred to the Schoolmen's porridge.

A MIDSUMMER NIGHT'S DREAM.

In 'Midsummer Night's Dream,' Act II, 1, 54, we are nightmared by a hideous bug of a word, which, although it appears in all the original copies, and has found its way into all the editions, and has not been, so far as I am aware, challenged or suspected by any of the commentators, I am persuaded never formed part of Shakespeare's Dream, nor passed through his brain, nor was authorized by his pen; born of carelessness and ignorance, fostered by diffidence and credulity, it is high time that this monster should be examined, exposed, exorcised from the text, and be replaced by the legitimate offspring of the poet's fancy, whose pretensions I shall now put forward for the first time, and whose rightful title I shall hope to make good, not, I admit, by any direct and positive proofs, but by negative testimony and circumstantial evidence, which in my opinion well deserves to be pondered. The reader will readily call to mind those well-known drolleries spoken by Puck,

> The wisest aunt, telling the saddest tale,
> Sometime for three-foot stool mistaketh me;
> Then slip I from her bum, down topples she,
> And 'tailor' cries, and falls into a cough;
> And then the whole quire hold their hips and laugh,
> And waxen in their mirth and neeze and swear
> A merrier hour was never wasted there.

Now what explanation has the annotator, what explanation has the antiquary to offer of this 'tailor'-cry? Dr. Johnson, the very mention of whose name raises our expectation, a man of indefatigable industry, and extraordinary intellectual ability, who, when he had anything to the purpose to say, both knew how to say it, and said it, has nothing more to communicate to us on this matter than is contained in the following note: 'The custom of crying 'tailor' at a sudden fall backwards I think I remember to have heard. He that slips beside his chair falls as a tailor squats upon his board.' Upon this Mr. Aldis Wright, who would be sure to give us some additional information, if it were possible to give it, drily remarks, 'If this is not the true explanation, it is at least the only one which has been proposed.' And this is all—positively all—not a jot besides! But this is in reality *nothing*; and, when a man like Dr. Johnson can say no more than that '*he thinks he remembers to have heard,*' we may be pretty sure that he had no very great confidence himself in the only explanation which he had it in his power to offer. Is it conceivable—is it likely that, if this cry of 'tailor' had been customary under certain circumstances, and had been sufficiently well-known to have been apprehended at once by an Elizabethan audience, when only thus incidentally alluded to, it would have so utterly died away, as not to have left an echo behind it? that no one should have heard it? no one should know it? Why I venture to say that this is just one of those little bits of fun, which, if it had once been in vogue, would not have been easily forgotten; it would have been talked about, and laughed over, and occasionally practised; it would have passed from sire to son, and been familiar as a household word; instead of which there is no such practice—no trace—no tradition of such practice; it is as if it had never been. Marvellous obliteration indeed! I am little disposed, as a rule, to blench from the undoubted reading of the copies, but I cannot hold fast to the Folio version here. The high probability is that 'tailor' is a spurious word, which through inadvertence has got possession of the place of some other word, not altogether unlike it, but more forcible, and more appropriate. The original genuine word I believe to have been 'traitor.' Such an astounding metamorphosis will not be so much as listened to by many—I cannot expect it to be credited by any without something more than the bare affirmation of the writer. I invite the reader's close attention, therefore, to the following dry but most significant particulars.

In 'Richard II,' Act I, 1, 102, we have an undoubted instance of 'traitor' being spelt in the first Quarto 'taitour.' It is true that in the latter part of the word we have a *t*, and not an *l*, but the second letter of the word, viz., *r*, has been accidentally omitted. In other words, we have a very near approach to 'tailor'; we have a 'traitor' almost dressed up in the disguise of a 'tailor'; and yet no one would be silly enough in *that* passage to say that 'taitour' was meant for 'tailor,' and not rather for 'traitor.' And in this passage in 'Midsummer Night's Dream,' had we 'taitour' rather than 'tailor, no one,. I conceive, would have dreamed of adopting 'tailor' rather than 'traitor.' But, as a matter of fact, we have 'tailor'; we have an *l* in the latter part of the word, and not a *t*. Now a *t* may be so mis-crossed as to be almost a facsimile of *l*. Between a mis-crossed *t* and an *l* there is scarcely any difference; and yet this is all that my conjecture needs to obtain for itself credibility.

I may add that *r* is a letter not unfrequently omitted, when it holds the second place in a word; if the reader will take the great trouble to search, he will certainly find that 'beast' is set down in one place, where there can be no question that 'breast' is intended; that 'fiends' has displaced 'friends'; and that 'Fance' stands for 'France.' As instances of *l* being used, where *t* should have been, we have 'Calues,' where 'Cato's' ('Catue's') is acknowledged to be the true reading; 'succedaul' for 'succedant,' (1 Henry VI); and contrariwise 'untimety' in 'Pericles' is a mistake for 'untimely.' The letters *l* and *t* being frequently confounded, I am supposing no greater error on the part of the copyists, than has actually been made in numbers of places elsewhere. Thus much, then, for the anatomy of the words and the possibility of their having changed places: as regards suitability to the passage, in my opinion, there can be no doubt which should have precedence. Is it likely that this superlatively wise aunt, who had just met with a stunning catastrophe, and who instantly fell a-coughing to hide her confusion, would have compared herself ridiculously to a squatting tailor? Would it not be much more consistent with her disposition, her age, her dignity, and, I may add, with the serious nature of her story, to raise against her invisible foe that fierce cry of 'traitor,' which was wont to be raised against suspected political malcontents? 'Traitor' rests on a distinct historical basis; 'tailor' has for its foundation the great lexicographer's 'I-think-I-remember-to-have-heard'; 'traitor' is intelligible; 'tailor' inexplicable and unaccountable; 'traitor' is full of strength and 'spirit'; 'tailor' is feeble and languid.

In striking the balance between the two, it should not go for nothing, that the first edition of this play, which contains on the whole the best reading, and was possibly, we are told, taken from the author's MS., was *carelessly printed*.

Shall, then, this low squatting word, this word of needle and thread, this long-time impostor, this ridiculous antic which starts up and struts its ugliness before us, be allowed any longer to express the real indignation of a highly dignified deeply injured lady, whom I must think that Shakespeare with inimitable fun made attribute to her fantastic foe a word very different—one, which, at that period, on the occasion of every political peril, was in every one's mouth—of deep political significance and tremendous meaning; as frequently abused as it was frequently used; a terror to the innocent no less than to the guilty—the word 'traitor,' in using which the 'wisest aunt' associated herself with kings and queens and empresses of the earth.

The few small knots that remain may easily be untied, or cut asunder. To begin with a trifling matter of punctuation: in Act III, 2, 13-15, it may be an open question, whether we should point, as the 'Globe' editors do, reproducing, I presume, the punctuation of the Folios,

> The shallowest thick-skin of that barren sort,
> Who Pyramus presented, in their sport
> Forsook his scene, and enter'd in a brake,

or whether we should set the comma after 'sport' rather than after 'presented,' to which mode I myself rather incline; but in Act IV, 1, 150, where the same learned editors put a full stop at the end of the line, I own I have a decided preference for a hyphen, or at any rate for the first Quarto's comma; for no sooner had Lysander uttered the words,

> Without the peril of the Athenian law,

than, having incriminated himself, he is roughly and sharply interrupted by Egeus, who exclaims,

> Enough, enough, my lord ; you have enough :
> I beg the law, the law, upon his head.

A little below, the 163rd line seems to be short of a syllable, not to the detriment of the sense—for Demetrius might well have said that 'his love for Hermia *melted* '—but to the detriment of the metre. What should we do here ? Not surely introduce some fresh word at the beginning of the line before ' melted,' as some have proposed to do, but borrow from the preceding line a syllable which it has in excess of its requirements. The linear boundary is broken up, line melts into line, the words unite their streams, in order that we may have more vividly impressed upon us the dissolution and evanescence of Demetrius' love. The reader, who is accustomed to mark with his eye the division of the lines, may miss a syllable before 'melted,' but, as the actor, entering into the spirit of the poet's conception, disregarded the artificial boundary, and repeated without a moment's pause the words, ' love for Hermia melted,' the metre was as complete to the ear as the most exacting rhythmist could desire. A similar poetic artifice, I think, may sometimes be found elsewhere ; in each case the metre is subordinated to the sense and spirit of the passage. I do not, however, recommend that any alteration should be made in the *writing* of the lines, which may remain just as they are.

A word has, in all probability, been lost in Act V, 1, 56—60,

> 'A tedious brief scene of young Pyramus
> And his love Thisbe; very tragical mirth.'
> Merry and tragical! tedious and brief!
> That is, hot ice and wondrous strange snow.
> How shall we find the concord of this discord?

Sense demands, if scansion does not, that there should be some epithet of 'snow,' as startlingly opposite to the nature of snow, as 'hot,' the epithet of 'ice,' is to the nature of ice. The word, which has no doubt been lost in transcription, was probably a very small one, perhaps with letters, or a sound, corresponding to the termination of the word preceding it. The final letters of 'strange' are *ge*; what word more fully and fairly satisfies the conditions required than the little word 'jet,' used by Shakespeare in 2 Henry VI, Act II, 1, in three consecutive lines,

> *Glou.* What colour is my gown of?
> *Simp.* Black, forsooth; coal black as jet.
> *King.* Why, then, thou know'st what colour jet is of.
> *Suff.* And yet, I think, jet did he never see.

In 'Romeo and Juliet' we read of 'palfreys black as jet.' Perhaps, however, it would be too much to expect editors boldly to print

> That is, hot ice, and, wondrous strange! jet snow,

seeing that 'swart,' 'black,' 'hot,' 'red,'—the poet Claudian makes the snow *blood*-red—might equally fill the gap in the text.

A little further down in the same Act and scene exception has been taken to the 92nd line,

> And what poor duty cannot do, noble respect
> *Takes it in might, not merit,*

on the ground that the antithesis is not sufficiently well sustained. This is not the only passage in Shakespeare where the antitheses have been adversely criticized. Perhaps the critics would do well to consider, whether they themselves may not sometimes be in error in expecting the contrasts to be as sharply defined in a dramatic effusion, as they might not unreasonably expect in a mathematical or philosophical treatise. Anyhow, what Shakespeare says, is one thing; what the critics think he ought to have said, is another. The main drift of the passage is unmistakeable. When persons of feeble power, from a sense of duty, do their best to please, men of noble and generous nature regard not so much the *worth* of the performance, as the *strength*, or perhaps rather the *mighty effort*, of the performers; they accept all in good part, not because it is in the least degree *meritorious*, but because it is the *most* that the actors are capable of. The pith of what is said is summed up in the text, 'she hath done what she could.' A line from 'Julius Cæsar,' Act IV, 3, 261, deserves to be quoted,

> I should not urge thy duty past thy might.

Compare also what is written a few lines above, 78-80,

> And it is nothing, nothing in the world;
> Unless you can find sport in their intents,
> Extremely stretch'd and conn'd with cruel pain,
> To do you service.

THE MERCHANT OF VENICE.

In the 'Merchant of Venice' there is not the least occasion to make any fuss about the little phrase 'worth this' in Act I, 1, 35, as if the meaning were obscure, or a line had been lost! If Salarino chose to indicate the untold wealth, which lay in the noble vessel's bottom, by the modest method of a demonstrative pronoun and a significant gesture, rather than by an enumeration of so many ducats, who but an Income Tax Commissioner has any right to complain? 'It is not worth *that*' is a phrase as common as it is intelligible. Our appraisement of the rich freight of silks and spices is enhanced rather than otherwise by the indefiniteness with which it is described. And yet, as compared with 'nothing,' 'this' has almost an appreciable value. Plays were written for the stage, not for the study. The actor could give a good account of 'this,' if the annotator cannot. The deictic use of the pronoun is eminently dramatic.

Nor in Act II, 7, 69, is there any need, either for the prosody, or for the syntax, to foist into the text Dr. Johnson's conjecture 'tombs' in lieu of

Gilded *timber* do worms infold.

If it be objected that the second syllable of 'timber,' occurring in the central pause of the verse, violates the cæsura, and is a metrical superfluity, how, then, are we to deal with those numerous lines in Shakespeare, where the termination of 'father,' 'brother,' 'daughter,' 'spinster,' 'speaker,' 'sworder,' 'thunder'—all quotations—is equally censurable or equally justifiable? What is admitted in a decasyllabic line, must be admitted in a heptasyllabic. The termination of 'timber' may be so slurred—'timbre'—as to be almost annihilated in pronunciation; or 'timber' may form part of a dactyl in the second place, or an Anapæst in the third; the melody of the verse is not marred by such occasional variations. As for the concord, the plural idea contained in 'timber' justifies the use of a plural verb following it. Even in itself the word strikes me as preferable to the great Lexicographer's. It is simple, quaint, original, expressive; it has a smack of the antique, and a sepulchral significance.

I am not sure that a little irony was not intended by the rich coffin being described as mere 'gilded timber.' All the copies both of the Quarto and of the Folio have it. Their combined authority should have been sufficient to save it from being ostracized from the text.

With more reason it has been asked, how are we to understand the words that are printed in italics

in the passage that I shall next quote from Act III,
2, 97-101 ?

> Thus ornament is but the guiled shore
> To a most dangerous sea ; the beauteous scarf
> Veiling an *Indian beauty;* in a word,
> The seeming truth which cunning times put on
> To entrap the wisest.

The beauteous scarf raises a presumption that the figure veiled by it is a thing of beauty; the context requires that it should be *no beauty at all*, or, if a beauty, one of such a questionable kind, that, notwithstanding her beauty, she would be not an object of **desire**. It has been thought that '*Indian*,' parted off by a semicolon from 'beauty,' would satisfy the conditions required, but that 'Indian *beauty*' cannot. Is this so? The stress is on the epithets; it was not the sea in itself that was objected to, but the kind of sea; nor yet the beauty, but the kind of beauty; the sea was dangerous; the beauty 'Indian,' and 'Indian' was synonymous with 'coloured,' and colour was detested — many yet living know how cordially—by a white-skinned race. But in the reign of Queen Elizabeth the prejudice against colour far exceeded any thing that we can dream of in these more civilized and catholic times; '*Indian* beauty' would be received with disappointment, with aversion, with disgust. In this very play Portia says of the Prince of Morocco that, even if he had the condition of a saint, in respect of his complexion, she should regard him as a *devil*. Colour alone, be it observed, would be sufficient to damn him. Would facial beauty redeem, when moral beauty could not? Not the grandest contour of countenance, not the most finely-moulded features, not the most pleasing expression would compensate in the eyes of Shakespeare's contemporaries for that fatal stain in the skin, which nothing could obliterate. The most celestial seraph, if of the wrong colour, if dusky, would be pronounced a spirit of darkness. 'Sooty bosom'—'tawny front'—'swarthy complexion'—'woman coloured ill'—such are some of the expressions which attest the feeling in Shakespeare's day. The beauteous scarf indeed would well beseem an Indian *beauty*; the scarf would strike the eye at once, and raise the expectation; but, the moment it was withdrawn, what a contrast! the '*beauty*' would be lost in the *colour of her skin*.

This explanation seems to me sufficient, but to those who are not yet satisfied I will offer, as an alternative, another explanation, which is formed on considerations derived from Indian idiosyncracy. I shall suppose that the physiological rather than the physiognomical features are alluded to; the Indian's soul was as dark as his body; his character as evil-hued as his complexion—such at least was the vulgar prejudice. It is not a little curious that, whenever Shakespeare makes mention of *Indian*, he

almost invariably does so in terms of disparagement!
'Savages and men of Ind' are coupled together in
the 'Tempest'; in 'Love's Labour's Lost' we read of
'rude and savage men of Ind ;' in 'Othello,' 'base' is
the epithet attributed to him; in 'King Henry
VIII' the allusion is disgustingly contemptuous.
Now, if such were the estimation in which the Indian
men were held, is it likely that the Indian *women*
would be more highly accounted? Where the men
are bad, the women are generally worse. And the noted
beauty—she who was admired, courted, beautifully
scarved and apparelled—*she* would be sure to have
her full share of feminine weakness, and feminine
wickedness—aye, and would be credited with having
it. Deceitful as the serpent, stealthy as the tiger,
their natures hot and fiery, their sunshine uncertain
and transient, their tempers liable to sudden and
violent outbursts, their rage like the hurricane, their
passions like the tempest—these eastern Jezebels
might not unnaturally be regarded as not less dangerous than the dangerous sea with its guiled
shore, which had just been previously mentioned.
It was some such a one as this, albeit a 'brow of
Egypt,' who wrang from Antony the cry,

         Betray'd I am.
O this false soul of Egypt! this grave charm,—
Whose eyes becked forth my wars, and call'd them home;
Whose bosom was my crownet, my chief end—
Like a right gipsy, hath, at fast and loose,
Beguiled me to the very heart of loss.

If, then, 'Indian' may hold its place by reason of the infamy which was usually associated with the name by Shakespeare's contemporaries, much more may 'Indian beauty' be tolerated, because such a one might be regarded, and justly regarded, as a dangerous body, an arch and subtle seductress, a very mouth of hell, and dark pit of perdition. If, however, 'beauty' may not pass, taken in connexion with 'Indian,' not all the acting and authority of Mr. Irving will induce us to retain it, divorced by Theobald's semicolon from that adjective.

Notwithstanding the strictures of certain critics, I cannot see anything that is amiss in the following lines from Act III, 2, 160—167,

>   But the full sum of me
> Is sum of *something, which, to term in gross,
> Is an unlesson'd girl, unschool'd, unpractis'd;
> Happy in this, she is not yet so old
> But she may learn; happier than this,
> She is not bred so dull but she can learn;
> Happiest of all is that her gentle spirit
> Commits itself to yours to be directed,
> As from her lord, her governor, her king.

Portia's meaning is clear enough. Whether we read 'something' with the Quarto, or 'nothing' with the Folio, will depend on whether we reckon an 'unlesson'd girl, unschool'd, unpractis'd,' to be a small entity, or an utter nonentity. Either is tolerable,

---

* So Q.

but there is more sense in the former, to which, therefore, I give the preference. The occurrence of a short line in the passage affords no reasonable ground for suspecting its integrity. While, as for the sentences, in which the ascending scale of happiness is described, if they are not modelled in that precise form, which has since become common, they are none the less likely on that account to have been Shakespeare's, as his patterns, his style, his workmanship almost invariably bear the impress of originality.

Different opinions have been entertained concerning the punctuation in Act III, 3, 26—29. I conceive that Antonio was intended to say that the duke could not refuse to let the law take its course, because of the commercial dealings which strangers had with the Venetians; if law were denied, the *denial* would greatly reflect on the justice of the state. Accordingly, the colon, which I find at the end of the first line, I transfer to the middle of the third;

> The duke cannot deny the course of law
> For the commodity that strangers have
> With us in Venice : if it be denied,
> Will much impeach the justice of his state.

It was the omission of the pronoun-subject in the last line, which caused editors to punctuate otherwise: they could only find a subject for the verb 'impeach' in the noun 'commodity;' yet they might have recollected such texts as

> By my troth, 's not so good;
> > 'Much Ado About Nothing,' Act III, 4, 9, 19;
>
> 'Tis his own blame; hath put himself from rest;
> > 'King Lear,' Act II, 4, 293;
>
> *Brut:* Has said enough.
> *Sic:* Has spoken like a traitor, and shall answer
> As traitors do.
> > 'Coriolanus,' Act III, 1, 161—62;

and 'Merchant of Venice,' Act I, 1, 98; 'King Henry VIII,' Act III, 1, 119; 'Pericles,' Act II, 1, 60. Capell, I find, long ago proposed the same arrangement; only he, at a loss for a nominative case for the verb 'impeach,' fabricated one, reading ''Twill impeach.' This interpolation vitiated an otherwise faultless proposal.

Am I too easily satisfied, or are the critics too fastidious, I in accepting, they in rejecting the little phrase 'mean it' in the following passage?—Act III, 5, 78-83—

> It is very meet
> The lord Bassanio live an upright life;
> For, having such a blessing in his lady,
> He finds the joys of heaven here on earth;
> And if on earth he do not mean it, then
> In reason he should never come to heaven.

Why should not 'mean it' refer to the words contained in the second of the above lines, and be a concise mode of saying, 'mean to live an upright life.'? The expression is one which is in common parlance, and I need scarcely say that the theatre echoes the language of the people.

All the Folios and all the Quartos have 'masters' in Act IV, 1, 50,

> For affection,
> Masters of passion, sways it to the mood
> Of what it likes or loathes.

Yet in many editions 'mistress' is the established reading. Perhaps 'masters' was a typographical error for 'master,' the masculine form serving equally for both genders—Portia speaks of herself as '*master* of her servants'—perhaps 'masters' may be not a noun at all, but a verb, followed by the preposition 'of,' just as 'like,' 'bear,' 'determine,' 'desire,' and many other verbs are in Shakespeare. We may allow for the use of an archaism, if it is authorized by all the copies, if it is susceptible of explanation, if it can be fortified with analogous examples. Our smooth and uniform emendations poorly replace the rough, vigorous, oft-varying phraseology of the great master whose works we presume to criticize.

The last passage that I shall notice is in Act IV, 1, 379, where I demur both to the punctuation and to the explanation given by the Cambridge editors, and I acquiesce in Mr. Knight's more correct arrangement.

> So please my lord the Duke and all the court
> To quit the fine for one half of his goods;
> I am content, so he will let me have
> The other half in use, to render it,
> Upon his death, unto the gentleman
> That lately stole his daughter.

Antonio intercedes with the Duke to remit the public fine altogether, expressing himself as satisfied, if his adversary would let him have the portion, which the law awarded *him*, in *use*. To have said that he was content that the Duke should remit the fine would have been to impertinently interfere with the Duke's prerogative.

But what does he mean by his having the other half in *use*? Does Antonio suggest that Shylock should lend him *gratis* that half of his fortune, which he (Antonio) might legally have appropriated, but his legal right to which he had waived on the understanding that it should fall to Lorenzo and Jessica at Shylock's death? But this would be a queer sort of '*favour*'—the word is Antonio's own—and would be neither very disinterested, nor very generous. Was it Antonio's wish, then, to be a sort of trustee of the money for Lorenzo and Jessica—for this view has been taken by some—not, I suppose, letting it lie idle, but making it productive, either by lending it out at interest, or, if it be thought that Antonio would not do that, by trading with it—anyhow reserving it, whether the principal only, or both principal and interest, for Shylock's son-in-law and daughter at Shylock's death? But neither can I see in what sense *this* would be a *favour* done to the Jew.

What, then, was the favour which the Jew and his race would both understand and thoroughly appreciate? Why, plainly, that the half, which Antonio might have alienated from him, should be *his* still, not in respect of the principal, but in respect of the interest, which Antonio, using the principal, undertook to pay him, promising to hand over the whole to the young people at Shylock's death. But it has been objected that such an arrangement would be opposed to Antonio's principles and practice. True; but Antonio himself tells us, that he would 'break a custom,' and pay Shylock interest, in order to supply the 'ripe wants of a friend;' and he would not scruple to 'break the custom' yet again, in order to ensure a provision for Lorenzo and Jessica—a provision quite independent of what Shylock possessed, which, though settled on the young couple by deed, could not be said to be *certain*, as Shylock, though he would not squander it, might by misadventure lose it. Antonio's wish was to let Shylock have a life-interest in what, as having been given back to him, could only be regarded as his; yet at the same time to secure the principal for the Jew's kith and kin, lest, taking vengeance on them, he should disinherit them. What advantage, then, it has been asked, what present advantage had Lorenzo and Jessica; I might answer that they had expected none—they wanted none. Jessica was Lorenzo's golden treasure, more precious to him than argosies and ducats. But, though he had no *present* advantage, he had a fortune in prospect; he was sure of what was in

Antonio's safe-keeping; he was entitled also by deed to what Shylock might die possessed of. Hence, when Nerissa says,

> There do I give to you and Jessica,
> From the rich Jew, a special deed of gift,
> After his death, of all he dies possessed of,

Lorenzo replies,

> Fair ladies, you drop manna in the way
> Of starved people.

AS YOU LIKE IT.

There is no question about the meaning— there should be none about the punctuation and construction of the opening lines of 'As You Like It' (Act I, 1, 1-5). We have merely to put a semicolon after 'fashion,' and to suppose that the pronoun, the subject of the verb 'bequeathed,' has been omitted, not accidentally by the transcriber, but designedly by the author, and the play will commence in that easy familiar colloquial style, which is characteristic of Shakespeare, and as might be expected in an interchange of words between an old servant and his young master:

> As I remember, Adam, it was upon this fashion; bequeathed me by will but poor a thousand crowns, and, as thou sayest, charged my brother, on his blessing, to breed me well: and there begins my sadness.

Some have fancied, because the initial letters of 'bequeathed' bear a near resemblance to the pronoun 'he,' that the pronoun may have been omitted in the copying by mistake, but I have already hinted that there is *reason*, and I may now add that there is abundant Shakesperian *precedent*, for the ellipse, while there is neither authority *here*, nor yet absolute necessity for its expression.

In Act II, 4, 1, Rosalind's exclamation, 'How *merry* are my spirits!' has been changed by editors into 'How *weary* are my spirits!' Such a radical change, if not demanded by urgent necessity, cannot be too strongly reprobated. I confess that I cannot see sufficient justification for taking so great a liberty with the text. We may grant that Rosalind was as weary as any of the little band, but between feeling weary and making an avowal of weariness there is a vast difference. It is scarcely credible that Rosalind would be the first to show the white feather, and demoralize by her example the whole company; her character as a woman, the character which she assumed as a man, forbid us to think so; she made light of difficulty, and laughed at misfortune; and *this*, quite as much because she was the high-spirited girl that she was, as because she felt that it devolved upon her to encourage the others. It is true that she said to Touchstone—

> I could find in my heart to disgrace my man's apparel, and to cry like a woman;

but this admission, itself redolent of fun, and provocative of laughter, was wrung from her sympathy by a plaint which he had uttered—and marvellously well was it timed to brace him up, and make him speak and act like a man—but immediately after, as

if repenting of her own confession, she justified her
first utterance by adding,

> But I must comfort the weaker vessel, as doublet and hose
> ought to show itself courageous to petticoat.

Why, then, have editors altered the reading of the
Folios? I presume, because Touchstone in his
answer happens to mention the word 'weary.' But
Touchstone's confession of leg-weariness is no proof
that Rosalind complained of spirit-weariness; the
most that Touchstone's words can prove is that
Rosalind made some allusion to the state of her
spirits: *she* struck a cheerful note; *he* a mournful
one; this chimes in with her *finale* to Touchstone,
'Aye, be content, good Touchstone,' which I may
here parody by saying, 'Be content, good *critics*.'

But the passage in the play, which of all others
has excited the most lively discussion, and has
occasioned the greatest diversity of opinion, and
which certainly requires comment, perhaps change,
occurs in Act II, 7, 53-57, in the course of a famous
speech of Jaques:

> He that a fool doth very wisely hit
> Doth very foolishly, although he smart,
> Seem senseless of the bob; if not,
> The wise man's folly is anatomized
> Even by the squandering glances of the fool.

Here the critics, chafing at what they are pleased to
call the 'halting sense and limping metre,' change
'seeme senselesse,' which is the exact reading of the

Folios, into '*Not to* seem senseless,' which is Theobald's conjecture; but not even Theobald's great name can reconcile us to to such a startling innovation, unless it be dictated by imperious necessity. Does, then, the line really need Theobald's crutch? may it not stand without any such artificial prop, and *that*, without resorting to the questionable ruse of connecting 'very foolishly' with the subordinate clause that follows? It is not at all surprising that '*very wisely*' should be applied to the fool, seeing that, with an arrow shot at a venture, he had well hit a weak joint in the wise man's harness; but it does seem at first sight a little strange that '*very foolishly*'—which is plainly opposed to '*very wisely*'—should be attributed to the wise man. It certainly was *not* foolish of the wise man to counterfeit insensibility; for it would certainly never have done for him to lay himself open to a fool, who would have covered him with mud, and crowed over him eternally, on the strength of having, at a chance gathering, by a chance utterance of the moment, touched some exceptional weakness in his character; nor can the allusion be to any awkwardness, or sheepishness, as we sometimes term it, of look and manner on the part of the wise man, while he strove to hide the workings of his heart; for this would not have escaped the sharp eye of the fool, and would only have made him more than ever a butt for ridicule. No; the force of the words lies not in the *fact* of his dissembling, but in the *fashion*—the *manner* of it. He is hit, yet he cries, 'Ha! ha! ha!' he smarts, yet he smiles; he is lashed, yet he laughs; any amount of castigation he is ready to face out with any amount of cachinnation; no one knows it but himself; but, if it were possible for one, after observing his face and manner, to look into his heart, and see there the true state of the case, how that his laughter was forced and his mirth simulated; that he was a masquer and mummer for the nonce, in order not to be made a fool of to no purpose by a fool, would he not admit that, though there was wisdom in the dissembling, there was *very foolishness* in the *manner* of it; yet this show of folly, this foolishness of laughter, was his only chance, situated as he was. Well, then, he made a virtue of necessity—put a fool's vizor on his face, and acted like a wise man. The end justified the means.

A little further down, in Jaques' speech, there is another line, which has been turned and twisted in every imaginable way by the emendators, without having been straightened to the satisfaction of any of them. It is the last line of the following passage,

> Why, who cries out on pride
> That can therein tax any private party?
> Doth it not flow as hugely as the sea,
> Till that *the wearie verie meanes* do ebb?

In this case the critics do not quarrel with the *short* line of the passage; what they object to is the 'words' printed in italics, and yet not so much the words themselves, as the peculiar collocation of them —the interposition of the adjective 'very' between 'the weary' on the one hand, and 'means' on the other. But, supposing that it were intended to lay special emphasis on 'means,' where could 'very' have stood more fitly than where it now stands? Had it been placed immediately after the definite article, and before the adjective 'weary,' it would most certainly have been taken for nothing more than an adverb intensifying the adjective 'weary.' As it is, there is no possibility of any such misapprehension; there is no ambiguity; its position effectually ministers to its purpose, which is to emphasize the noun 'means,' and the noun 'means' requires emphasization. For is it not strange that the great sea should have its limits, its billows should weary and break, its swellings should subside; yet of *pride* there should be no abatement, weariness, or cessation? Not from want of *will* does it fail, but only from want of '*means*'—'means' referring partly, perhaps, to the person's physical powers, but also, as the context shows, to his purse and property. Now the eccentric position, and undoubted force of 'very,' cause the necessary stress to be laid on 'means.' The very means of pride must weary and ebb, ere its great swelling flood subside. Not much unlike is the position of 'very' in the phrase, '*this same very day*,' which actually occurs in ' King

Richard III.' The explanation which I have given seems reasonable and sufficient; yet the notion, that the line is faulty, has got such a grip on the critics, that probably a new generation must arise, before the mists of prejudice will be dissipated, and the place will have a chance of being looked at in the clear atmosphere of an impartial judgment.

I cannot go with Mr. Aldis Wright, when, in annotating on Rosalind's words, 'one inch of delay is a South-sea of discovery,' in Act III, 2, 207, he says, 'If you delay the least to satisfy my curiosity, I shall ask you in the interval so many questions, that to answer them will be like embarking on a voyage of discovery over a wide and unknown ocean.' It seems to me that, just as we, when on the tiptoe of expectation, are wont to say, 'Every minute seems an age,' so she, taking, however, jocularly as her unit of measurement inches rather than minutes, protests that she is so eager to know, who the forest poet is, that a single *inch* of further delay would be to her as a vast unmeasurable distance, involving infinite unconscionable delay—in fact, (and here there is an allusion to one of the great wonders of the day,) it would be to her as it were a '*South sea of discovery.*' Such, and no less, would be the delay, as measured by Rosalind's impatient eagerness.

We need not start, as some have done, at a phrase used by Silvius in Act III, 5, 7, where he appeals to Phebe thus touchingly,

> will you sterner be
> Than he that dies and lives by bloody drops?

He who 'dies and lives' means 'he who spends his whole life long in such and such a way.' The order of the words may seem somewhat preposterous; yet that Chaucer should have so ordered them is a conclusive proof that it is both old and genuine; and that Shakespeare should have observed the order is a further proof that in his day it was neither quite obsolete, nor thought by him unworthy of preservation. *We* may look upon the phrase as an archaism, and explain it as a hysteron-proteron, but we may not condemn it as a solecism, much less as a corruption. Such vagaries of the English language are to be noted, not branded. I need scarcely say that Shakespeare elsewhere uses the expression in its usual reversed form, '*lives and dies.*'

Further down, in the 23rd line, where Phebe says,

> lean but upon a rush,
> The cicatrice and capable impressure
> The palm some moment keeps,

'capable impressure' can only mean 'the impression which can be received from so soft and weak a substance as a rush.' The word 'capable' is used frequently in Shakespeare—in 'The Tempest,' Act I, 2, 352-53,

> Abhorred slave,
> Which any print of goodness wilt not take,
> Being capable of all ill,

where 'capable' asserts positively, what in the

previous line had been asserted negatively, and signifies 'able to take a print'—whether of good, or of evil, being determined by the context; in 'Hamlet', Act III, 4, 126,

> His form and cause conjoin'd, preaching to stones,
> Would make them capable,

i.e., 'able to receive the doctrine preached,' and so 'impressionable'; in 'Winter's Tale,' Act IV, 4, 791,

> If thou beest capable of things serious,

i.e., 'able to receive,' and so to comprehend them; and in 'King Henry IV' Northumberland was advised that his son's flesh was 'capable of wounds and scars'; and in 'All's Well that Ends Well,' Act I. 1, 106,

> heart too capable
> Of every line and trick of his sweet favour.

On the other hand, it is used differently in 'Hamlet,' where an actor is said to be 'capable of nothing,' *i.e.*, *'able* to do nothing,' 'but inexplicable dumb shows and noise.' Differently still it must be used in the phrase 'capable impressure,' where, however, 'capable' is added, in order to express the amount of power or force exerted by the rush; the impression was just as much as was possible, where none, it might be thought, was possible. 'Capable,' therefore, is no mere otiose epithet, but is both significant

and potential. For 'impressure' we may go to
'Troilus and Cressida,' Act IV, 5, 131,

> by Jove multipotent,
> Thou shonld'st not bear from me a Greekish member
> Wherein my sword had not impressure made
> Of our rank feud.

The last passage that I shall notice in this play is in Act V, 4, 4, where the meaning is clear, though the expression is a little cloudy,

> I sometimes do believe and sometimes do not,
> As those that fear they hope, and know they fear.

Here we have as striking an example of what is called 'pregnant locution' as we can find anywhere. They *know* that they *fear*; but, as touching their *hope*, they are *not certain*; nay, they have considerable doubt; and, inasmuch as in their doubt fear predominates, the poet, without any circumlocution, goes to the pith of it, and says tersely, albeit perhaps somewhat darkly, *they fear they hope.*

THE TAMING OF THE SHREW.

In the Induction of the 'Taming of the Shrew' a little word occurs in the 17th line of the first scene in connection with the name of a hound, which is a puzzle alike to the sportsman and the scholar,

> Huntsman, I charge thee, tender well my hounds:
> Brach Merriman, the poor cur is emboss'd;
> And couple Clowder with the deep-mouthed brach.

The last 'brach' is intelligible enough, but what is the meaning of the first? It can hardly be used in its ordinary Shakesperian sense of a bitch-hound, firstly, because Merriman is immediately after designated as the 'poor cur,' which would seem of itself a sufficient designation of him, and, secondly, because it is highly improbable that Shakespeare would have introduced the same not very common word without cogent reason in two consecutive lines.

Unless, therefore, it is surmised that 'brach' is an old verb, no traces of which remain, indicating some remedial operation which was applied to embossed hounds, we are driven to the region of conjecture to find the word which was in all probability intended by the author.

If, as some would have it, embossment was a swelling of the legs or joints from overrunning, it might have been customary to bandage the poor beast that was so afflicted, and 'brace' in this sense would approximate to the reading of the copies; or, if a fomentation of salt and water were prescribed by the veterinary surgeons of the day, there is an old verb 'brack,' which would come nearer still. 'Drench' would be a licentious and rambling conjecture, but not an impossible injunction.

For my own part, I think that we have a clue to the meaning in the line which follows, where we read,

    And couple Clowder with the deep-mouthed brach.

I imagine that Merriman had been coupled with the deep-mouthed brach, and now, that Merriman was disabled, it was intended that Clowder should take his place; it was necessary, therefore, to unfasten Merriman's coupling chain—to part him off, that Clowder might be coupled in his stead. I think that 'break' may very well have been used in this sense; and, as regards the spelling, even if there were not a phonetic relationship between it and 'brach,' it would not be surprising, considering the spelling to be found from time to time in the Folios and the Quartos, if 'break' or 'brake' had been spelt 'brach' just as elsewhere 'eke' is printed 'ech,' and 'ache' 'ake.' Upon the whole, then, I am inclined to read,

    Break Merriman, the poor cur is embossed,
    And couple Clowder with the deep-mouthed brach.

A little further on in the same Scene, there is some doubt as to what should be the reading in the 64th line,

> Persuade him that he has been lunatic,
> And, *when he says he is*, say that he dreams.

If these words are to stand, they can only mean, that Sly, amazed at the outward transformation of himself and all around him, when told that he had been beside himself, replies that he must be so still. This, however, he does not do, nor perhaps was it contemplated that he should do. The easiest way of unravelling the difficulty is to suppose that 'that' has been shifted from its proper position, and that the words originally stood thus,

> And when he says *that he is*, say he dreams,

'that he is' being, of course, equivalent to '*who he is.*' A kind of resemblance, however, between 'Sly' and 'say' has led some to conjecture

> And when he says he is *Sly*, say that he dreams,

and in support of this view, it has been urged that Sly does say 'I am Christophero Sly.' But a question like this will be thought too frivolous to discuss, save by those, who are determined that nothing, if they can help it, shall be set down in an edition of Shakespeare, which was not in all probability authorized by Shakespeare. Passing from the Induction to the body of the play, we stumble upon an extraordinary word in Act I, 2, 6-7, which has for its first two syllables the dative case of a well-known Latin noun, and for its last the termination of an English past participle! Grumio says to Petruchio,

> Knock, sir! whom should I knock? Is there any man has *rebused* your worship?

The most that can be said for this hybrid verb is, that it is vulgar Grumian for 'abused'; but, as there is not a single other instance in the whole play of Grumio speaking in the Dogberry-and-Verges dialect, we have no right to shuffle out of the difficulty so. In all likelihood, the error is a typographical one. 'Rebused' is a horrible jumbling together of the two well-known words, 'robbed us,' the termination (ed) of the participle having been carelessly misplaced after 'us' instead of after 'rob.' 'Rob-us-ed' became corrupted to 'rebused,' and then 'your worship,' which properly is the nominative of address, came to be regarded as an objective case governed by that monstrous imposture 'rebused.' I have little doubt that Grumio said,

> Is there any man has robbed us, your worship?

Twenty lines lower down Grumio has again, I think, the misfortune to be misunderstood owing to inaccurate pointing: what I conceive he *should* say, is

> Nay, 'tis no matter, Sir, what he 'leges in Latin. If this be not a lawful cause for me to leave his service! Look you, Sir, he bid me knock him and rap him soundly, Sir.

I have placed a note of exclamation after 'service' instead of the usual comma, because I believe that the conditional clause is used elliptically, just as it very frequently is in common conversation, and as we might expect it to be sometimes used in dramatic dialogue; the same construction occurs in 'Merchant of Venice,' Act II, 2, 166,

> Well, if any man in Italy have a fairer table, which doth offer to swear upon a book I shall have good fortune!

and thus too some think we should point—though I am not of the number—in another passage in 'Merchant of Venice,' Act III, 2, 321,

> All debts are cleared between you and I. If I might but see you at my death!

and thus too we certainly should point in '2 Henry IV,' Act II, 4, 409, where Doll should say,

> I cannot speak; if my heart be not ready to burst! Well, sweet Jack, have a care of thyself.

The next passage that I shall notice is Act III, 2, 16, where a seeming incompleteness of metre, rather than an impossibility of finding a meaning, has excited a suspicion that there is some imperfection in the text. The metrical difficulty, however, has been exaggerated. In scanning the line

> Make friends, invite, and proclaim the banns,

the easiest way is to make 'and proclaim' pass as an anapæst, just like 'and I challenge law' in 'Richard II,' Act II, 3, 134; 'which torments me' in

'Cymbeline;' 'or perform my bidding' in 'Pericles;' 'he desires,' 'art thou certain,' and many other instances, which the critic is **compelled** to respect, because *they* cannot possibly be otherwise dealt with; nor would it be wonderful, if we had a short line here, just as we have a little lower down in this same scene in the 233rd line;

> She is my goods, my chattels; she is my house,
> My household stuff, my field, my barn.

But there is another *possible* mode of scanning the line, by pronouncing 'friends' in the time of a dissyllable, in which case 'invite' will be accentuated on the penultimate, just as 'congealed,' 'excuse' (the verb), 'oppose,' 'infect,' 'confirmed,' 'expire,' sometimes are in Shakespeare. It is a curious coincidence, which I will give the critic to chew, that there is another line in this very play, having 'friend' in it, where the verse seems to halt for lack of a syllable. By giving a dissyllabic value to 'friends' in Act I, 2, 190,

> No, say'st me so, friend? What countryman?

we manage to get over a seeming difficulty there also. This mode of solving the problem cannot be deemed absolutely impossible in Shakespeare, where so many monosyllables are similarly treated; but for my own part I prefer to scan in the fashion which I first indicated. As regards the meaning, which is the next thing that we have to settle, we may either accept the punctuation of the Folios, interpose a comma betwixt 'make friends' and 'invite,' and understand the words to mean that Petruchio led every one to believe that he was a *bona fide* suitor, not only by his attention to the lady he was courting, but by making friends among the kinsfolk and acquaintance of her family, or we may disregard the Folios' comma, and take 'make friends invite' as all belonging to one sentence, in which case the meaning will be that Petruchio caused the friends of the various ladies he wooed to issue invitations, as if for the wedding; and this is what Petruchio seems to have done; for does he not say in Act II, 1, 318,

> Provide the feast, father, and bid the guests?

Upon the whole, considering the licence which Shakespeare allows himself in his versification, and the many rare quaint and curious phrases which are to be found in his plays, I should not have thought it necessary so laboriously to defend this line, as it stands in the first Folio, were it not that it has been set down in the proscription-list of the critics.

Once more, in Act IV, 2, 59-62, where Biondello exclaims,

> O master, master, I have watched so long
> That I am dog-weary; but at last I spied
> An ancient angel coming down the hill,
> Will serve the turn,

the critics regard 'angel' with Sadducæan distrust; but is not Biondello true to his character for merriment and fun, when, to the amusement and laughter of the audience, he declares that a special providence—a sort of *Deus ex machina*—an *angel* from heaven, had come to do what?—to enable Tranio to make good his personation of Lucentio, and to enable Lucentio to carry through his love intrigue! Or Biondello might simply have meant to intimate that, in the extremity of his weariness, the ancient coming down from the high hill was in his eyes as an angel coming down from heaven. These angelic comparisons frequently recur in Shakespeare. Anyhow, whatever were Biondello's thoughts, when first he spied the venerable father, it is certain that, at the time of his speaking, the human being who was wanted, rather than the superhuman who was *not*, was uppermost in his mind; for in right matter-of-fact business fashion, if with some lack of reverence, he says, 'he will *serve the turn*. Better retain 'angel,' and explain so, than exchange it for either 'angel,' a lure, or 'engle,' a gull.

ALL'S WELL THAT ENDS WELL.

In 'All's Well that Ends Well' I cannot but think that the Cambridge editors have gone a little beyond the mark, when in a note on the line,

> Not my virginity yet,

in Act I, 1, 179, they go so far as to say, ' it cannot be doubted that there is some omission here.' It cannot be doubted that there is a somewhat abrupt transition from one theme to another, which may displease scholars, accustomed rather to regular argumentation and logical conclusion than to desultory conversation, and who perhaps hardly make sufficient allowance for the quick and sudden evolutions of feminine cristics; but, if Helen could explain her own meaning, she might insist that there was a very real connection between speech on her virginity and speculation on Bertram's court amours; possibly she meant to intimate that *she* was content to remain a spinster, till *Bertram* ceased to be a bachelor; though there was every probability of his becoming entangled in engagements, where there would be so much to engage him, still she would *wait and see.* If this were her meaning, the thread of her discourse would hardly be broken at all. But suppose that it were otherwise; can we wonder that she should not desire to prolong conversation on a subject so delicate, and touching herself so nearly, with a fellow like Parolles, whose rollicking style and libertine utterances were neither very elegant, nor very edifying? She shifted her ground, therefore. Grant this, and what was she to talk about? What topic more natural for *her*, what more likely to divert and interest *Parolles* than that of Bertram's reception, the sensation that he would cause, the flirtations, intrigues, love-makings, heart-burnings, jealousies, quarrellings, in fact, all the sunshine and shade, the sweets and bitters of the court? A short line here is surely not out of place, where the subject is cut short—where there is a break, a pause—perhaps a silent wish, a secret sigh; where at any rate there is a marked crisis in the conversation, and Helen has to extemporize another more appropriate, but not less engaging topic. To what particular portion of Parolles' speech she referred, when she said, 'Not my virginity yet;' whether the balance inclines in favour of 'I will not anything with my virginity yet,' or 'Not a withered pear is my virginity yet,' or 'I will not off with my virginity yet,' let those decide who have the eye to discern.

I will pass on from such a nice question to two passages in the latter part of the same scene—in both cases Helen is the spokeswoman—where the editors of the 'Globe' Shakespeare again hoist their danger signals, and make us enquire, what is the matter.

We are told that our progress is seriously blocked in the 237th and 238th lines,

> The mightiest space in fortune nature brings
> To join like likes and kiss like native things.

In both these lines literary engineers have consulted long and anxiously as to what had best be done, and various alterations have been proposed, where, perhaps, after all none may be required. I can see two ways of clearing the passage without so much as altering a letter.

In the first place, 'space,' a *singular* noun, may be treated as an *accusative of measurement, space, distance*, rather than, as it is usually supposed to be, the direct object governed by the transitive verb 'brings;' the noun which that verb governs has to be supplied; whatever we take it to be, whether 'objects,' or 'beings,' or what, *nature brings them across, or through, the mightiest space*, to join, just as if they were likes, nay, to kiss, just as if they had had but one original.

Or, in the second place, 'space' may be treated as virtually a *plural*, according to that well-known canon, which allows the plural of words ending in *se, ss, ce,* or even *ge*, to be at times assimilated to the form of the singular. In this case, the meaning of the word is accommodated to the sense that is required; the abstract is put for the concrete; the 'mightiest space' will signify not the interval which separates, or the various portions of it which are effaced as the two bodies move towards each other, but *the objects themselves which are so separated*, whose junction and osculation nature effects. A fine Catholic doctrine, which no doubt Shakespeare as much commended as Helen at the time cherished. In the words that follow,

> Impossible be strange attempts to those
> That weigh their pains in sense and do suppose
> What hath been cannot be,

it has been assumed that the *negative* clause, 'what hath not been,' must have been in some form in the original, rather than the *affirmative* one, 'what hath been.' But why should not Shakespeare have intended to intimate that some refuse to believe that a thing can be, which, in point of fact, has already been, although *they* may not have seen or heard it? It is man who cries, 'Impossible;' nature proclaims, 'It hath been—it can be!' The old saw—'the thing which has been, it is that which shall be.' Man's miracles are Nature's laws.

And here it may not be amiss to transcribe one or two examples from Shakespeare, where nouns are used as plurals without possessing the plural suffix:

Than other *princess* can,
> 'Tempest' Act I, 2, 173.

As blanks, *benevolence*, and I wot not what,
> 'Richard II,' Act II, 1, 250.

A thousand of his people butchered ;
Upon whose dead *corpse* there was such misuse,
> '1 Henry IV,' Act I, 1, 42—43.

Where are the *evidence* that do accuse me ?
> 'Richard III,' Act I, 4, 188.

But to resume: there is a passage in Act I, 2, 31-45, where the King thus finely describes the character of Bertram's father:

> In his youth
> He had the wit which I can well observe
> To-day in our young lords ; but they may jest
> Till their own scorn return to them unnoted
> Ere they can hide their levity in honour ;
> So like a courtier, *contempt nor bitterness
> Were in his pride or sharpness* ; if they were,
> An equal had awaked them ; and his honour,
> Clock to itself, knew the true minute when
> Exception bid him speak, and at this time
> *His tongue obey'd his hand*; who were below him
> He used as creatures of another place
> And bow'd his eminent top to their low ranks,
> Making them proud of his humility,
> In their poor praise he *humbled*.

Not a line of this portrait but has been drawn by the hand of a consummate artist; yet parts of it have not escaped criticism, as wanting in distinctness, or as inappropriate, or as having been tampered with by an inferior hand—the parts which I have underlined, for instance—the 36th line, where, however, I think I read the great limner's meaning aright, when I understand him to tell us, that Bertram's father was such a model of courtesy, that he could be *proud* without being contemptuous, *sharp* without being bitter—the 41st line, where, however, I recognize the strictest *horological* accuracy in the expression, 'his *tongue* obey'd his *hand*'—and lastly the 45th line, where in the sentence 'he humbled' I catch the *ipsissima verba* of the humble poor—their own poor way of expressing their appreciation of the great good man's condescension. Yes, scholars and grammarians, you might doubtless command correcter grammar by the addition of the reflexive pronoun, but, what you would gain *so*, you would more than lose in originality, in character, in point, in force, in brevity. Not for one moment would I barter this poor man's homely phrase for Mr. Staunton's turgid compound '*behumbled*'; nor can I tolerate Malone's gloss—'he being humbled'—much less agree with those who would brand the expression as corrupt. Critics must learn to bend their ears to this not altogether inharmonious cottage note; possibly Shakespeare heard it; possibly he invented it; certainly he was pleased with it.

A stigma too has been attached to the following line—Act I, 3, 141—

> Such were our faults, or then we thought them none;

yet a poor exchange it would be, were Warburton's *O*, or Mr. Collier's '*for*,' or Hanmer's '*though*' to supplant the good sound expressive idiomatic conjunction 'or,' which leaves it undecided, which of two possible ways of putting a case is the more correct. I see nothing to stigmatize here.

In Act II, 1, 3, it has been suggested that we should read,

If both gain, *well*,

on the ground that it would be impossible for both to gain '*all*'; the absence of a comma after 'all' in the Folios has induced, I suppose, the editors of the 'Globe' Shakespeare to connect it with '*gift*' in the following line. This seems to me rather a shirking of the difficulty, than a successful solution of it. The natural connection of 'all' is with '*gain*,' and in that connection I think it should be explained. May not the meaning be that, if both the *young* lords, and those who were separately addressed as '*you, my lords*—or if both those who were going to join the Senoys, and those who had chosen to espouse the cause of the Florentines, appropriated to their advantage the advice in all its fulness which the king had given them, that gift of advice would not be diminished by being diffused among so many; it would be all-sufficient for all of them, whether they fought with this side or with that, and the value of it could only be measured by the receptivity and appreciative capacity of those to whom it had been given. *Its usefulness would depend on themselves.* But this clumsy and common-place prose would poorly replace Shakespeare's neat, but more recondite, mode of expressing the same sentiment. I confess, however, that the phrase, 'I am kept a coil with,' is hard of digestion, nor can I either parallel or explain it. A friend has hinted that perhaps a hyphen should be interposed between the preposition and the noun, and 'a-coil' should be classed with such adverbial compounds as 'aboard,' 'afield,' 'afire,' 'akimbo,' and the like. Of the general meaning there can be no dispute.

I am now going to touch a passage in Act II, 1, 175—177, where it is all but impossible to ascertain either the precise reading or the precise meaning. Helen, having been challenged by the king to say, what she durst venture on her certainty and confidence, replies

Tax of impudence,
A strumpet's boldness, a divulged shame
Traduced by odious ballads; my maiden's name
Scar'd otherwise, *ne worse of worst* extended
With vilest torture let my life be ended.

The words which I have italicized are set down, I believe, exactly as they appear in the first Folio. In the other versions of the Folio 'no' takes the place of 'ne.' It has been thought that 'ne' was meant to represent 'nay'; to all intents and purposes, then, *'no'* and *'nay'* are the two words which have to be taken into account, and, according as we prefer the one or the other, we shall have to regulate and vary the sense of the passage.

I assume, in the first place, that '*nay*' is the genuine word, and I may *either* punctuate thus,

> Sear'd otherwise ; nay, worse—of worst extended
> With vilest torture let my life be ended,

that is, she will submit to be not only foully *slandered*, but, worse still, foully *slain*—to be reckoned as '*of*,' or belonging to, the very worst of her kind, and, as such, to end her life only after a long extension of the vilest torture ; *or*, by a different arrangement of the stops, from the same words we may get a different, perhaps a preferable, meaning :

> Sear'd otherwise ; nay, worse of worst extended
> With vilest torture let my life be ended,

where 'worse of worst' would be an adverbial phrase, qualifying the participle 'extended' and indicating successive degrees in the process of torture, the '*worst*' for the time being being always followed by something 'worse,' till life could endure it no more—a hyperbolic expression, which may be matched with Milton's

> And in the lowest deep a lower deep.

But what talk I of 'Milton' ? Have we not in 'Timon' Act IV, 3, 247, ' *worse than the worst* ' ?

and have we not also in 'Measure for Measure,' Act III, 1, 126,

> To be worse than worst
> Of those that lawless and incertain thought
> Imagine howling?

In fact, what *here* is expressed by an adverbial phrase, in 'Antony and Cleopatra' is expressed by the sentence, 'Let worse follow worse'; or we may get a flash of light from a passage in the 'Tempest;' just as *there* we read in Act III, 3, 77,

> *Lingering perdition, worse than any death*
> *Can be at once, shall step by step* attend
> You and your ways,

so here we may read,

> Sear'd otherwise, nay, worse of worst, extended
> With *vilest torture* let my *life be ended,*

the adverbial phrase 'worse of worst' being taken as a sort of summing up by anticipation of what is more fully expressed in the remainder of the sentence, '*worst*' referring to the 'death' which she imprecates upon herself, to use the word of the 'Tempest,' or the 'life ended,' as it is expressed in this play; the '*worse*' than that worst referring to the 'lingering perdition,' as it is expressed *there*, or the 'extension with vilest torture,' as *here*.

But in the second place, I have to assume that the writer of the second Folio knew well what he was about, when he changed 'ne' into 'no': the passage will now have to be interpreted very differently:

> Scar'd otherwise ; no worse of worst ; extended
> With vilest torture let my life be ended,

where 'no worse of worst' may either be considered as more or less connected with the words that immediately precede; 'my maiden's name scared otherwise—no worse-wise of the worst than of me;' or it may be taken as indicating yet another step in her denunciation of herself—a further and separate aggravation of the curse with which she would have herself stricken—'let there be no person reckoned worse of all who come under the denomination of worst.' Such, then, being some of the interpretations, which the words, as they are given in the Folios, are capable of bearing without much wrenching, I would not discard the reading of the Folios, doubtful though it may be, for the notion of this or that commentator's private fancy, which must be much more doubtful.

We must on no account listen to those who would have us believe that there is something wrong with the words—Act II, 5, 52—

> I have spoken better of you than you have or will to deserve at my hand ;

the occasional insertion in Shakespeare's time of the sign of the infinitive after auxiliary verbs I have already illustrated with copious examples ; if

I add one example more, it is because we have in this very play,

> 'To belie them I will not.'

Shall I be accused of splitting a hair, if I advocate the shifting of a stop in Act IV, 1, 17-21,

> Now he hath a smack of all neighbouring languages; therefore we must every one be a man of his own fancy; not to know what we speak one to another, so we seem to know, is to know straight our purpose.

The authorized position of the semicolon is after '*another*,' not after '*fancy*.'

With regard to the 38th line of Act IV, 2,

> I see that men make *ropes in such a scarre
> That we'll forsake ourselves,

the precise meaning has not been ascertained—perhaps is not ascertainable. Possibly, there may be an allusion to the rope-ladder, by which young gallants made it easy for their loves to forsake themselves—*facilis descensus Averni*—the ladder, however, here referred to would be not a material, but a metaphorical one; if this view is correct, it may be a question whether the last word of the line were not originally '*stair*,' agreeably to that dictum in 'Romeo and Juliet,'

> And bring the cords made like a tackle *stair*;

possibly the phrase 'make ropes' may be a nautical

---

* rope's—so the first Folio.

metaphor tantamount to what is nowadays more usually expressed by its kindred phrase, '*to spin a long yarn*;' and some such sense it might bear in 'The Taming of the Shrew,' where we read

<blockquote>He'll rail in his rope tricks,</blockquote>

and in 'Romeo and Juliet,' where the nurse says,

<blockquote>What saucy merchant was this that was so full of his ropery?</blockquote>

but I feel here that I have no sure ground to stand upon; I will hasten on, therefore, to the 31st line of the 4th scene, where our first operation must be to see that the stops are in their right places: I set them thus:

<blockquote>
Dia: Let death and honesty
Go with your impositions, I am yours
Upon your will to suffer.

Hel: Yet, I pray you;
But with the word—'The time will bring on summer,
When briers shall have leaves as well as thorns,
And be as sweet as sharp.'
</blockquote>

The whole of the last sentence stands in apposition to the noun '*word*,' pretty much as is the case in 'Measure for Measure,' Act I, 2, 126—127,

<blockquote>
The words of heaven—'On whom it will, it will;
On whom it will not, so'—yet still 'tis just.
</blockquote>

'Suffer a while *yet*'—says Helen, and I need not say that '*yet*' is repeatedly used as a particle of time, *one* instance, which seems to have given a deal of trouble at any rate to past scholars, occurring in 'King Henry V,' Act IV, 3, 49,

> Old men forget ; yet all shall be forgot,

and so here—'suffer awhile *yet*, but withal remembering the proverb, which tells of leaves as well as of thorns, of summer's sweetness as well as of winter's sharpness.'

'Blade of youth,' the reading of the copies in Act V, 3, 6, is neither unnatural, nor unintelligible, nor, I believe I may add, unexampled; but, standing where it does, it seems incongruous and out of place, like a cockle in the wheat. The word, which has found most favour with critics, is 'blaze,' which has been introduced into most, I believe, of the published editions; yet, I am not at all sure that we should not give the precedence to '*blood*,' which, as pronounced by some, sounds almost exactly like 'blade' (cf. 'bled'), and, if spelt '*blode*' or '*blude*,' is within a letter of it. I read, therefore,

> And I beseech your majesty to make it
> Natural rebellion, done 'i the *blood* of youth ;
> When oil and fire, too strong for reason's force,
> O'erbears it, and burns on.

The '*blood*' first, the '*blaze*' is afterwards expressed. The following passages may give some colour to my conjecture :

> The strongest oaths are straw
> To the fire 'i the blood.
>
> 'Tempest,' Act IV, 1, 52-53.

The *blood of youth burns not* with such excess.
'Love's Labour's Lost,' Act V, 2, 73.

It hath the excuse of *youth and heat of blood.*
'I Henry IV,' Act V, 2, 17.

A little below, in the 66th line, should we read with the editors of the 'Globe' Shakespeare,

Our own love waking cries to see what's done,
While *shame full late* sleeps out the afternoon;

or should we stand to '*shameful hate,*' the phrase of the Folios? The former is ingenious and plausible; but it is an innovation, and one that is not varnished by the pretence of necessity. The latter is sufficient, is countenanced by the testimony of the best copies, and, in my opinion, seems most suitable to the context. It must have been some great 'displeasure' indeed—something very much akin to **hate**—which could have wrought so fearfully as to '*destroy*' a 'friend,' and bring him to the '*dust.*' When love awoke and cried, that spirit of evil, whatever it was—'hate,' as we believe, and as the Folios indicate—slept. But love only awoke in the decline of the man's life, after the worthy one, who should have been loved, had passed away; 'hate,' having had the morning and noon all to itself, and as it were exhausted with its half or three quarters of a day's hard hearty work, instead of being cast into durance, and made to do painful penance, had a lazy time of it in cushioned ease—'sleeping out the afternoon' is said to the disparagement of

Falstaff—while love, awake at last, was bitterly crying. Love and hate are the two opposite extremes, and may well stand in counterpoise to each other. Antitheses, it has been remarked, frequently occur in rhymed lines. *'Laissez faire'* must be our principle here.

Some change, however, must be made in Act V, 3, 216, where the reading of the Folios is arrant nonsense; for what can be made of '*insuite comming*' in the passage that follows?

> She knew her distance and did angle for me,
> Madding my eagerness with her restraint,
> As all impediments in fancy's course
> Are motives of more fancy ; and, in fine,
> Her *insuite comming*, with her modern grace,
> Subdued me to her rate.

Shall we not snatch at such a conjecture as '*infinite cunning*,' which is charmingly ingenious, and seems pretty appropriate, to say nothing of the adjective bearing a rough resemblance in form, the noun in sound, to the word of the copies? Yet there is some difference between the two versions; we have to suppose that not one word only, but two consecutive ones have been falsely rendered ; nor am I aware that 'infinite,' a common word enough, is commonly miswritten; can the critics, whose ears were hurt by the disagreeable assonance of 'talked' and 'walked' in two consecutive lines of 'Julius

Cæsar,' endure here—here, where joking must be out of the question—the jarring sound of '*in fine*,' and '*infinite*'? There is another emendation possible, which is neither unsuitable to the passage, nor inimical to the reading of the copies, and which may be brought forward to compete with that which has found favour in the cloisters of Cambridge. The point, which Bertram was seeking to explain, was how he had been induced to part with his monumental ring. We *know* how it was. It was not done *proprio motu*; it was no thought or wish on his part; nor was there any particular act of cunning on hers; it was her own request — her '*own suit*'—' Give me that ring' are her very words, as given in Act IV, 2, 39; and this I think that Bertram, for all that he was so great a liar, in order to screen himself spoke here truly enough :

> Her own suit, coming with her modern grace,
> Subdued me to her rate ; she got the ring.

It may be a moot question, whether '*summing*' may not have been in the original *vice* ' comming '; but every one can see how easily ' in ' and ' own ' may have been confounded, just as ' in ' and ' on ' continually are. To this emendation it may be objected, that it is out of keeping with what is previously attributed to her; it may be replied that her suit for the ring would not be inconsistent with her coy reluctance to gratify her lover. The most subtle harlot, who had opposed restraint to eagerness, and impediment to fancy, would not scruple to ask for a precious ring which sparkled in her eyes, nor is it easy to see how Bertram could palliate his having given it, without pleading that he had been compelled to do so, because she had actually sued for it. It suited the purpose of the liar *here* to speak the truth.

I may add, by way of postscript, that, on looking at the foot-notes of the 'Cambridge' Shakespeare, after I had made a fair and concluding copy of my notes on this play, I found to my surprise that '*her own suit*' had been already conjectured. I cannot, therefore, claim to be the first inventor of this version, some one else having patented it before me.

TWELFTH NIGHT; OR, WHAT YOU WILL.

In 'Twelfth Night,' Act II, 5, 71, it has been considered questionable, whether Shakespeare wrote, what he is represented in the copies as having written,

> Though our silence be drawn from us with *cars,* yet peace,

or some other word, of which 'cars' is only a false adumbration.

In this very play, Act III, 2, 64, we have

> I think oxen and wainropes cannot hale them together,

where the form of expression is somewhat similar, but both the cattle and the tackle are specifically mentioned.

In 'The Two Gentlemen of Verona,' Act III, 1, 265, Launce says,

> A team of horses shall not pluck that from me,

where again there is a certain resemblance; the draught animals are expressed, but the traces to draw with are left to be supplied. May not, then, in 'Twelfth Night' the simple word 'cars' stand not only for the vehicle, but for the harnessed horses and requisite tackle? It is true that horses draw, as do oxen with wainropes, but cars and carts are drawn; yet it is equally true that Hector's corpse was drawn or dragged by the chariot of Achilles. *Verbum sat.* No traction-engine, of how many horse power soever, should move them to speak.

Of conjectures, the most noteworthy of the *serious* ones are 'cords' and 'scars'—the latter word intended, I presume, to express the wounds inflicted on the soul by the sharp sword of the tongue—of the *comical* ones, 'curs.'

In Act III, 3, 13—16, unless we have one of the short lines which are occasionally to be met with in Shakespeare—a possible, but not, I think, here a probable circumstance—a lacuna occurs in the text, through the carelessness of the transcriber, or the printer.

> My kind Antonio,
> I can no other answer make but thanks,
> *And thanks and ever oft good turns*
> Are shuffled off with such uncurrent pay.

I need scarcely say—every critic can see—that 'thanks' was in all likelihood the word that originally was repeated for the third time after 'ever'; but I may be permitted to observe, what it has occurred to no critic that I know of to note, that, that done, the verse is mended, the metre is completed, no further insertion is necessary, none must be tolerated. For this is one of those instances, where a pause occurs in a line, and that pause is equivalent to a syllable. It is not necessary that I should cite examples of this well-known peculiarity of Shakespearian prosody; but, inasmuch as there are passages elsewhere, where the same peculiarity occurs, but where emendations have been essayed, as though the metre were defective, I will avail myself of this opportunity to quote one or two such passages, not, it must be distinctly understood, as vouchers for, but merely as illustrations of, the limited alteration, to which in the present instance I insist that we should confine ourselves.

In 'All's Well that Ends Well' we read, Act II, 3, 140,

>That is honour's scorn,
>Which challenges itself as honour's born
>And is not like the sire : honours thrive,
>When rather from our acts we them derive
>Than our foregoers.

Here, though the wanting syllable is capable of being supplied either by pausing after 'sire,' or by making 'sire' pass as a dissyllable, would it be believed that some editors have actually foisted into the text '*our* honours thrive'!

Take another instance from 'Timon,' Act V, 4, 35,

>All have not offended ;
>For those that were, it is not square to take
>On those that are, revenge ; crimes, like lands,
>Are not inherited.

Here the 'Globe' editors read 'revenges,' which no doubt Shakespeare uses elsewhere, but which they have no authority for supposing that he used here; nor is the correction necessary.

Lastly in 'King John,' Act V, 7, 35,

> Poison'd—ill fare—dead, forsook, cast off,

the footnotes of the 'Cambridge' Shakespeare will show how some would have botched where there is really no need for mending at all. But it is no botching to write

> Thanks, and ever *thanks: oft* good turns.

With respect to technicalities of punctuation, there is room for considerable divergence of opinion. Yet I cannot but think that, when a sentence is not broken off altogether, but merely interrupted by a parenthetical remark, and after that resumed, its continuity as a sentence should be marked, as far as possible, by means of the stops. This does not seem to me to have been done in Act III, 4, 86—91, which is thus set down in the 'Globe' Shakespeare:

> *Mal.* Why, everything adheres together, that no dram of a scruple, no scruple of a scruple, no obstacle, no incredulous or unsafe circumstance—What can be said? Nothing that can be can come between me and the full prospect of my hopes.

According to this mode of pointing, it would seem that a sentence was left unfinished, a question asked, and a fresh sentence commenced with the words,

'Nothing that can be;' but, as a matter of fact, these last words are merely a continuation of the sentence which had been interrupted by the bye-question, 'What can be said?' Dram, scruple, obstacle, circumstance, all these are too feeble to express what Malvolio is hammering at; he pauses, therefore, and asks, 'What can be said?' How can he put it more forcibly? The words that follow—'Nothing that can be'—are his continuation, his climax, his last best stroke of words. A comma, then, should be placed after 'circumstance;' 'what can be said' should be armed with brackets or hyphens; 'nothing,' should lose the capital, which is now its initial letter; and Malvolio's words will be fitly presented thus:

Why everything adheres together, that no dram of a scruple, no scruple of a scruple, no obstacle, no incredulous or unsafe circumstance,—what can be said?—nothing that can be can come between me and the full prospect of my hopes.

To attach too much importance to the words of a fool would be the acme of folly; but, when fools utter, albeit in a quaint and silly fashion, such sound sense, as Shakespeare's fools frequently do, we are not warranted in pooh-poohing what we do not fully understand, and passing it by as mere foolery. What, then, does the Clown mean, when in Act IV, 1, 14, 15, he says,

I am afraid this great lubber, the world, will prove a cockney?

It is somewhat against us that we are unable to ascertain either the origin or the precise meaning of 'cockney.' All that we can assert positively is that it was wont to be used in no very complimentary sense. Perhaps our best chance of unravelling the meaning is to examine closely the texture of the passage. Sebastian had used a word, which to the fool's ear was new-fangled, far-fetched, affected, heard used by great men, and then borrowed, and straight applied to a fool's folly. 'What will happen next'—cries the fool—'now that Cesario'—for such he must have imagined Sebastian to be—'instead of using the good rough homely language of mother wit, takes upon him to spout in this high fantastic style! By and by, not your picked men only and your fine fellows, but *every lazy hulking chap* will give himself airs, and affect the same singularity of diction.' The fool sees the evil spreading, like an epidemic, from individual to individual, till it becomes a general plague, and the huge world is nothing more or less than a lazar-house of cockneyism. Such I venture to think is the gist of a passage, which, if not as clear as it might be, is very far from deserving the condemnation of editors. 'Cockenay' is used in Chaucer, but this is the only passage, if I mistake not, in which it is to be found in Shakespeare.

THE WINTER'S TALE.

When a sentence is interposed between the protasis and the apodosis of a hypothetical sentence, without being dependent on either of them, surely some more distinctive mark of separation than a comma is required to isolate it from the two portions of the sentence which on either side enclose it. In Act I, 2, 273-76, of 'The Winter's Tale' a couple of hyphens—a sign which has been used by the 'Globe' editors with much effect in the six previous lines—must have been omitted involuntarily, and, for clearness' sake, should surely be substituted for the two commas which at present stand there,

> If thou wilt confess—
> Or else be impudently negative,
> To have nor eyes, nor ears, nor thought—then say
> My wife's, &c. &c.

Further on, the correctness of the text has been challenged in the latter part of the 324th line where Leontes says to Camillo,

> Make that thy question, and go rot;

but it is not so much a revision of the text that is here wanted, as an interpreter of the meaning.

Singer is of opinion that 'that' refers to the queen's infidelity, and that the King of Sicilia as good as says, 'If you treat *that* as a matter of doubt, and not of absolute certainty, to the dung-hill, to the crows with you!' But is not the sentiment much about the same as that which was expressed on a memorable occasion in those well-known words to a manifest traitor, 'What is that to us? See thou to it,' Leontes insinuating that Camillo must be false in his professions of loyal attachment, because he had not revealed to him the secret of the queen's alleged infidelity? Probably the King had no wish to be turned from his subject by the introduction of this bye-question of Camillo's loyalty.

Further on still, in the same Act and Scene, lines 457-460, there is a passage, which has miserably embarassed the critics, but the difficulty of which I cannot but think has been greatly overestimated. It occurs in the latter part of one of Polixenes' speeches, where he says,

> Fear o'er shades me :
> Good expedition be my friend, and comfort
> The gracious queen, part of his theme, but nothing
> Of his ill-ta'en suspicion !

Dr. Johnson affirmed that he could make nothing of the words, 'part of his theme, but nothing of his ill-ta'en suspicion ;' and, if Theobald had said so, we might be chary of giving any opinion; but Johnson does not hold the same rank as a Shakespearian expositor as he does as an English lexicographer. The two phrases seem to me to stand in a sort of appositional relation to the 'queen.' 'Part of his theme,' of course, means that she equally with Polixenes was the subject of the King's reflections; but the meaning of the other phrase, 'nothing of his ill-ta'en suspicion,' is not so apparent. If it can *only* mean that the queen was *not* suspected by the King, it is utterly unsuitable, and must be pronounced corrupt; but may it not bear another meaning more agreeable to the sense required?

In 'Antony and Cleopatra,' Act II, 2, 79-80, the words,

> Let this fellow
> Be nothing of our strife,

can only mean, 'Let him give no occasion to us to quarrel;' and 'This fellow *is* nothing of our strife' would mean 'This fellow gives no occasion to us to quarrel;' and similarly 'The queen is nothing of the King's suspicion' may mean, 'She gives no occasion to the King to suspect, however much he may suspect;' she does nothing to *promote* it; and in *that* sense she is 'nothing of it.' As for the words 'comfort the queen,' I dismiss Warburton's conjecture 'the queen's,' which, though it satisfied Dr. Johnson, is a mere shirking of the difficulty, and I conceive that Polixenes expresses a wish that the good expedition, which he prays may befriend *him*, may 'comfort the queen.'

I put it thus: where he was, he was already a doomed man, without a chance of vindicating his character, or escaping the King's vengeance. To get away as fast as he could, was his only hope; well then he might pray for himself, '*Good expedition be my friend.*'

But, while he was thus providing for his own safety, what of the queen? His presence at court would certainly not avail her during the short space that he would be suffered to bide there; protest his innocence as much as he might, the ears of jealousy would be deaf to his protestations. What then? His speedy withdrawal—his disappearance from the scene—beneficial to himself, would benefit also the queen; would be the best arrangement not indeed for her justification—for that was impossible—but for her 'comfort.' It was what she herself would have him do under the circumstances. Well then he might further pray that his expeditious departure might 'comfort the queen.'

The Cambridge editors suggest that they would have expected Polixenes to say that his flight without Hermione would be the best means of dispelling Leontes' suspicion; but *that* he well knew that he could not hope to do; the fire of jealousy is not so easily extinguished. The utmost that he could do was not to fan and fuel the flame by his presence; not to add to the queen's already great discomfort, but go, and leave it to time to prove both his innocence and hers. It was the best course for *both*: for *him* it was *life*; for her *his* prayer was that it might be '*comfort*.'

There is a passage in Act II, 1, 133—36, where Antigonus declares that, if it should turn out that the queen has gone wrong,

> I'll keep my stables where
> I lodge my wife; I'll go in couples with her;
> Than when I feel and see her no farther trust her.

A mere bubble of a difficulty this! The last line expresses in plain language what the former lines had expressed in the language of metaphor. Nothing but the testimony of his senses should convince him that his wife was faithful to him. He must have ocular, nay, tangible testimony. The chase was his delight; he must look to his horses; but, while looking after them, he could not have an eye upon his wife. Well—one building shall serve for both—'he will keep his stables where he lodges his wife.' Does the declaration sound monstrous? Not a whit more monstrous was it in his estimation than the monstrous suspicion that the King had harboured concerning the queen. But further; he must look to the coupling of his hounds; this operation supplies him with a figure expressive of yet closer watchfulness; a coupling chain shall be reserved for his wife, that, by having her at his elbow, he may know that she has not given him the slip.

So then the emendation of 'stabler' or 'stablers,' proposed by the Cambridge editors, though involving a minimum of change, is objectionable for the simple reason, that it *is* a change, where no change is required.

Six lines lower down Antigonus protests that the King had been deceived by some putter-on, and that, if *he* knew the villain, he would '*land-damn*'[*] him. This strange compound has perplexed the most learned and sagacious commentators. All that we can venture to pronounce positively is, that it must denote some punishment, adequate to the magnitude of the crime, which it was in the power of the speaker to inflict in this flesh-and-blood world. Would he damn him *from* the land by throwing him into perpetual durance? or into the sea? or into the fire? or would he damn him *to* the land by burying him quick in it? or is it possible that the term is borrowed from feudal nomenclature, and that by land-damning he meant taking from him the land he held and his personal freedom, and condemning him and his posterity to servitude and the degrading occupation of cultivating the land of another? Or is it possible that we can cast a glimmer of light on this dark and mysterious compound from the following passage in 'Cymbeline,' Act I, 2, where

---

[*] Land damne—so the first Folio.

Cloten and some lords are talking of a duel, which had just taken place between the former and Posthumus Leonatus:

Clo. The villain would not stand me.

Sec. Lord. [*Aside*] No; but he fled forward still, toward your face.

First Lord. Stand you! You have land enough of your own: but he added to your having; gave you some ground.

Sec. Lord. [*Aside*] As many inches as you have oceans. Puppies!

Clo. I would they had not come between us.

Sec. Lord. [*Aside*] So would I, till you had measured how long a fool you were upon the ground.

'*Land-damn him*' in the light of this passage would contain a deal in a small compass—the challenge which Antigonus would have sent him; the duel which he would have fought with him; the resolution with which he would have held his own ground; the fiery vigour with which he would have forced him to give him some of *his* ground; the stunning blow which he would have dealt him till he had measured his length on the ground, and, having left him no ground to stand upon, whether he would damn him further, and forbid his body interment, we need not pursue— the land-damning would have been thorough and complete. The illiterate multitude of Shakespeare's day (and we are no better off than they, so far as accurate knowledge of this word goes) would understand the meaning and significance of the *last*, if they could not of the first portion of this mysterious compound.

But there is another mode of smoothing the difficulty which deserves to be mentioned. 'Land-damn' was the title of a high magistrate in a Swiss canton, and might have been used to indicate the sort of authority which the Sicilian officer desired, to warrant his infliction of a punishment of exceptional severity. As its final syllable emphatically repeated the 'damn' of the preceding line, it gave room for a *double entendre*, with which the author condescended not unfrequently to divert his audience. The entire word, with the true meaning of it, would occur to the statesman and to the scholar, and would satisfy their sense of judicial propriety; but the second half of the word, with its delusive sound, would be rapturously caught at by the inerudite multitude, and would be hailed by them with revengeful vociferations. '*I* would be his judge—*I* would deal with him, with a *vengeance*'—such would be accepted as the drift of Antigonus' exclamation.

In '2 Henry IV,' Act I, 2, when the Chief Justice says to Falstaff,

> I sent for you, when there were *matters against you for your life,* to come speak with me,

Falstaff answers,

> As I was then advised by my learned counsel in the laws of this *land-service*, I did not come.

I pass on to a passage, which has caused some dispute, in Act III, 2, 60-62, where Hermione says,

> More than mistress of
> Which comes to me in name of fault, I must not
> At all acknowledge.

The expression is peculiar, and the order of the words equally so; but neither is repugnant to Shakespearian usage; the fellow-line we have in 'As You Like It,'

> I show more mirth than I am mistress of.

It is, of course, possible—it has actually been conjectured—that the letter *m*, preceded by an apostrophe, may have been omitted before 'mistress' —the latter word beginning with an *m* would facilitate the omission—and even that the pronoun itself [*I'm*] may also have been omitted. The addition would not incommode the metre. But we must not recast Shakespeare's sentences to please the fastidiousness of modern readers; the ellipse is not incredible; the sense is perfectly clear; the passage might have been more explicit, it would not have been more forcible, had the words been

> I must not acknowledge more fault than I am mistress of.

There remains to be accounted for the little clause, 'which comes to me in name of fault.' This is what is called a relative proposition, limiting something, which is stated in general terms. Such parenthetical clauses are frequent in ancient classical literature. To the explanation, then, which I have already given, I have merely to add, 'at least so far as relates to that which comes to me in the category of fault,' and I have said enough on this passage to remove not perhaps the suspiciousness of a Leontes, but, I trust, of every unbiassed critic.

There is seemingly a slight flaw in Act IV, 3, 98, where we read

> They cherish it (*i.e.* virtue) to make it stay there, and yet it will no more but abide.

'But' seems out of place. There are many words which might be substituted for it, *e.g.* 'jot,' or 'whit,' or even 'bit,' a little word often used by rural folk, and not unlikely to drop from a Clown's mouth. 'More bit' would be like 'more requital'—'King John,' Act II, 1, 34—and 'our more leisure'—'Measure for Measure,' Act I, 3, 49; lastly — and this remark may make us pause before we commit ourselves to any change at all— 'but,' having itself at times a negative signification, may have been used, or misused, to fortify the negation. But what am I saying? The Clown is represented as a poor simple silly fellow. Should we, then, weigh his nonsense in the scales of reason and sense?

There is another word which proceeds from the Clown, in the 250th line of the 4th Scene of the same Act, which has confounded the learned. '*Clamour* your tongues, and not a word more,' if right, has not yet been shown to be so. Perhaps it was a slang term in olden time, which has long since been defunct, and which needs not now be exhumed; but I should not be surprised if it were an error of the copyist, miswritten for '*Shame o'* your tongues.'

I read in the 'Globe' edition in Act IV, 4, 590-92,

> My good Camillo,
> She is as forward of her breeding as
> She is i' the rear our birth.

Notwithstanding that ''our' is the reading of the Folios, ''our' and 'o' her' have such a strong phonetic resemblance, and the latter here is so far preferable to the former, that I would stretch a point for once, and read 'o' her.' 'She is as forward in respect of her breeding, as she is backward in respect of her birth.' As said Buckingham in 'King Richard III,' 'So cunning and so young.'

I had all but dropped my pen, when my eye fell on a word in a speech of Autolycus in the 760th line, where we read

> Thinkest thou, for that I insinuate, or* *toaze* from thee thy business, I am therefore no courtier?

---

* The first Folio has '*at* toaze.'

Singer thinks that we have the same word here, as in the phrase 'to toaze wool,' which he says is to pluck or draw it out. The only approach to a parallel that I can recollect in Shakespeare is in 'Measure for Measure,' 'I'll touse you joint by joint.' 'To toazle' hay—I can vouch for the use and the sound, but not for the spelling—is used in Devonshire meadows for shaking out the hay, in order to scatter and expose it to the burning rays of the sun. There are numbers of words and phrases current in provincial and rural districts— becoming more and more rare, as intercommunication increases—which have no place in a Latham's or a Webster's Dictionary. A vagabond like Autolycus might have picked up some of these unconsidered trifles in country lane or village fair.

As for Leontes' speech in Act V, 1, 56-60, I am quite willing to leave it as it is found printed in the first Folio,

> One worse
> And better used, would make her sainted spirit
> Again possess her corpse, and on this stage,
> (Where we offenders now appear), soul-vex'd,
> And begin, Why to me?

The meaning here is tolerably clear without inserting '*are*' before 'offenders,' as the 'Globe' editors do, and making '*and*' connect the two verbs '*possess*' and '*appear*'—'*and* on this stage' is both idiomatic and Shakespearian English.

KING JOHN.

In the first Scene of the second Act [Act II, I, 183-90] of 'King John,' by way of prelude to the great battle, which is about to be fought before the walls of Angiers between the French and the Austrians on the one side, and the English forces on the other, there is a smart skirmish of tongues—a sort of Gynækomachia—between Elinor and her daughter-in-law Constance, the two champions respectively of the two rival candidates for the English crown, in which the latter with her two weapons 'sin' and 'plague' presses her adversary so persistently, and in such a rapid dashing shifting fashion, that, though we can see clearly enough the aim and effectiveness of her general strategy, we have not a very distinct notion of the force and bearing of her particular evolutions and assaults. The passage is in every sense a *plaguy* one; the punctuation has first to be settled—then the explanation. I should imagine that the stiffest stickler for Folio pointing would be willing in this instance to acquiesce in the pointing adopted by the editors of the 'Globe'

Shakespeare, where the various clauses are thus divided:

> I have but this to say,
> That he is not only plagued for her sin,
> But God hath made her sin *and her the plague
> On this removed issue, plagued † for her
> And with her plague; her sin his injury,
> Her injury the beadle to her sin,
> All punished in the person of this child,
> And all for her; a plague upon her.

There are two ways in which children may suffer by their fathers—either *indirectly*, by their fathers' sins being visited upon them, or *directly*, by their fathers' grossly ill-using them. Now in both these ways Constance, the mother of Prince Arthur, avers that Elinor, his grandmother, has been a plague to him.

Not only has she, by her *general* wickedness, entailed upon him an inheritance of woe, according to the denunciation of the decalogue; but, in the superfluity of her naughtiness, she is actually in her own person doing him a *particular* injury, in that she is leagued with her son John, who is a usurper, to deprive her grandson of that goodly inheritance, which is his by right of primogeniture. The latter sin was worse than the former: for in the former case the ill might have fallen upon him without her

---

* and her, Ff,
† For her,
And with her plague her sin; his injury Ff.

having ever *intended* it, albeit she were the *cause* of it; but in the latter it was inflicted by her consciously, deliberately, and as it were with her own hands belabouring him.

With these two clues to guide us, we shall not have much difficulty in threading our way through the intricacies of the passage. For clearness' sake I will present my explanation in the following form:

'I have but this to say, that he is not only plagued for her sin '—that is, for the general sin committed by her, which, according to the canon, is visited upon him—' but God hath made her sin and her '—aye, not only her sin, but actually *her*, her personally, the very grandmother herself—'the plague on this removed issue, plagued for her '—*this* refers to the canonical denunciation—' and with her plague '—*this* to the grandam's present direct ill-usage of him, in conspiring with her son John to rob him of his rightful inheritance—' her sin his injury'—that is, she has done him grievous wrong in having lived such a life as to bring down upon him the divine chastisement, but, as if that were not enough,—' her injury the beadle to her sin '—she is actually now herself inflicting a wrong upon him, which with beadle-like severity scourges him; in a word, her past wickedness, and her present unnatural cruelty, her injury of him indirectly, and now also directly, 'all' are now visited with the divine chastisement, but not unfortunately on the head of her the wrong doer; but all are 'punished in the person of this child'—not for anything which he has done to deserve it, but 'all for her; a plague upon her!'

After getting out of this labyrinth, we pursue a straight and easy course, until we come to Act III, 1, 259, where it is not a little tantalizing that we have in the Folios a word, which is as nearly right as it possibly can be without being exactly right. 'A *cased* lion' may have been intended either for 'chafed' —so Theobald—or for 'chased'—so Pope—or for 'caged'—so Collier. It does not follow, because we have in 'King Henry VIII,' Act III, 2, 206,

> So looks the *chafed* lion
> Upon the daring huntsman that has galled him,

that 'chafed' was certainly the word used by Shakespeare here; a passage in 3 'Henry VI,' Act I, 3, 12, 13,

> So looks the *pent-up* lion o'er the wretch
> That trembles under his devouring paws,

may give some countenance to 'caged,' a word which I need not say is used by Shakespeare, and is not an unlikely one, as *s* and *g* are somewhat similarly formed, and are not unfrequently confused—*e.g. corasio* for *coragio*. But why quibble about a word, when we have, if we can, to unravel the elaborate web of Cardinal Pandulph's subtle casuistry—a marvellous sample of priestly sophistry—which extends from the 263rd line to the 297th, though the most knotty part is contained in the 279th to the 285th line :

> It is religion that doth make vows *kept ;
> But thou hast sworn against religion,
> By what thou swear'st against the thing thou swear'st,
> And makest an oath the surety for thy truth
> Against an oath : the truth, thou art unsure
> To swear, swears only not to be forsworn.

To say that Shakespeare intended Pandulph's speech to be subtle, and his logic close and intricate, is right enough ; that he intended it to be incomprehensible, cannot be allowed. I make no question that the lines as we have them are as the poet composed them ; all we have to do is to ascertain the punctuation ; that done, the explanation will follow. I have transcribed the passage pretty much as I have found it in the 'Globe' Shakespeare, because, after turning it well over in my mind, I am persuaded that the arrangement there adopted is in the main correct. For the elucidation of the speech I shall make the following expansion of it.

Thou art setting faith against faith, oath against oath, tongue against tongue (263-265). Thy first vow was to be the champion of the church ; it was made to heaven ; it was advantageous to thyself ; to heaven it should be performed. Thy second vow was to be true to thy compact with England's king ; it

---

* In the first Folio the passage is punctuated thus :
Kept, religion : thy truth, an oath the truth, not to be forsworn,

was contrary to thy interest; it was contrary to religion; it may not be performed (265-69). For, if a man swears what is wrong, it is *not wrongly* done —that is to say, it is *rightly* done—when it is done *truly*, and it is done *truly*, when it is *not done at all*, because, if it is done, it tends to evil (269-73). The better plan is, when purposes are mistaken, that they should be again mistaken, that is, that they should be reversed, so that they should be as if they had never been. Indirection, instead of being persisted in, should be made direct by indirection. The crooked course should be trodden back again, till the foot stands where it did before. There is a sort of homœopathy in ethics, as well as in physics; falsehood cures falsehood, as fire cools burns (273-78). Vows are only obligatory, in so far as they conform to the canons of the church—'it is religion that doth make vows kept, but thou hast sworn against religion by what thou swearest against the thing thou swearest,' that is to say, by swearing two things which are irreconcilable with each other, the one being fidelity to the King of England, the other, fidelity to the Church; and so thou art making an oath a surety for thy truth against an oath. Surety for thy truth indeed! *The truth*, as to which thou art so unsure—for how canst thou with all thy vacillation and equivocation give any suretyship for it— the truth, the tongue of truth, the man of truth, swears only not to be forsworn; truth's sole object is truth, but thy object is falsehood—thou dost swear only to be forsworn. The Cardinal concludes with an exhortation to Philip to repudiate his second, and, return to his first vow, to which end he says he will pray; but, if his prayers should prove ineffectual, he has in reserve a heavy load of curses to heap on Philip's head, which will weigh him down to desperation and the dust.

Having extricated ourselves from the Cardinal's meshes, we meet with no hindrance in our course until we come to the following passage in Act III, 3, 37—39, which is obelized by the 'Globe' editors,

> If the midnight bell
> Did, with his iron tongue and brazen mouth,
> Sound on into the drowsy race of night.

The obelus seems to me unnecessary. Certainly 'on' must not be cast out for the little word 'one.' The correctness of '*sound on*' is guaranteed by the occurrence of such phrases as 'say on,' 'go on,' 'run on'; a line in '1 Henry VI,' Act I, 2, 42, is very much to the purpose,

> Their arms are set like *clocks, still to strike on.*

'Drowsy race of night' refers, I think, to the slow progress of the night, as 'her jades with drowsy slow and flagging wings' pursue their course: elsewhere Night is called the 'cripple tardy-gaited'; and in 'Midsummer Night's Dream,' Act V, 1, 375, we have 'the heavy gait of

Night': in 'Pericles' a 'glorious walk' is assigned to the day. The only instance that I remember of 'race' being used at all similarly in Shakespeare, is in 'Measure for Measure,' Act II, 4, 160,

> And now I give my sensual race the rein.

The next passage which catches my eye is in Act IV, 2, 40—43,

> Some reasons of this double coronation
> I have possess'd you with and think them strong;
> And more, more strong, then lesser is my fear,
> I shall indue you with.

Here it is difficult to state positively what the precise meaning is, because we are not at all sure what the reading should be. The little clause, 'then lesser is my fear,' is our *crux*.

I am inclined to think that 'then' is a mistake for 'than'—the two words are repeatedly interchanged by the copyists—and that the comparative 'lesser' is a Shakespearian redundancy—numbers of such redundancies will occur to the reader—where we should rather use the simple comparative 'less'; unless, as is quite possible, the construction here is formed after the model of a well-known Greek and Latin idiom, of which the following example from Livy V, 43, will be a sufficient illustration,

> Bella fortius quam felicius gerere.

The king tells the peers that he has 'more' reasons, and 'more strong' reasons for his double coronation than he has yet disclosed; and it would be not unreasonable to expect him to add, that his fears had *diminished* in consequence. But I am not at all sure that this is what he says. Men, timid and irresolute, who have been agitated by fears, are not so easily reasoned out of their fears. The king was full of fearful foreboding. I understand him to say that *his reasons are stronger than his fears are less*, which is another way of saying, that his fears were not lessened in proportion as his reasons were numerous and weighty. The utmost had been done, but the terror had not passed. This avowal might have been merely the outcome of a heart conscious of its own guilt, but I think that it was rather prompted by the suspicious attitude of the peers towards him, to whom he thus conveys a hint that he is not ignorant of their disaffection. As a slight confirmation of this interpretation, it is noticeable that, in the short remainder of his speech, the King expresses himself as willing to agree to such measures of reform, as they should deem expedient.

I shall next notice a pretty emendation which has been introduced into the text in Act V, 6, 12, where Hubert, having met the Bastard in the darkness of the night and failed to recognise him, on being made aware who it was that he had failed to recognise, exclaims,

> Unkind remembrance! thou and endless night
> Have done me shame: brave soldier, pardon me,
> That any accent breaking from thy tongue
> Should 'scape the true acquaintance of mine ear.

I have written 'endless' night, because 'endles' —'endlesse'—'endless' is the reading of the Folios; yet 'eyeless,' which Theobald adopted, has become the *textus receptus*. We must admit that an 'endless' night is a physical impossibility; yet the expression is not an impossible one: it may be regarded either as a loose popular way of speaking, or as the natural though hyperbolic language of impatience or intense anxiety. People say there is no end to a business, trouble, journey, period of time, when the business, trouble, journey, time are more lingering and tedious than they either wish or expect. And so Hubert, walking in the black brow of night to find the Bastard, impatient and eager to find him that he might communicate to him the stunning intelligence of the poisoning of the king, having all but missed him through the prevailing darkness although close to him, may, inaccurately indeed from a physical, but correctly enough from a popular or metaphysical point of view, apostrophize the night as 'endless.'

A difficulty also has been made of '*invisible*' in Act V, 7, 15-17,

> Death, having preyed upon the outward parts,
> Leaves them invisible, and his siege is now
> Against the mind.

But 'invisible' may be used here for 'invisibly,' the adjective for the adverb—a well-known Shakespearian peculiarity. Personify the King of terrors, give him a kind of body and the power of making himself visible or invisible, and the adverbial adjective is neither inappropriate nor destitute of force. Yet there is another mode of smoothing the difficulty which is not incompatible with the reading of the Folios. The exact word of the copies is '*inuisible*.' This may have been intended not for 'invisible,' but for 'inusible'—a strange form, no doubt; yet 'inteniblc,' which we find in 'All's Well That Ends Well,' Act I, 3, 208, and 'inaidible' in the same play, Act II, 1, 122, may both match and justify it. Granted its admissibility, its applicability is incontrovertible. Death, having preyed upon the outward organs and made them utterly useless, proceeds next to make havoc of the powers of the mind.

Below in the 21st line, where the editions have '*cygnet*,' the Folios have '*Symet*;' the converse happens in 'Macbeth,' Act V, 3, 55, where '*cyme*' of the copies is very properly printed 'senna' in the editions.

KING RICHARD THE SECOND.

The Cambridge editors tell us that the Quarto is the best authority for the text of 'King Richard the Second;' yet in Act I, 2, 67-70, where that copy has

> Alack, and what shall good old York there see
> But empty lodgings and unfurnish'd walls,
> Unpeopled offices, untrodden stones?
> And what *cheere* there for welcome but my groans?

they reject 'cheer,' and give the preference to 'hear,' which is the reading of the Folios. Unquestionably 'see' and 'hear' more closely correspond to each other than 'see' and 'cheer,' and 'hear' is the word that we should naturally have expected; but, in calculating the probabilities of what Shakespeare wrote, it is not always safe to build too much on what a modern critic would expect. Shakespeare is as fond of varying his diction as he is of observing correspondences. The occurrence of such a word as 'welcome' would in this particular instance have facilitated a change, 'cheer' and 'welcome' being reciprocally suggestive. Copyists do not usually set down the rarer word by mistake in lieu of the more common one. Besides, the *idea* of hearing is contained in the phrase 'what cheer there for welcome.' Whether 'hear' were inserted by Shakespeare, when he revised the play, as is certainly possible, or were a correction by Shakespeare's friends, when they undertook to collect his works, we cannot now decide, but I think it not improbable that 'cheer,' which is set down in the first Quarto, *the earliest and most trustworthy impression*, was the word that Shakespeare *originally* introduced.

Nor would I be positive, as some critics are, that in Act I, 3, 128,

> And for our eyes do hate the dire aspect
> Of *cruell* wounds plough'd up with neighbours' sword,

'civil' was intended, where 'cruel' is copied. 'Ploughed up with neighbours' sword' is sufficient to indicate that the contest was a civil one. What we have here is not a possible contingency suggested to the *mind*, but a ghastly spectacle—'dire aspect' is the royal phrase—presented to the *eye*. Under these circumstances, 'cruel' is no mere common descriptive epithet; it is a sentimental one, expressive of the shocked feelings of one who as it were saw with his eyes the furrowed wounds; how cruelly intestine war is wont to be waged, has been drawn by the masterly hand of Thucydides. 'Civil' is the word of the historiographer and of the critic, but is not 'cruel' the feeling exclamation of the eye-witness, and the vivid expression of the poet? In 'Troilus and Cressida,' Prologue, line 5, we read,

> Fraught with the ministers and instruments
> Of cruel war.

I shall next say a word on the arrangement of the text in Act II, 1, 246-48, where some can see nothing but broken and imperfect remains. I do not agree with them. It is not uncommon, when some statement is made, which is intended to be particularly emphatic, to give it point and prominence by putting it in an isolated position. Thus, in 'As You Like It,' 'Thou hast not loved' is three times introduced (Act II, 4, 36, 39, 42), and each time it is made more impressive by being set in a line by itself. The same is done in 'Hamlet,' Act I, 1, 129, 132, 135. And so here; the one fact which of all others was sure and certain was that Richard had forfeited the affections of all classes of his subjects. Accordingly the fact is emphasized by the special position which is assigned to it:

> The commons hath he pill'd with grievous taxes,
> And quite lost their hearts:
> The nobles hath he fined for ancient quarrels,
> And quite lost their hearts.

There is also disagreement among editors as to the way in which the stops should be set, and consequently as to the exact meaning to be given to the Queen's words in Act II, 2, 39, 40. I allow but of one way of punctuating the passage, which, however, has not been approved of by the 'Globe' editors:

> But what it is that is not yet known what,
> I cannot name; 'tis nameless woe, I wot.

Further down—108th and following lines—a portion

of a speech of York's has incurred the suspicion of the same learned editors:

> Gentlemen, will you go muster men?
> If I know how or which way to order these affairs
> Thus disorderly thrust into my hands,
> Never believe me. Both are my kinsmen:
> The one is my sovereign, whom both my oath
> And duty bids defend; the other again
> Is my kinsman, whom the king hath wrong'd.

The second of the above lines is the one which is actually obelized; why, I can hardly say; not surely from any dislike to the phrase 'how or which way,' the frequent recurrence of which in Shakespeare is a pledge that it is genuine; thus in 'All's Well That Ends Well,' Parolles says, Act IV, 3, 156,

> I'll take the sacrament on't, how and which way you will;

and in 'Two Gentlemen of Verona,' Act III, 1, 87, we read,

> How and which way I may bestow myself;

and in 'I Henry VI,' Act II, 1, 71-73,

> Then how or which way should they first break in?
> *Puc:* Question, my lords, no further of the case,
> How or which way; 'tis sure they found some place.

Is it then because the line is an Alexandrine? but the tedious length of an Alexandrine is neither out of place nor destitute of force in this passage, throughout the whole of which York shows, by his abrupt, laboured, hesitating, perplexed utterances, in what an extremely difficult position he suddenly finds himself, and how utterly unable he is to choose with resolution and act with energy. The first three words of the line,—'If I know'—must be taken as an anapæst, just as we have elsewhere 'If I were,' 'If our betters,' &c., &c.; so that it is not necessary, although it would be easy, to take the words, 'if I,' and tack them on to the end of the shorter line that immediately precedes, in which line, as is not uncommon in Shakespeare's versification, 'gentlemen' is equivalent to a dissyllable. One alteration I am sure that we must not make; we must not attempt to give an easier flow and more smoothness to the *third* line of the above passage by placing 'disorderly' after 'thrust,' instead of, as it stands, with all its rough strength and vigour, alike in all the Quartos and in all the Folios, before it. The order of the words ministers to the scene of disorder. 'Disorderly' has as much right to its place, as 'detestable' has in the lines, which no one *would*, and no one *could* alter,

> And I will kiss thy detestable bones ;
> Thou detestable man :

Any interference of the metre-mongers here is as unnecessary, as it is mischievous. Even in the last line, the emphasis, which was intended to be laid on 'whom,' gives it the time of a dissyllable, though Shakespeare would probably have pleased some critics better, had he written,

> The other again,
> *He* is my kinsman, whom the king hath wrong'd.

'Something,' it has been said, 'has doubtless dropped out' in Act III, 2, 175-77, where my text book has

> † I live with bread like you, feel want,
> Taste grief, need friends ; subjected thus,
> How can you say to me, I am a king ?

But here again, the lack in the measure of the verse may have been intended by the poet, in order to bring out into striking relief the lack of means complained of by the King. 'Something is wanting,' the critics cry; 'something is wanting,' is King Richard's lament; the expression matches the matter; the effect is impressive and significant. If, however, it were necessary to excogitate an emendation, I should certainly not side with those who affirm that the 'best suggestion is that of Sydney Walker,' who after 'needs friends' thrusts in 'fear enemies.' I really think that, without assuming too much to myself, I can offer something more plausible than that. If Shakespeare had written,

> I live with bread like you, *like you* feel want,
> Taste grief, need friends *like you;* subjected thus,
> How can you say to me, I am a king ?

the very repetition and close proximity of the underlined words might have facilitated the omission of them. Some such arrangement we have in 'The Winter's Tale,' Act IV, 4, 138,

> When you sing,
> I'd have you buy and sell *so, so* give alms,
> Pray *so.*

but I hear the judicious critic cry, 'Ohe, ohe!'— Enough, enough! This is like mending of high ways in summer, when the ways are fine enough.

It matters not a straw, so far as the sense is concerned, whether in Act V, 1, 25, we read 'stricken' with the Folios, or 'thrown' with the first four Quartos. On the supposition, however, that the Quarto is the most reliable authority, there is no *metrical* reason why we should not follow it here, as elsewhere. In Shakespeare's prosody 'thrown' is as good for a dissyllable as 'stricken.' I need not present it in the form of 'throwen,' after the analogy of 'wreathen,' 'shotten,' 'strucken,' 'foughten,' 'fretten,' 'droven,'—all used by Shakespeare—I need not point to the use of other monosyllables as dissyllables, in order to support my contention; I will merely quote a line from 'Pericles,' Act V, 3, 23, where 'thrown' is actually used, just as, according to the Quartos, it is here:

Thrown upon this shore, I oped the coffin.

Aye, 'thrown'—and I am not sure that 'thrown,' though passed over by some for 'stricken,' is not the more ponderous and forcible, and therefore preferable word here. Accordingly I write

Which our profane hours here have thrown down.

Does not the critic hear the thud?

KING HENRY THE FOURTH.

Part I.

In 'The First Part of King Henry the Fourth,' at the very commencement of the play, a word of common use and simple meaning, by the connexion in which it stands, forces itself on the attention of the reader, and fills him with surprise and perplexity. As he repeats the lines—Act I, 1, 5-6—

> No more the thirsty entrance of this soil
> Shall daub her lips with her own children's blood,

he hesitates at the word 'entrance,' and sceptically inquires, whether *that* is the reading of the copies, whether it can be correct, what other word it is possible and probable that Shakespeare may have written. Nor is he singular in his perplexity. Pages have been written on the passage; numerous emendations have been proposed; I shall add one page more, not for the purpose of starting one more emendation, but to defend the reading of the Quarto, and to indicate one or two meanings, which it seems to me that it is capable of bearing.

And the first in order of mention will probably be reckoned first also in merit. According to it, 'entrance' is used to designate an organic part of the earth's personified body. The lips are the portals of the mouth; through them the 'entrance' into it is effected; the streams of blood that were drunk, as they passed into the mouth, surged over through the narrowness of the 'entrance,' and daubed the lips; and thus, what in reality was caused by the gory fluid, may be said to have been occasioned by the 'entrance' through which it was admitted. This explanation is in keeping with the imagery, and makes the epithet 'thirsty' apply to the earth, as having craved for, or at any rate copiously imbibed the horrid drink.

Or secondly, 'entrance' may not denote a vital and constituent part of the earth's body at all, but something extraneous to and independent of it. We still regard the earth as a person; her habitation is coextensive with the soil from which she derives or to which she gives her name; as the sea-God is masked by the sea, as the river-Gods by the waters, so the earth is concealed by a layer, more or less thick, of the soil under which she dwells—it is this outer stratum, this 'entrance' as it were of the soil, through which the blood that is shed upon it quickly sinks, to be drunk, whether she wills it or not, by the great subterranean mother herself. The rapidity with which it permeates the superficial crust justifies perhaps the application of 'thirsty' to 'entrance' rather than to the earth, to whom, strictly speaking, it would more properly belong.

There is a third mode of treating the passage, which varies considerably from the two preceding ones, and which, in default of them, may perhaps deserve a place. The 'thirsty entrance of this soil' may be a bold periphrasis for an invader setting foot on the land, thirsting for one or other of those many objects which usually influence such adventurers, and which may be summed up under the two heads of private interest or public utility; it is even possible that 'entrance' may be used for the *person who enters*, just as elsewhere 'conduct' stands for 'conductor,' 'revolts' for 'revolters,' 'medicine' for 'medical practitioner,' 'liberties of sin' for 'sinful libertines,' and in 'Much About Nothing,' a certain person is said to be 'turned orthography.' But, be this as it may, it is certain that the King is referring to recent events in the national history, and it is possible that he may be excusing the part which he himself had taken therein, and lamenting the *necessity*—such is the common plea of all these scourges of their kind —which had compelled him to disembark on the coast of Yorkshire, unfurl the banner of rebellion, and pollute his country with blood. As a slight confirmation of this view of the passage, it may be mentioned that, after the King had referred to the *first landing* on the soil (supposing that 'entrance' may allude to that event), he proceeds to mention the march into the *inland country*, where the fields were channelled with trenching war, and the flowers bruised by the armed hoofs of hostile paces. The regular progress of the invader would thus be delineated.

The next passage which I shall notice requires, I think, to be emended, rather than explained. It occurs in Act IV, 1, 31, where Hotspur is commenting on the contents of a letter which he had just received from his father, who politicly excused himself on various pretexts from joining at that critical moment the insurgent army.

> He writes me here, that inward sickness—
> And that his friends by deputation could not
> So soon be drawn.

Here there is a violation both of the metre and the syntax. The most that can be said for the first line, as it stands, is that Hotspur just reads enough of the sentence to get the pith of it, and then, leaving it unfinished, hurries on, impatient to hear what comes next. Such hot-headed haste, it must be admitted, would be eminently characteristic of the speaker, who, much as he was concerned that the Trent should run on straight and even, for the straightness and evenness of the grammar would care not a groat. In my opinion, however, there is a surer, easier, more natural explanation. Allow for a little illegible writing—allow for a little confusedness, consequent on the words having been jumbled together rather too closely, and 'sickness' and 'sick-he-is' are all but identical. Unfortunately the former word has usurped the place of the latter, but the latter have a metrical and grammatical right to it. That Shakespeare did not disdain to end a line with some part or other of the substantive verb may be seen from the following examples,

> Which harm within itself so heinous is.
> 'King John,' Act III, 1, 40.

> From helmet to the spur all blood he was.
> 'King Henry V,' Act IV, 6, 6.

> For by my mother I derived am.
> 'I King Henry VI,' Act II, 5, 74.

With some confidence, therefore, I restore to the passage what I believe to be Shakespeare's own line,

> He writes me here that inward sick he is.

I am not aware what amount of objection has been raised to Act V, 2, 8, where editors seem to have settled to their own satisfaction that 'supposition'—such is the reading of the copies—is a mistake for 'suspicion,' and so 'suspicion' they have printed. But Worcester had only a moment before said,

> *He will suspect us still* and find a time
> To punish this offence in other faults,

and I hardly think that Shakespeare would have made him repeat himself immediately afterwards, by adding,

> *Suspicion* all our lives shall be stuck full of eyes.

May not that long awkward word 'supposition' have been intended for a yet longer word 'supposititious,' which was a critic's gloss, expressive of his opinion that the whole line was an interpolation? Certain it is that, if the line were omitted, it would not be missed. The words of the speaker would flow on just as continuously and just as connectedly. If it be said that the phrase is undoubtedly a Shakespearian one, I answer, 'Undoubtedly, and perhaps borrowed from one of those passages where it actually occurs?' But mark how differently it is used here from what it is elsewhere. In 'Measure for Measure,' Act IV, 1, 60-61, where we have

> O place and greatness! millions of false eyes
> Are stuck upon thee,

and in 'A Lover's Complaint,' line 81, where we read

> That maidens' eyes stuck over all his face,

it is in the one case *the person desired*, in the other *the person gazed at*, who is said to be stuck all over with eyes; and by parity of expression we should have expected here not 'Suspicion stuck full of eyes' —Suspicion's eyes are never wanting—but the persons who were the objects of suspicion, who in this particular instance were Vernon and Worcester. If the whole line is not a forgery, rather than suppose that 'supposition' was intended for 'suspicion,' I would remove the former word altogether, as a parasitical fungus which had got attached to the original line, and I would substitute for it the pronoun 'we,' which continually recurs throughout the speech, and may have been accidentally omitted. This would give us

> We all our lives shall be stuck full of eyes,

a line of the normal length, Shakespearian in expression, and unexceptionable as regards meaning. For, if once it were whispered that the King suspected them, numbers of eyes, other than the King's, would be constantly upon them. But, although I have nothing more than 'supposition' on which to found my opinion, I have a strong 'suspicion' that the line is 'supposititious?

In conclusion, I may notice a singular ellipse of a verb in Act V, 2, 77-79,

> Better consider what you have to do
> Than I, that have not well the gift of tongue,
> Can lift your blood up with persuasion.

The verb, of which 'I' is the subject, is not actually expressed in any part of the sentence, but has to be taken out of the verbal phrase, 'lift up with persuasion,' the construction being, 'than I persuade'—*i.e. attempt* to persuade—'you, who have not well the gift of tongue, which can lift your blood up with persuasion.' I am well aware, however, that this is not the only way in which it is possible to construe the sentence.

KING HENRY THE FOURTH.

Part II.

I shall now proceed to probe one or two passages in the Second Part of 'King Henry the Fourth,' which are suspected of unsoundness. In Act I, 3, 36-37, there is certainly corruption, though it is susceptible of treatment, if not of cure. 'Should expectations and hopes be taken into account in forming an estimate of military resources?'—this is the question on which the debate turns in a council of war held in the palace of the Archbishop of York. Hastings contends that they should;

> But, by your leave, it never yet did hurt
> To lay down likelihoods and forms of hope.

Lord Bardolph takes the opposite view, and states his case clearly enough, but the first two lines of his speech are clogged with difficulty, owing probably to a word having been set down by the copyist, which, though it resembled, did not reproduce the word of the original. The lines are thus given in the 'Globe' Shakespeare:

> Yes, if this present quality of war,
> Indeed the instant action : a cause on foot
> Lives so in hope as in an early spring
> We see the appearing buds ; which to prove fruit,
> Hope gives not so much warrant as despair
> That frosts will bite them.

It is manifest that in the first two lines some emendation is necessary, but none has yet been suggested which can be pronounced altogether satisfactory. What is wanted is some verb to take the place of the adverb 'indeed.' The verb 'induced,' used often enough and sometimes rather peculiarly by Shakespeare, may be the verb that we are looking for. To Hastings' assertion that it never yet did hurt to lay down likelihoods and forms of hope Lord Bardolph answers, 'Yes, it *did hurt*, if this present quality of war,' that is to say, this warring on hope, this dependence on a bubble, this speculative gambling spirit, ' *induced* the instant action '—were the covering to hide its nakedness, stuffed and padded its thin skeleton-like frame, were the blood to colour it, the soul to quicken it, the power in reserve to reinforce and renew it. 'Instant action,' which is the more particular expression, indicates a battle on the very eve of being fought, just as in '1 Henry IV,' Act 4, 4,20, we have

> I fear the power of Percy is too weak
> To wage an instant trial with the king ;

'a cause on foot'—the more general term—refers to a war already proclaimed and begun. The sense, which I have given to 'indued,' is somewhat analogous to that which it bears in 'Othello,' Act III, 4, 146,

> For let our finger ache, and it indues
> Our other healthful members even to that sense
> Of pain.

So far as resemblance to the word of the copies is concerned, 'indued' can hardly be bettered. We have merely to erase the comma after 'war,' and in the room of 'indeed' introduce 'indued.'
In Act IV, 1, 50, the commentators are in doubt, whether

> Turning your books to *graves*

is the exact phrase which Shakespeare indited. It has been thought that 'greaves' would be more suitable. The change would be insignificant, the meaning unexceptionable,—the leather which bound the Archbishop's books being capable of being manufactured into that particular part of a soldier's equipment. Moreover, it is credible that 'greaves' was sounded like 'graves.' Notwithstanding, the word of the copies is not inappropriate, and I am not sure that it is not preferable. When it is said that the Archbishop turned his ink to blood, it is not meant that the ink *became* blood, but merely that he was intent on dipping into blood, and *not* into ink: and similarly his pen was not *turned* into a lance, but the pen was dropped, and the lance poised in its stead: and so with the tongue; and so with the trumpet: when, then, the Archbishop is said to be turning his books to 'graves,' it is not necessary to suppose that his books or any portion of them were actually *used* for military purposes, but simply that he left his study and his books, to deal with the battle-field, the slaughter, and the burial of the dead.

Or I might put it thus: the Archbishop, instead of taking up his *pen*, and dipping it into *ink*, and composing a learned *book*, which would be a monument to his memory, was poising the *lance*, and going to dip it into the *blood* of his countrymen, and the work, which he would be thus engaged in and which would be remembered as his, would be not a *book*, nor a library of books, but a *grave*, or rather a yardful of graves: a grave-maker he would be, and not a bookmaker. That 'graves,' rather than 'greaves,' is the genuine word, is rendered further probable by the *order* in which the several things referred to stand relatively to each other. To begin with the last first, and proceed in retrograde fashion, we observe first the military arrangements—'a point of war'; next, the signal for battle—the 'trumpet'; after that, the charge and the combat—the 'lance'; then the slaughter—the 'blood'; last of all, what should, what *must* come? What but the burial of the dead—the 'graves'? 'Greaves' here would be out of place, and would spoil the picture of the battle. There is reason, therefore, for the editors *not* departing from the reading of the Folio.

A little further on in the same Act and Scene we come to a spirited dialogue between the Duke of Westmoreland on the King's side, and the Archbishop of York on the side of the insurgents.

> *West:* When ever yet was your appeal denied?
> Wherein have you been galled by the king?
> What peer hath been suborn'd to grate on you,
> That you should seal this lawless bloody book
> Of forged rebellion with a seal divine
> And consecrate commotion's bitter edge?
>
> *Arch:* † My brother general, the commonwealth,
> To brother born an household cruelty,
> I make my quarrel in particular.

I must not omit to mention here that the *last* line of Westmoreland's speech, and the *second* of the Archbishop's, are not in the Folios, nor in every copy of the Quarto: their obliteration would greatly reduce, if it did not annihilate, the difficulty. Notwithstanding, as they are found in that particular copy, of the Quarto which is declared to be the most trustworthy authority for this play, we must not refuse to take them into account; for, to use the words of Bacon, we must not 'reject difficulties for want of patience in investigation.'

On taking a general survey of the whole passage, what strikes me first and foremost, is the different cast and character of the two speeches: the contrast is very striking—in the one, indignant interrogatory, repeated fervid appeal, angry upbraiding, flowers of rhetoric; in the other, a cold calm concise dry judicial statement. The Archbishop's reply has been thought wanting in clearness, confused, corrupt. Various efforts have been made to elucidate, to emend it. I admit that it embarasses, and almost staggers us at first; the arrangement is preposterous; the phraseology peculiar; yet I do not believe that the Archbishop has been misreported; nor can I allow that his words are ill-placed or ill-chosen, or that they are otherwise than lucid. We have to examine them in close connexion with Westmoreland's chidings; we have to consider the effect, that such ideas as Westmoreland's would be likely to have on one of the Archbishop's spirit, discernment, and high pretensions; we must call to recollection, too, certain facts of history.

Westmoreland had proceeded on the supposition that the Archbishop felt personally aggrieved and was seeking for personal satisfaction; he had twitted him with ingratitude, and branded him as a rebel and apostate; but he had not said one syllable of the *public welfare, or the cause of humanity*. The Archbishop, cool, calm, collected, perceived his advantage, and seized it. He occupied at once the lofty summit of patriotism and humanity, and in three lines confounds his adversary. The interests of the commonwealth—the late King's violated majesty—these he places, and purposely places, and proudly places, in the very fore front of his reply, in order to contrast with, and stand directly opposed to,

Westmoreland's miserable grovellings. *These* were the Archbishop's motives: *these* touched him personally; these were his grievances; these his quarrel. The measured tone, the air of lofty superiority, with which he uttered the words,

> I make my quarrel in particular,

can be better conceived than expressed. If we had heard the Archbishop's own elocution, there would have been no possibility, I think, of our misunderstanding his meaning.

To come now to particulars, 'the commonwealth' he calls his 'brother-general,' just as in 'Coriolanus,' Act II, 3, 102, a certain one is ready to call the people his 'sworn brother,' though the expression, coming from an Archbishop's mouth, may be thought to have a more comprehensive significance, and to savour somewhat of Christian theology. The act of 'cruelty' referred to is *Bolingbroke's treatment of Richard*; 'household cruelty' it is called, to distinguish it from 'commonwealth cruelty'; 'brother-born' is an additional aggravation; for, if the Archbishop were bound to the people at large by the tie of a general brotherhood, by a dearer and nearer relationship was Bolingbroke bound to Richard—was not a 'brother-general' merely, but a 'brother-born,' seeing that they had both sprung from the same blood royal.

The same two capital reasons are elsewhere alleged as the pretext and justification of the rebellion. In

Act I, 1, 200-209, Morton says to Northumberland,

> But now the bishop
> Turns insurrection to religion :
> . . . .
> . . . .
> And doth enlarge his rising with the blood
> Of fair King Richard, scraped from Pomfret stones ;
> Derives from heaven his quarrel and his cause ;
> Tells them *he doth bestride a bleeding land,*
> Gasping for life under great Bolingbroke.

It has been thought by some more likely that the Archbishop refers to the death of his own brother, Lord Scroop—'1 Henry IV,' 1, 3—and that Westmoreland would most certainly have so understood him; but it should be borne in mind, that, however much the Archbishop might desire to revenge his brother's death, he could not decently proclaim *that* to the public ear as the cause of his uprising; it would be more politic to dissemble his private wrongs, to smother his personal resentment; but the safety of the state, the cruel treatment of the King—these were more specious pretexts. And that this was the Archbishop's meaning is evident from Morton's account of the Archbishop's public manifesto, as given in the passage I have just quoted. Nor am I here 'catching at shadows of resemblance.'

KING HENRY THE FIFTH.

The first passage that I shall notice in 'King Henry the Fifth' consists of a couple of lines in the second Scene of the first Act, at the end of a long and learned dissertation delivered by the Archbishop of Canterbury, in support of his thesis that the King of England could rightfully claim the crown of France:

> Howbeit they would hold up this Salique law
> To bar your highness claiming from the female,
> And rather choose to hide them in a net
> Than amply to imbar their crooked titles
> Usurp'd from you and your progenitors.

The puzzle here is to find a meaning for the verb 'imbar'—spelt 'imbarre' in the Folio—which the word will bear, and which the passage seems to require. It may help to clear the way somewhat, and be of advantage to us, if we explain in the first instance what is meant by the French hiding them in a net.

The Archbishop argues that, in their eagerness to vitiate King Henry's title, the French had hunted up an old law, called the Salique law, which excluded from the succession all those who claimed, as the English King did, from the female. This law, according to the Archbishop, did not touch the question at all, as the Salian land was a distinct configuration from the French land. He supposes, however, that it were otherwise, that the lands were one and the same, and that the law was applicable, and he proceeds to show that the effect of it would be to vitiate the title not of the English King only, but of a large number of the French Kings as well—the reigning Monarch among the number—forasmuch as they held in right and title of the female. It was in this way, then, that the French had hidden them in a net; they had taken shelter in a law in the meshes of which they themselves had been caught. And this they had chosen to do rather

> Than amply to imbar their crooked titles.

These words, it is obvious, must be antithetical to those which immediately precede them. Whatever be their meaning, of this we may be sure, that the sum and substance of the Archbishop's counsel to the French must be that they should have done with their artful chicanery, and submit to have the question decided in a fair and straightforward manner according to the recognised law of succession. Now supposing that 'amply' contains the idea of large and handsome dealing, which is pretty much the sense that it bears in the phrases, 'ample amends,' 'ample security,' the spirit indicated by it will be directly opposed to the sly trickery attributed to the French in the previous line; and, if 'imbar' may be allowed to mean, what Mr. Knight informs us that an anonymous expositor declares that it may mean, '*to bring to the bar of judgment*,' we have already a sense which fulfils the antithesis which the passage requires. As, however, there is no instance, that I know of, of 'imbar' ever having been used in this sense, and as I am by no means sanguine that it can be so used, I venture to offer another, and, unless I am mistaken, a better explanation. I shall assume that 'imbar' is used here in pretty nearly the same sense as the simple verb 'bar,' just as 'pawn' and 'impawn,' 'paint' and 'impaint' are used elsewhere almost indifferently. When, then, it is said that the French did not choose to imbar their crooked titles, it is merely another way of saying—it is an abridged and perfectly allowable way of saying—that they did not choose to *rest on a law which would imbar* those titles; what would be done by the *law*, is said to be done by *themselves*—a well-known figure of speech, which, though it has embarrassed all the expositors, would be quite intelligible to the learned congregation which the Archbishop was at the time addressing. Thus interpreted, the two lines stand in capital antithetical relation to each other. This mode of dealing with the passage is surely better than to entertain such a word as 'imbare,' or to read, as Pope wished to do, 'openly to embrace' in lieu of 'amply to imbar.' Were there room for conjecture, I would far rather shape out something from the Quarto's word 'imbrace,' and regard it as a corruption of 'abase,' so as to make the Archbishop say, that the handsome thing for the French to have done would have been to lower their pretensions—to *abase* their crooked titles, or rather to *erase* them altogether. But I hold fast to the explanation which I have given above, as, upon the whole, a fair solution of a problem which is by no means free from difficulty.

A little further on, in the same Act and Scene, we find Westmoreland and Exeter urging the King to proclaim the war, which the Archbishop had declared to be lawful. Exeter having said

> Your brother kings and monarchs of the earth
> Do all expect that you should rouse yourself
> As did the former lions of your blood,

Westmoreland continues—125, 27—

> They know your grace hath cause and means and might;
> So hath your highness—never king of England
> Had nobles richer and more loyal subjects.

The usual mode of pointing these last lines is to put a semicolon after 'highness,' the effect of which is to emphasize 'hath,' which consequently would have for its object the nouns 'cause and means and might' understood from the preceding line. I have punctuated differently, and I construe and interpret differently. I place a hyphen rather than a semicolon after 'highness,' and consider that Westmoreland, having either intended to say, or made a feint of intending to say, 'so hath your highness rich nobles and loyal subjects,' suddenly breaks off, as not satisfied with that mode of expressing himself, or as having been struck with a more appropriate and felicitous one; anyhow, this breaking off of his, whether a courtly ruse or not, rivets the attention more than ever to what he is going to say of the King, whom with exquisite adulation, the more telling because seemingly unpremeditated, he pinnacles above all the monarchs who had preceded him. Grammatically, then, 'hath' borrows for its object 'rich nobles and loyal subjects' from the sentence which follows; dramatically, it has no object; the finishing stroke is given in a fresh and finer combination.

This view of the passage, though quite tenable, and eminently Shakespearian, is yet so different from that which is ordinarily taken, that I shall make no apology for introducing here a few examples, taken from other plays, which may serve to illustrate and confirm what seems at first sight a very improbable interpretation. Thus in this very play we have, Act I, 1, 3,

> My lord, I'll tell you; that self bill is urged,
> Which in the eleventh year of the last king's reign
> Was like, and had indeed against us pass'd;

where the full expression would have been 'was like to have passed';

'Richard II,' Act V, 5, 27,

> Who sitting in the stocks refuge their shame,
> That many have and others must sit there;

that is, 'many have sat, and others must sit';

'Troilus and Cressida,' Act I, 3, 288-89,

> And may that soldier a mere recreant prove,
> That means not, hath not, or is not in love;

i.e. 'means not to be, hath not been, or is not';

'All's Well That End's Well,' Act II, 5, 51-52,

I have spoken better of you than you have or will to deserve at my hand,

which is equivalent to 'better than you have deserved.'

Reserving for future notice a much more startling illustration, I shall merely add here, that, although the examples which I have given do not of course prove conclusively that my mode of stopping and explaining the passage is the right one, they go to show that it is not repugnant to Shakespeare's usage—that it is possible—I go farther and say, that it is not only probable, but preferable to any other.

A word, which occurs in a speech of King Henry's in the same Act and Scene, lines 273-75, must next be considered.

> But tell the Dauphin I will keep my state,
> Be like a king and show my sail of greatness,
> When I do rouse me in my throne of France.

'Sayle' is the exact word which is found in the first, second, and third Folios, for which some have desired to write 'soul,' which they think was certainly Shakespeare's word, and much more appropriate. The conjecture is plausible; the change insignificant; the sense yielded unexceptionable; yet, if emendation is to be thought of, there is another word, which may fairly be put in to compete for the place. The Dauphin, having taunted the English King with low tastes and mean ambition, the latter might not inaptly bid tell the Dauphin that he would be

> Like a king, and show his zeal of greatness.

This change, though at first sight it seems considerable, is in reality hardly a change at all. The letter *s* is continually sounded like *z*, and *z* like *s*; *ea* was more often pronounced like long *a* in Shakespeare's time than it is in our own; '*meat*' was '*mate*,' and in 'King Henry VIII,' Act III, 1, 9-10, 'sea' rhymes to 'play,'

> Everything that heard him play,
> Even the billows of the sea:

We may be pretty sure, then, that 'zeal' was pronounced like the French zèle, and probably by not a few exactly like 'sail'; the error once written was little likely to be challenged, when so many other more serious ones escaped detection.

I have so far humoured the suspicions of the critics, as to notice a plausible conjecture, and to suggest another possible one; but I am not disposed in this particular instance to part with the *litera scripta* of the copies for the guess-word of any emendator. That nautical phraseology should be current among an island people, at a time when nautical enterprise was enormously stimulated by startling discoveries and dashing sea-fights which yielded rich prizes, needs surprise no one. The gallant and glorious deeds of naval heroes, which were talked of in the streets, were glanced at in the theatres, and were received with great gladness and enthusiastic clappings; hits of this kind Shakespeare well knew how to make; 'sail' he uses in two senses—in the more limited one as part of a ship's tackle, and in its larger signification of a ship's course. In the latter sense it occurs in

'King John, Act V, 7, 53,'

> And all the shrouds wherewith my life should sail,
> Are turned to one thread, one little hair;

'Othello,' Act V, 2, 268,

> And very sea-mark of your utmost sail;

Sonnet,

> The proud full sail of his great verse.

According to this sense of it, the king would intimate that, though France might be to him a sea of trouble, and its horizon might lour with tempests, yet he would sail on his course day by day, and give proof of that greatness, for his supposed lack of which the Dauphin had taunted him. If, however, the other meaning of 'sail' be thought preferable, we can abundantly illustrate it by such passages as follow:

2 'Henry IV,' Act V, 2, 17-18,

> How many nobles then should hold their places,
> That must strike sail to spirits of vile sort!

3 'Henry VI,' Act III, 3, 5,

> No, mighty King of France: now Margaret
> Must strike her sail and learn awhile to serve.

3 'Henry VI,' Act V, 1, 52,

> I had rather chop this hand off at a blow,
> And with the other fling it at thy face,
> Than bear so low a sail to strike to thee.

I conclude, then, that '*sail*,' authorized as I believe it to be by the Folios, should on no account be discarded.

As little reason is there for swerving from the track of the Folios in Act II, 2, 138-40, where the King, upbraiding Lord Scroop with his ingratitude and treachery, says

> And thus thy fall hath left a kind of blot
> To make the full-fraught man and best indued
> With some suspicion.

Place a comma, nay, only conceive a comma placed after 'man,' and another after 'best,' and, where is the difficulty? What possibility is there of mistaking either the construction or the meaning? That Pope should have abstained from meddling is proof enough of itself that Theobald's proposed change of 'make' to 'mark' is quite unnecessary; yet even when Theobald slips many follow.

It has been deemed incredible that in Act III, 3, 35, where the King warns the citizens of Harfleur of the terrible consequences that would ensue, if they rejected his proffered mercy, Shakespeare could have written

look to see
The blind and bloody soldier with foul hand
Desire the locks of your shrill-shrieking daughters.

What! nothing more terrible than '*desire*' from an infuriated soldiery, let loose, like so many hell-hounds, on a stormed city! Rowe was the first to throw a little more devilry into the text by changing 'desire' into 'defile.' Carried away by the unanimity with which all the critics condemned 'desire,' yet not quite satisfied with Rowe's conjecture, I at one time cast about for something better, and, remembering that, when a messenger brought ill-tidings to Cleopatra, the ungovernable passion of the Egyptian Queen vented itself in the ferocious threat—the unparalleled expression—'I'll unhair your head'—I ventured to ask myself whether here too a special word might not have been coined for a special occasion—a word without a parallel—a horrible compound—the word '*dishair*,' the faint echo of which I fancied I caught in 'desire'; but, after further consideration I have come to the conclusion that the word, which we have, may possibly be the word that Shakespeare wrote. 'To desire with the hand'—what is it but to stretch out the hand for, to lust to seize a booty, almost within reach, but not yet actually grasped. 'To defile with the hand' is to have the booty already in their filthy grasp. The one is a picture of the virgins flying with shrill shrieks from their bloody pursuers, who with outstretched hands are eager to seize their flowing locks; the other is a picture of them already in the hands of the ruffian soldiers. Both are equally picturesque — equally terrible. Perhaps the former is more delicately touched and more exquisitely wrought; the latter is certainly ruder and more masterly; in spite of the savagery of the scene depicted, it is not impossible that the artist-poet may have given expression here to the former.

There is a fine passage in the 4th Act, beginning at the 257th line of the first Scene, where the King, soliloquizing on the vanity of kingly greatness, addresses ceremony as a living personal entity, and questions her as to who, or what she was, and why such extraordinary value was set upon her, such extraordinary worship was paid to her. 'Place, degree, and form' he could conceive her as being, but he exclaims,

> What are thy rents ? what are thy comings in ?
> O ceremony, show me but thy worth !
> What is thy soul of adoration ?

It is the last line which has a mark set against it by the 'Globe' editors, and I have printed it as they have, disregarding the note of interrogation after 'what,' and also 'Odoration'—which is merely a copyist's mode of spelling 'adoration'—both of which disfigure the first Folio. Now if adoration had been something more than an attitude—a gesture; if it had been something capable of being apprehended and appraised, the royal querist might have said simply 'what is the adoration that is accorded to thee'? But, inasmuch as he craves for something more than an empty name or idle motion, inasmuch as he labours to get at the heart of the matter and to find out something definite and precise about her, he does not put it so, but he says 'What is the soul of the adoration that is paid thee, which can be said to be truly thine?' What is there which is, and not merely appears? which has a real and sterling, and not merely an ideal and nominal value? which is constant and abiding, not ephemeral and fleeting? What is there which has a principle of vitality, and is no mere cold dead form? He seeks, in a word, to find the *soul*, and refuses to be mocked with a fine fantastic shape. As a soul is attributed to adoration here, so elsewhere to joy, beauty, goodness.

KING HENRY THE SIXTH.

Part I.

There is very little indeed that requires special comment from me in any one of the three parts of 'King Henry The Sixth'; what revision has been necessary, and at the same time possible, has been fairly accomplished by the assiduous industry of successive critics. Yet in Act I, 1, 56, there is still a line left unfinished, a word wanting, a gap in the text to be filled; and, although it is of course impossible to say for certain, what the word was that originally completed both the metre and the sense, in this instance we happen to have a better chance than usual of making a lucky guess, as we are circumscribed in our selection by three considerations. In the first place, the word must be a proper name; in the second place, it must be such as the metre will admit; in the third place, it must be recommended by historic fitness. We have to discover, if we can, in the vast expanse of the political horizon a soul-star that may shine by the side of the *Julium sidus*. The brilliancy of Charlemagne's career has been thought by some to entitle him to the place, and 'great Charlemain' actually occurs in 'All's Well That End's Well.' I give the preference to Constantine, whom Gibbon—and his testimony in this instance is above suspicion—has not hesitated to pronounce 'great.' Like Cæsar, Constantine was famous for military activity and successful achievement; both triumphed over domestic rivals and a barbarian foe; both founded a dynasty and an empire; both were exalted to divine honours in a pagan, and Constantine in a Christian heaven as well. In this very play—Act I, 2, 142—the name of Constantine figures conspicuously:

> Helen, the mother of *great Constantine*,
> Nor yet St. Philip's daughters were like thee,
> *Bright* star of Venus, fallen down to the earth.

If, therefore, as I think probable, Shakespeare completed the line, the Duke of Bedford may well have been made to couple together the two great luminaries of the Eastern and the Western world, of Byzantium and of Rome.

It is a matter of infinitesimally small consequence, whether, in the 62nd line of this same Act and Scene, the note of interrogation stands at the end of the line, or in the middle of it, although I confess I have a decided preference for

> What say'st thou, man? Before dead Henry's corse
> Speak softly, &c.

but it is not a matter of small consequence, how we place the stops—I am now taking a long jump—in Act IV, 6, 42-47. By substituting a note of exclamation for the ordinary comma, I venture to think that I not only simplify a somewhat complicated sentence, but I give clearness to the meaning, and throw spirit and fire into a soldier's utterance.

> The sword of Orleans hath not made me smart ;
> These words of yours draw life-blood from my heart :
> On that advantage, bought with such a shame,
> To save a paltry life, and slay bright fame !
> Before young Talbot from old Talbot fly,
> The coward horse that bears me fall and die !

A sentiment and a spirit worthy of the gallant son of a gallant sire ! The infinitives, 'to save,' 'to slay,' like Virgil's

> Mene incepto desistere victam !

are infinitives of indignant remonstrance ! That Shakespeare well knew how to turn them to account, the following examples will show,

> Louis marry Blanche !
> Thou wear a lion's hide !
> This lord go to him !
>   She, in spite of nature,
> Of years, of country, credit, everything,
> To fall in love with what she feared to look on !

I add to the list the words that were spoken by young John Talbot.

We might read the 70th and 71st lines of Act V, Scene 3, without being in the least aware that we had come to a part of the play, which had exercised the ingenuity of commentators, but a glance at the foot-notes in the Cambridge Shakespeare shows us that, where the copies have

> Ay, beauty's princely majesty is such
> Confounds the tongue, and makes the senses rough,

even Capell would have altered to 'makes the senses crouch,' Collier to 'mocks the sense of touch,' another to 'wakes the sense's touch,' and generally editors seem to be under the impression that the fag end of the line is faulty. But the fault lies with the would-be emendators; Shakespeare knew well what he was about, when he set down what the copies ascribe to him. There is, an allusion to the confusion and awkwardness, the rudeness and want of self-possession, which are occasionally observed in some—not usually so affected—when they are ushered into the presence of some great personage, or confronted by the gaze of some world-famed beauty. The following quotations may be read with advantage.

'As You Like It,' Act I, 2, 269,

> What passion hangs these weights upon my tongue?
> I cannot speak to her, yet she urged conference.

'Merchant of Venice,' Act III, 2 177,

> Madam, you have bereft me of all words,
> Only my blood speaks to you in my veins;
> And there is such confusion in my powers,
> As, after some oration, &c.

Compare also 'Midsummer-Night's Dream,' Act V, 1, 93.

A little below in the 193rd line the first Folio reads '*mad* natural graces,' which editors have changed to '*And* natural graces'; possibly Shakespeare wrote

Maid-natural graces that extinguish art,

a compound formed after the analogy of 'maid-pale,' which is found elsewhere.

I shall only add that in Shakespeare's versification 'contrary' may be pronounced in the time of either a trisyllable or a quadrisyllable, and the quantity of its penultimate is sometimes long, sometimes short. The reader, then, may scan the 64th line of Act V, Scene 5,

Whereas the contrary bringeth bliss,

as he likes, provided he is content to let it alone.

KING HENRY THE SIXTH.

Part II.

I pass on to the second Part of 'King Henry The Sixth,' where critics might have saved themselves the trouble of trying to mend the metre in Act I, 3, 153,

> She's tickled now ; her fume needs no spurs,

if they had recollected that 'tickle' in particular, and words of similar termination generally, are repeatedly used by Shakespeare as trisyllables, so that all corrections here are nugatory.

But in Act II, 1, 26, where Gloucester says to the Cardinal,

> Churchmen so hot ! Good uncle, hide such malice ;
> With such holiness can you do it.

a word of comment is not out of place; a full stop at the end of the last line is right, a note of interrogation wrong. For Gloucester does not so much twit the Cardinal for inconsistency, as he sneers at him for his hypocrisy, as though it were easy for *him* to use his holiness as a cloak of his malice; and he distinctly intimates that the Cardinal would have no compunction in so using it. Let the learned critics rail at the little phrase 'do it' as much as they will, it is one that is used so repeatedly in conversation in the great theatre of the world, that it is surprising that any should doubt the probability, or question the propriety, of its being used in the course of a dialogue in the tiny theatre in which 'King Henry the Sixth' was acted. The critics are too crotchety. I grant that the line seems to halt, but the slow deliberate measured way, the peculiar tone of voice, with which this stinging insult would be conveyed, may account for its shortness, and make it quite equal in length to one of ordinary measure.

There is one more passage in this Second Part, on which I am anxious to say a word: it is in Act IV, 10, 56, where Alexander Iden is represented as saying to Cade,

> Thy hand is but a finger to my fist,
> Thy leg a stick compared with this truncheon;
> My foot shall fight with all the strength thou hast;
> And if mine arm be heaved in the air,
> Thy grave is digg'd already in the earth.
> As for words, whose greatness answers words,
> Let this my sword report what speech forbears.

The difficulty is confined to the last two lines, and is partly of a textual, partly of an interpretative character. As touching the text, I hold it to be so certain that the pronoun 'thy' has been omitted by the merest accident in the last line but one—do not the 'thy,' 'thy,' 'thou,' 'thy,' of the previous lines sound in the reader's ear, and cry for the repetition?—that I marvel that it has not occurred to the commentators, and been installed in its rightful position in the text; specially as in the 'Tempest,' Act I, 2, 58, they have not hesitated to introduce 'thou,' on the authority of Steevens, in order to complete the sense and perfect the metre. I assume, then, that the lines should be printed

> As for *thy* words, whose greatness answers words,
> Let this my sword report what speech forbears,

and I proceed in the next place to show in what way the couplet should be interpreted. Surely he is a bad interpreter who would refer 'whose' to 'words;' it should be referred to 'combatants.' The following paraphrase will illustrate both the construction and the meaning. 'As for thy words, which of the two's greatness, mine or thine, corresponds to, or matches, words, let this my sword report; for with my tongue I would fain not utter it.' Blows, not boasts, suit Alexander Iden best. Of the use of 'whose' in this way we have not a bad example in another part of this very play,

> And poise the cause in justice' equal scales,
> Whose beam stands sure, whose rightful cause prevails.

For the sentiment we may go to 'Macbeth,' Act V, 8, 7,

> I have no words:
> My voice is in my sword;

and 'Cymbeline,' Act IV, 2, 78,

> Have not I
> An arm as big as thine? a heart as big?
> Thy words, I grant, are bigger, for I wear not
> My dagger in my mouth.

KING HENRY THE SIXTH.

Part III.

I have considerable misgivings, whether I ought to write a single word on the one only portion of the Third Part of 'King Henry the Sixth,' which seems to provoke the pen of the speculative critic—I allude to Act I, 4, 152-53,

> That face of his the hungry cannibals
> Would not have touch'd, would not have stain'd with blood,

for such is the reading of the passage in an edition, which, though for convenience and uniformity's sake it is called by the Cambridge editors a Quarto, is, they tell us, in point of fact an Octavo. There is no fault to be found with the lines either in respect of metre, rhythm, or sense : cannibals would not have *hurt*, much less *slain*, the fair-faced boy. But there are suspicious circumstances connected with them, which ought to be fairly met and debated. In the first place, they are arranged in the first Folio in three lines instead of in two :

> That face of his
> The hungry cannibals would not have touch'd,
> Would not have stain'd with blood ;

a discrepancy this, which would not be worth noting, were it not that in the second, third, and fourth Folios, which are usually no more than reproductions of the first, or of each other, with just occasional variations, there is a variation, which is *not* slight or immaterial, but considerable and important; there is, in fact, a distinct addition to the text,

> Would not have stain'd *the roses just* with blood—

not fresh *words* merely, but a fresh *idea;* and that too, where there seemed neither room nor reason, so far as metre and meaning were concerned, for any innovation whatever—the fresh idea, too, has a poetic colour, and is full of Shakespearian fragrance; for I am struck with such passages as 'Measure for Measure,' Act I, 4, 16,

> Those cheek-roses;

'I Henry VI,' Act II, 4, 49-62,

> Meantime your cheeks do counterfeit our roses;

'Richard III,' Act IV, 3, 12,

> Their lips were four red roses on a stalk;

'Titus Andronicus,' Act II, 4, 24,

> Thy rosed lips;

'Romeo and Juliet,' Act IV, 1, 99,

> The roses in thy lips and cheeks shall fade;

not to mention many others. Be it observed, too, that the added words are not, like most interpolations, ill-chosen and ill-placed; they are particularly appropriate as applied to young Rutland. Whence, then, came these words originally? Did the copyist turn poet for the nonce, and set them down in the exuberance of a playful fancy? I do not believe that this is the true account of them; my belief is that they were Shakespeare's own, and were originally interwoven with the text, but were either discarded by him some time or other when he revised the play, and were re-inserted by a copyist in the later Folios, *or* (which I think much more probable) they were discarded by the *copyist*, or by the editors of the first Folio, because they could not decipher and understand them, though they managed to keep their place in the later impressions. Now, if this theory is correct, the words ought not to be relegated any longer to a footnote, but should be reinstated in their rightful position in the text. But what, it will be asked, is 'roses just with blood?' I had long ago conjectured, what *long long* before me Theobald had conjectured, that 'just' was merely another way of spelling 'juiced.' 'Juiced with blood' is a participial enlargement of 'roses,' and is both forcible and fitting. Understand 'blood' in its natural sense, and it marks the distinction between the vegetable and the human flower; make 'blood' refer to the life-juice of the flower (just as in 'Richard II,' Act III, 4, 59, it is applied in common with the sap to the life-juice of trees), and it is a fine dash of colour pourtraying to the life the fresh and beautiful complexion of the rosy-faced boy. Where cannibals are mentioned, the mention of blood is specially significant. Blood might have tempted them, but beauty deterred them. A cannibal would have spared, a Clifford did not. The lines, then, with the added words in them, will stand thus,

> That face of his
> The hungry cannibals would not have touch'd,
> Would not have stain'd the roses juiced with blood.

It is just possible, however, that the words 'would not have stained,' coming immediately after 'would not have touch'd,' are merely a commentator's gloss, and have been interpolated, and that the lines originally stood thus,

> That face of his the hungry cannibals
> Would not have touch'd, the roses juiced with blood,

where there would be two objects, the one introductory and general, the other descriptive and particular, or the latter simply standing in apposition to the former. Thus much for young Rutland: in the language of Chaucer,

> He was so fair and bright of hue,
> He seemed like a rose new
> Of colour, and in flesh so tender.

KING RICHARD THE THIRD.

The tragedy of 'King Richard the Third' has come down to us singularly free from mutilation and corruption. It is true that the Cambridge editors tell us in their preface, "that the respective origin and "authority of the Quarto and the Folio is perhaps the "most difficult question which presents itself to the "editor of Shakespeare; that the Quarto contains pas-"sages which are not in the Folio, and *vice versa*; and "that passages, which in the Quarto are complete and "consecutive, are amplified in the Folio, evidently "by Shakespeare;" yet one thing is incontestable— they have not found it necessary to brand with their usual obelus a single line or word throughout the play. Such being the case, I have asked myself, whether there could possibly be any portion of it, which needed comment from me; for the reader would not thank me for starting minute or imaginary questions, such, for instance, as whether, in Act I, 2, 64-66, 'heaven' should be regarded as a nominative, or vocative case; or whether, in the 101st line of the same Scene, we should read
        Didst thou not kill this king?
Glou.   I grant *it* ye.
Anne. Dost grant *'t* me, hedgehog? Then, God grant me too
    Thou mayst be damned for that wicked deed.

To no purpose should I plead in the former case, that, two ways being possible, one must be preferable; in the latter, that the addition of the pronoun, which might have been accidentally omitted, would not impair the force of the dialogue, and might even improve the metre; the reader would turn with contempt from such paltry speculative minutiæ, and would tell me, that I was making mountains of mole-hills, or even myself raising the mole-hill. Yet I am bold to say that the following passage in the third Scene of the first Act, lines 62-69, deserves just a passing notice, not that there can be any question either as to the reading or as to the meaning, but simply because of the very peculiar relation in which a nominative case stands to its verb:

> Brother of Gloucester, you mistake the matter.
> The king, of his own royal disposition,
> And not provoked by any suitor else;
> Aiming, belike, at your interior hatred,
> Which in your outward actions shows itself
> Against my kindred, brothers, and myself,
> Makes him to send; that thereby he may gather
> The ground of your ill-will, and to remove it.

Here the ostensible nominative of the verb 'makes' is undoubtedly the noun 'king,' but the real nominative is rather the disposition and aim of the king, as expressed in a number of consecutive clauses—it was *this*, which 'made him to send.' The confusion which we trace here *might* reasonably be attributed to the shock which the Queen felt owing to Gloucester's furious upbraidings; but I will rather explain it as one of those irregularities, which occasionally occur in sentences over-long drawn out, and which are suffered to pass, when, as in the present case, there can be no possibility of the meaning being misunderstood. We have a passage somewhat resembling it in the very next play,—'King Henry the Eighth,' Act I, 1, 59-62—which, for the sake of comparison, I may very well by anticipation introduce here.

> For, being not propp'd by ancestry, whose grace
> Chalks successors their way, nor call'd upon
> For high feats done to the crown; neither allied
> To eminent assistants; but, spider-like,
> Out of his self-drawing *web, O, gives us note,
> The force of his own merit makes his way.

Here the subject of the verb 'gives' is not the pronoun 'he,' which the 'Globe' editors have unwarrantably forced into the text to the exclusion of the interjection 'O,' nor is it any noun or pronoun understood, but a succession of participial and other clauses contained in the four and a half lines preceding, which, taken together, form a sort of cumulative nominative.

But, to revert to the passage from 'King Richard III,' in the last line I have written 'and *to* remove it,' which I believe is the reading of the copies, rather than 'and so remove it,' which is a **gloss** of the

---

*The first Folio has 'web. O gives us note'

editors. Whether you explain the construction as a change from a final adverbial clause to a final infinitive phrase, or (which I think more probable) as another instance, to be added to the many which I have mentioned in my notes on 'Measure for Measure,' of the sign (to) of the infinitive being inserted before the infinitive in consequence of the remoteness of the auxiliary (may) on which the infinitive depends—however you explain it, there is no necessity, there is no justification, for making any alteration. 'So' may be our idiom; but 'to' was tolerated by Shakespeare's contemporaries.

In this same Act and Scene—Act I, 3—there are two passages, where curiously enough the stops, at least in my opinion, should be the very reverse of what they are in the 'Globe' edition; in the one case, we do not want a note of exclamation, yet we have one; in the other, we want one, but we have it not.

For in the 113th line Gloucester does not so much express surprise at Queen Elizabeth's threatening him, as he resents the very idea of it, as if *he* were likely to be taken aback by anything that she could say, or the King could do:

> What threat you me with telling of the King?

he asks indignantly and defiantly, rather than

> What! threat you me with telling of the King?

On the other hand, in the 188th line, where Queen Margaret expresses astonishment that her political enemies should turn so soon from snarling at each other to join, one and all, in setting upon her, the punctuation should be

> What! were you snarling all before I came?

and not

> What were you snarling all before I came?

There is a very peculiar expression in Act III, 3, 23, in a line spoken by Ratcliff,

> Make haste ; the hour of death is *expiate*,

which must be tantamount to what he had said a few lines before, '*the limit of your lives is out*'; yet no parallel can be found for it in Shakespeare, unless it be in 'Sonnet XXII':

> Then look I death my days should expiate.

In Act V, 3, 173, a difficulty has been made of the words 'I died for hope,' but it hardly deserves to be called a difficulty. There are several ways in which the sentence might be explained, as the preposition 'for' has a wide grammatical scope. In '1 Henry VI,' Act I, 1, 85, 'I'll fight for France' means 'I'll fight to win it,' and so 'I died for hope' might mean 'I died while fighting to sustain it.' In 'Macbeth' 'dead for breath,' and in 'As You Like It' 'I die for food,' mean in each instance for the *want* of it; and so Buckingham might say he died, all hope of rescue having been lost. But there is yet another mode of construing the sentence, to which I am inclined to give the preference. The ambiguity of the expression arises from its conciseness. The principal sentence is left incomplete, because, in the subordinate clause which follows, are words which, when applied with the proper grammatical construction to the principal sentence, capitally complete it. It might not be too prolix for a prose-writer to say, 'I died for hope *of lending thee aid*, ere I could lend it thee,' but Shakespeare, who rejoices in brevity, writes simply

> I died for hope ere I could lend thee aid.

A *prægnans locutio:* what we lose in clearness, is more than made up to us in strength and spirit. I have given examples of this Shakespearian peculiarity elsewhere; so I need not tire any with the repetition here.

At the very end of the play—Act V, 5, 27-28— there seems to be a little doubt among the critics as to what the stops, and consequently what the sense should be. In the 'Globe' edition the passage is thus set down:

> England hath long been mad, and scarr'd herself ;
> The brother blindly shed the brother's blood,
> The father rashly slaughter'd his own son,
> The son, compell'd, been butcher to the sire :
> All this divided York and Lancaster,
> Divided in their dire division,
> O, now, let Richmond and Elizabeth,
> The true succeeders of each royal house,
> By God's fair ordinance conjoin together !

Mr. Grant White was of opinion that a full stop should be placed after 'Lancaster,' and the line, 'Divided in their dire division,' should be taken with 'Richmond and Elizabeth.' I am *sure* I am right, when I prefer to point thus:

> All this divided York and Lancaster
> Divided in their dire division?

The first 'divided' is a participle, the second a finite verb; the *subject* of the verb 'divided' is York and Lancaster'; the *object* dependent upon it is 'all this.' 'York and Lancaster, who were divided, divided in their dire division all this'; or, 'in their division caused all this division.' And what is meant by 'all this'? Plainly what has been just before lamentably described—brother being divided against brother, father against son, son against father.

KING HENRY THE EIGHTH.

I have already explained why I do not think it necessary to strike out the interjection 'O' from the 63rd line of the first Act and first Scene of 'King Henry The Eighth,' merely to make room for a nominative case to the verb 'gives'; I shall now state why I do not think it right to brand the 80th line of the same Act and Scene, where Buckingham thus gives vent to his indignation and disgust at Wolsey's high-handed dealing on the occasion of the King's visit to the French court:

> He makes up the file
> Of all the gentry ; for the most part such
> To whom as great a charge as little honour
> He meant to lay upon : and his own letter,
> The honourable board of council out,
> Must fetch him in he papers.

Buckingham charges Wolsey with having, at times when the Council were not sitting, or at any rate without consulting them and obtaining their concurrence, issued his mandates in writing, appointing to the ruinous honour of attending the

King any whom he chose to prick down on his list, or, as Buckingham scornfully expresses it, to '*paper.*' The language is too informal and simple, too homely and common, to please some scholars; yet it is old fashioned and Elizabethan, it is not unclerkly couched, it admirably expresses the unguarded impromptu outpourings, in familiar and confidential intercourse, of Buckingham's scornful heart. 'Paper,' a noun metamorphosed to a verb, is a special word for a special occasion; it is neither a Shakespearian impossibility, nor a linguistic one, and may be included by us without scruple in a vocabulary of Shakespeare's verbs formed from nouns.

Some words spoken by Brandon—the officer who came to arrest Buckingham—in the 204th and following lines I shall next notice.

> I am sorry
> To see you ta'en from liberty, to look on
> The business present : tis his highness' pleasure
> You shall to the Tower.

Such is the ordinary pointing; but should not a semicolon rather be placed after 'liberty,' and a comma after 'present,' and the infinitive phrase 'to look on the business present' be connected, not with the words that go before, but with those that come after? It was no part of Brandon's business to waste time in discussing, or hearing others discuss, *how* Buckingham had fallen under the King's displeasure, but to execute his commands, and dispatch a disagreeable duty with as much delicacy as he could; after expressing, therefore, his regret that he should have to be an eye-witness of such a scene, he gently reminds them of the object of his coming, of the 'present business,' which it behoved both himself and them to keep an eye on, and attend to. The business was that Buckingham should go to the Tower.

It was only after I had roughly sketched my views of these two passages, that I was informed that Singer had similarly explained the first, and Mr. Collier the last. The agreement—as Gibbon neatly expresses it—without mutual communication, may add some weight to our common sentiment.

The closing lines of the Scene, which are inexpressibly beautiful, are in Buckingham's more subdued manner, and finely contrast with the stout words previously spoken by him:

> My surveyor is false ; the o'er-great cardinal
> Hath show'd him gold ; my life is spann'd already ;
> I am the shadow of poor Buckingham,
> Whose figure even this instant cloud puts on,
> By darkening my clear sun. My lord, farewell.

'Figure' is, of course, the subject of the verb 'puts.' 'By darkening' should perhaps be taken not as two words, but as one compounded one; the same prefix is used by Shakespeare in 'by-peeping' and 'by-dependency.' Buckingham explains that he is no longer the man that he was; he is but a shadow of his former self; his figure, which but a moment before had been so conspicuous, at the very instant of his speaking is enveloped in a cloud, which throws into utter darkness his clear sun; he, who but now was the brightest in the political firmament, is now so totally eclipsed, that he is no longer even to be seen; a cloud had folded up his bright outshining beams. Surely commentators have perplexed themselves here with a passage that is sufficiently clear.

There is nothing now to interrupt our progress, till we come to the 92nd and following lines of Act II, Scene 2.

>   All the Clerks,
> I mean the learned ones, in Christian kingdoms
> Have their free voices—Rome, the nurse of judgment,
> Invited by your noble self, hath sent
> One general tongue unto us, this good man,
> This just and learned priest, Cardinal Campeius ;
> Whom once more I present unto your highness.

I have placed a hyphen after 'voices' rather than a colon, in order to indicate that the sentence is unfinished; the participle that should complete it is to be found in the sentence that follows. In my notes on 'King Henry the Fifth' I have quoted several passages to show, how fond Shakespeare is of this elliptic form of expression, which is sometimes used for conciseness' sake, but sometimes also for dramatic effect. Here it may serve both purposes. The Cardinal curtly and cursorily mentions the opinions of the learned clerks of Christendom, as knowing that the King would listen to that branch of the subject with comparatively languid interest, and that *they* had neither authority nor power to bind or to loose; with courtly expedition and tact he proceeds to that other branch of the subject, which the King might well be represented as straining to hear with impatient eagerness; it was only the Pope of Rome, who, in the estimation at any rate of Wolsey and the world, could settle the knotty question, whether the King were only a Bachelor after having lived upwards of twenty years in a state of supposed matrimony, or whether, if he contracted a second marriage, he should rather be called a bigamist; accordingly, without any curtailment, with all circumstance and ceremony, and with much complacency of tone and manner, the Cardinal presents the Pope's plenipotentiary, Cardinal Campeius.

In the next Scene—Act II, 3, 46—an old lady is introduced, rallying Anne Bullen for her mock modesty in being shocked at the very idea of being matched in marriage with a king. The two ladies thus prettily spar with each other:

Anne. How you do talk!
I swear again I would not be a queen
For all the world.
Old L. In faith, for little England
You'ld venture an emballing: I myself
Would for Carnarvonshire, although there long'd
No more to the crown but that.

Now what, according to the Old Lady, would Anne venture for even such a small portion of the world as little England? and what does she say that she herself would venture even for such a small strip as Carnarvonshire? 'An emballing,' says the text, but what is an 'emballing?' Some have supposed—for I make no account of numerous conjectures that have been started—that, instead of repeating the phrase, 'to be a queen,' she uses a word, which from the custom of carrying the ball in procession at coronations, alluded to in 'King Henry V,' Act IV, 1, 277, is in reality equivalent to it, and that, under cover of this word, she hints at a matrimonial, or at any rate a concubinal consequence, which every woman would instinctively understand. I do not quite agree with this view of the passage. I feel sure that the Old Lady used the word with a concubinal reference *only* —that she reiterates, in fact, what she had already said in the 25th line, which line in my opinion clenches the matter. There is not a little harmless satire in her use of the word 'venture'; whether in 'emballing' a pun—an execrable one—were intended on *Anne Bullen's* own name, I need not discuss; but the Old Lady was quite capable of it.

In Act III, 3, 2, 62-71, should the answer to Norfolk's question be, 'He is return'd,' or 'He is return'd in his opinions?' The latter phrase is certainly most peculiar—most unusual; there is nothing like it, that I can recollect, in the whole range of Shakespeare. It is true that the Folios so punctuate, but the punctuation of the Folios, we are assured by those who have had good opportunities of judging, is as likely to lead us wrong as right; we need not, therefore, be solicitous to enquire, how the Folios point, but rather which of the two modes of pointing is most consistent with Shakespeare's general style—which suits the passage best. In my opinion 'he is return'd' is simple, natural, Shakespearian. The words that follow describe the political consequences, or at any rate the future policy. Suffolk says that in virtue of, in accordance with, on the strength of, Cranmer's opinions, which have satisfied the King, and not the King only, but all the learned men of Christendom, the Queen is shortly to be divorced, and a new Queen installed in her stead. According to this interpretation the punctuation of the passage will have to be revised, and this is my revision of it.

Nor: But, my lord,
When returns Cranmer?

Suf: He is return'd; in his opinions, which
Have satisfied the King for his divorce
Together with all famous colleges
Almost in Christendom, shortly, I believe,
His second marriage shall be publish'd, and
Her coronation; Katherine no more
Shall be call'd queen, but princess dowager
And widow to Prince Arthur.

I have already had occasion to observe how fond Shakespeare is of condensing his matter, but I know of no more remarkable instance, at least so far as the syntax is concerned, than we have in Act III, 2, 190-92 of this play:

> I do profess
> That for your highness' good I ever labour'd
> More than mine own; that am, have, and will be.

No wonder that the grammarians stare with astonishment; no wonder that the text-doctors shake their heads, and refuse to see anything here but a shattered text. Yet have we here not so much dead stuff cumbering the line, but a skeletonized sentence, or rather a succession of skeletonized sentences, wherein we can yet recognise living specimens of the poet's creation. If we consider, who is the speaker, and what were the circumstances under which he spake, we shall be able to account for the obscurity, and grope out a tolerable meaning.

The speaker was Wolsey. Who more able than he to express in clear and vigorous language the conceptions of his soul? yet, like Tiberius, like Talleyrand, he could, when it served his purpose, hide by his words the secret counsels of his heart. It was a critical moment this for the Cardinal. Already he had asked himself, 'What should this mean?' His perplexity was not diminished, as the King continued to probe him with strange questionings. He had need of all his dissimulation; but the language of deceit is seldom pure and unadulterated. Consequently, with a deal of excellent matter, excellently expressed, we find in the Cardinal's speech some ambiguities, some twistings and turnings, much that is exaggerated, much that is extravagant. Those words, 'that am, have, and will be,' if they mean anything, must refer to what he had just been saying—'That I am, that I have been, that I will be, in the present, as in the past, and no less in the future, *a labourer for the King's advantage.*' Even supposing, Wolsey purposely cast his words in the form of a motto, and appropriated it as his motto descriptive of his devoted attachment to the King, could anything be more laboured, more confused, more perplexing, more obscure.' Read his words which next follow:

> Though all the world should crack their duty to you,
> And throw it from their soul; though perils did
> Abound, as thick as thought could make 'em, and
> Appear in forms more horrid—yet my duty,
> As doth a rock against the chiding flood,
> Should the approach of this wild river break,
> And stand unshaken yours.

What earnestness of protestation! what rhetorical flourishes! what verbal embellishment! It is not the efflorescence of nature; it is the embroidery of art.

A slight change of punctuation—these slight changes may not be unworthy of notice—I venture to throw out for consideration rather than for certain adoption in the 383rd line:

> The king has cured me;
> I humbly thank his grace; and from these shoulders,
> These ruin'd pillars, out of pity, taken
> A load would sink a navy.

Here I put a full stop, and continue,
> Too much honour—
> O, 'tis a burthen, Cromwell, 'tis a burthen
> Too heavy for a man that hopes for heaven!

The usual method is to put a colon after 'honour,' which is thus made to stand in apposition to 'load.'

Point as we will in Act V, 3, 1-2, the meaning is the same; yet I prefer as more after Shakespeare's manner,
> Speak to the business, master secretary,
> Why are we met in council.

There is a phrase in Act V, 3, 10-12, which has been needlessly cavilled at,
> But we all are men,
> In our own natures frail, and capable
> Of our flesh.

'Flesh' is here used, as it is in Pauline theology, for sinful indulgence. So understood, it should present no more difficulty to the interpreter than such phrases as 'capable of all ill' (Tempest), 'capable of evil' (Hamlet), 'capable of fears' (Richard III). It is the old doctrine of human fallibility put in Shakespeare's plain simple original effective fashion.

A little further on, is it an editorial, or is it not rather a typographical error, that at the end of the 108th line we find a note of interrogation rather than one of exclamation? 'Do you think, my lords,' says Norfolk,
> The king will suffer but the little finger
> Of this man to be vex'd?

to which the Chancellor's reply should unquestionably be pointed thus,

> 'Tis now too certain:
> How much more is his life in value with him!

To the printer, too, rather than to the editors, I would fain attribute the pointing that we have in the 'Globe' Shakespeare a little lower down in the 130th line,

> Good man, sit down. Now let me see the proudest
> He, that dares most, but wag his finger at thee.

It is true that the Folios omit the comma after 'proudest,' and that Shakespeare elsewhere uses the phrase, 'the proudest he'—*one* example we have in '3 Henry VI,' Act I, 1, 48—but even supposing that it makes no difference, as perhaps it does not, that, in the instance cited, the superlative and the pronoun are not cut off from each other by separate lines, I venture to think that there is more force in the King's words, if a comma is placed after 'proudest.' 'Now'—says he—'let me see the proudest, aye, the most daring'—superlative following superlative; for 'he that dares most' is virtually a superlative. How frequently Shakespeare explains, or amplifies, by the periphrasis of a personal pronoun and a relative clause, must have been observed by every attentive reader of his plays. That any objection will be raised on the score of the grammar, I do not anticipate.

CORIOLANUS.

The tragedy of 'Coriolanus' was first printed in Folio. The text, we are told, 'abounds with errors, due probably to the carelessness or illegibility of the transcript from which it was printed.' This may be so, but these are not the only errors in it which need rectification. In most of the editions of the play, which are to be found nowadays in bookseller's shop or private library, there are erroneous emendations smuggled into the text without license and without crying necessity; there are inaccuracies of punctuation, which obscure the sense and hoodwink the reader, attributable not to inadvertance on the part of the transcriber or printer, but to misjudgement on the part of the editor; there are also (to put it mildly) some very questionable interpretations, which should not be allowed to stand unchallenged, and which may have to be superseded by others more pertinent and truthful; besides all these, there are a number of passages, which admit of being explained in more ways than one, and which perhaps had better be left without note or comment of any kind to the unbiassed judgment of each individual interpreter; thus in Act I, 1, 195-198, where Coriolanus says of the multitude,

> They'll sit by the fire, and presume to know
> What's done i' the Capital ; who's like to rise,
> Who thrives and who declines ; *side factions* and give out
> Conjectural marriages,

why say that 'side factions' means '*take part in factions,*' unless *that* be the only tolerable, or decidedly the best meaning that the words can bear? As a matter of fact, it is neither the only possible, nor, in my opinion, the most probable one. These fire-side gossips affected to know the state of the political, just as they affected to know the state of the social world; they patched up imaginary parties, making this man belong to this side, and that man to that, just as they gave out conjectural marriages; faction-makers and match-makers were they, albeit their factions and their matches had no existence save in their idle imaginations and brainless babble. Minutiæ of this sort, though not altogether devoid of interest, are yet not of paramount importance; but it is important that there should be no mistake in such a passage as the 262nd line of this same Act and Scene—Act I, 1, 262—where the punctuation of the Folio, though not always to be depended upon, may be accepted with confidence; it certainly is not an advantageous exchange to put a note of exclamation, as some do, after

> The present wars devour him :

the tribunes are telling each other what they think of Coriolanus; how proud he was; how he had scorned and taunted them when they were appointed tribunes; they aggravate his offence by the remark, while perhaps they comfort themselves by the reflection, that even the gods themselves —those most high sacrosanct irresponsible arbiters —even the moon, the very ideal of modesty, he would not scruple to 'gird'—to mock at; what wonder, then, if *their* tribunitian majesty, *their* tribunitian modesty, he despised, he insulted! And now what further? Do they, as some would have it, invoke a curse on Coriolanus, and wish him perdition by the wars? No such thing. 'This' man,' they continue, 'who has no regard for God or tribune, what does he care for?' '*The wars*'— for the poet here, with a licence which is common to him, and which is perfectly well known to all those who have read his plays with attention, uses *the plural form as an exact equivalent of the singular*, an example of which we have in 'Cymbeline,' Act IV, 3, 43, where 'These present *wars*' is said of a *war then instant*—'the *wars*,' then, or, as we may express it, 'the *war*,' such as at that very moment was brewing with the Volsci—'this is his devouring passion; he is carried away, he is swallowed up, he is wholly absorbed by the *war*; and this is how he has grown—grown far 'too proud'; and the reason he is so proud is because he is so valiant.' Such I conceive to be a fair gloss on a much misconceived passage, though I am not quite sure that I have correctly expounded just the fag end of it. Trusting to the critics to make right my wrong, I proceed to the next psssage, my remarks on which, I wish it to be distinctly understood, are of a tentative rather than of a dogmatic character; nevertheless I fear I shall be scolded and smit by my tribunitian judges for presuming to stir up the dying embers of a past contention in Act I, 3, 46 — not that some emendation there is not absolutely necessary, but it will be argued that all that can be done has been done already, and that, where the *first* Folio reads

> The breasts of Hecuba,
> When she did suckle Hector, look'd not lovelier
> Then Hector's forehead, when it spit forth blood
> At Grecian sword.   Con!enning, tell *Valeria,* &c.,

and where the *second* Folio reads

> At Grecian swordes *contending* : tell Valeria, &c.

two ways, and two only are open to us—either that taken by Capell, who merely added to the line of the *second* Folio an apostrophe after 'swordes,' to indicate that it was a plural genitive, *or* that taken by Mr. Collier, who altered the line of the *first* Folio to

> At Grecian swords, contemning : tell Valeria.

There will be no lack of critics to correct me, if I err, but I cannot help thinking that the participle 'contemning'—Mr. Collier's participle—

coming immediately after such a strong expression as 'spit forth blood,' even if it be not slightly tautological, does not add much to the spirit and force of the passage; while, as for the emendation of the *second* Folio, *that* must, of course, claim our attention, but it cannot command our acceptance. And why? Because the second Folio was merely copied from the first, and not from an independent transcript; where, therefore, it differs from the first, the difference is due to transcriber, printer, prompter, press-corrector, no one knows whom, and it may be estimated accordingly. We are certainly not *bound* to follow it, specially if we can account in some other reasonable way for what appears in the *first* Folio. Now let it be observed that '*Contenning*' is cut off from the words that precede it by a full stop; secondly, that it is headed with a capital letter; and thirdly, that it is printed in italics: these three points can be gainsaid by none. Well now—this *exceptionally* printed, this obviously and avowedly misspelt word—what if it is no more than one of those numerous stage directions, like 'coming forward,' 'digging,' 'aside,' 'reciting to himself,' 'looking at the jewel,' 'to the gold'—all these taken at random from 'Timon' —which ever and anon interrupt the text, signifying that Volumnia had ceased speaking to Virgilia, and, in '*continuing*' her remarks—so the word should have been spelt—was addressing the gentlewoman in attendance. Thus the line shrinks from an Alexandrine to one of the ordinary measure, the full pause in the middle of it accounting for—some might think, necessitating, according to a well-known rule of Shakespearian prosody, the omission of a syllable; and so the metre, in spite of the ejection of a trisyllable, is as complete as the most sensitive rhythmist could desire. I shall only add that stage directions were usually printed in italics.

Our difficulty in the next passage—Act I, 4, 31—consists not so much in suggesting, as in selecting an emendation. The line, as given in the first Folio, is

> All the contagion of the south light on you,
> You shames of Rome! You Heard of Byles and Plagues
> Plaister you o'er;

this the editors of the 'Globe' Shakespeare, by changing the punctuation and the spelling, and supposing that Coriolanus was in such a towering passion, that he could not speak coherently, manage to retain, printing it thus,

> You shames of Rome! you herd of—Boils and plagues
> Plaster you o'er;

but, when a man, boiling over with rage, is hurling curses at a lot of runaways—a species of ammunition, by the way, of which Coriolanus had a goodly supply—he is not wont to falter with his tongue, or to be brought up with a jerk, even though it be to discharge a second volley of yet more bitter words.

I dismiss the method of the 'Globe' Shakespeare editors, then, as a clever shift rather than a correct solution; nor can I do more than commend Theobald's arrangement, for all that it is so neat and near,

> You shames of Rome, you! Herds of boils and plagues
> Plaster you o'er.

A word like 'sherds' would seem more appropriate than 'herds.'

If I could bring myself to believe that 'cowards' was spelt in the original 'Keardef,' and that the K of this 'Keardef' was misshapen, so as to be very much like an H, as might happen in a 'carelessly written and illegible transcript,' I could understand how such a corruption as 'Heard of' might have crept in, where Shakespeare had written,

> You shames of Rome! you cowards! Boils and plagues
> Plaster you o'er;

but I should be 'cooking a stone,' were I to try to persuade any that the line, as I have now tinkered it, was as the author manufactured it; some less violent change will reasonably be insisted on. Well then, in Act IV, 2, 11, of this play, we find the phrase 'the hoarded plague of the gods.' Here, then, is a word, viz. '*hoard*,' which bears a strong resemblance to 'Heard,' suits the context capitally, and derives a sort of sanction from the fact that it is used in connexion with plagues elsewhere in this very play. If we shift the stops, as Theobald dared to shift them, but for Theobald's 'herds' substitute '*Hoard*,' we have

> You shames of Rome, you! Hoard of boils and plagues
> Plaster you o'er.

Such, then, is my ultimatum. If it be objected that '*hoard*' is well enough, but that the antecedent '*you!*' sounds rather like a weak scream, unless a *hyphen* be placed after it, I answer that an exact parallel of this repetition of the pronoun may be found in Shakespeare; the fact I distinctly remember, the particular passage I cannot at this moment find for the satisfaction of the doubter. But the critics, who, in Act II, 1, 27, have not scrupled to transmute 'teach' to 'touch,' will not censure me for proposing to make *e* give way to *o* in this passage also.

On the next passage—Act I, 6, 76—I can only compare the notes of the commentators to clouds of dust, which hide from our eyes the very point of which we are anxious to get a clear and distinct view. The circumstances may be thus briefly narrated. Coriolanus, finding that the battle, which Cominius had fought with the Volsci, had terminated indecisively, asks for, and obtains, permission to call for volunteers to renew instantly the engagement. In answer to his appeal, not a few only, but the whole army rush forward with the most extravagant demonstrations of martial confidence and delight;

taken aback by this unexpected manifestation, he exclaims,

> O me alone! make you a sword of me!

These are the words—what are we to make of them? I take them to be partly a sort of gentle protest against the hero-worship that they were paying him, partly a preface to the remarks which immediately after he addresses to them. Who were these men who were now so eager for the fray? They were the very men who under Cominius had failed to beat the enemy; yet now that Coriolanus was to captain them, they made sure that they had a very engine of war, a talisman of victory—*they made a sword of him*—they regarded *him* as their sword, *him* as their confidence — him and him alone. Coriolanus says not a word to damp this newly kindled ardour; he credits them with it, and shifts the power from himself to them; or rather he shares it with them; if they were the men inwardly which they showed outwardly, no need to set their hopes on him, and him alone; they themselves were equally with him *swords*—terrors to the foe; not one but could be a match for four Volsci; not one but could front the redoubtable Aufidius himself, and push his shield with shield as hard. 'A certain number,' he continues,

> Though thanks to all, must I select from all: the rest
> Shall bear the business in some other fight,
> As cause will be obey'd. Please you to march;
> And four shall quickly draw out my command,
> Which men are best inclined.

Over the last line and a half there has been a deal of wrangling, a deal of conjecturing. 'Why four?' it has been asked. To which a learned annotator stoically answers, 'Why not four?' Yet, as if not quite satisfied himself with this method of meeting an adversary's objections, he refers to a passage in 'Hamlet' (which does not strike me as relevant) to show that 'four' was used of an indefinitely small number. I rather look for an explanation of the difficulty in the notion which Shakespeare entertained of the organization of the army. He speaks of the 'centuries'—the 'centurions'—of the *Volsci;* there cannot be a doubt that he conceived the *Roman* army as similarly divided; the number 'four' indicates with sufficient exactness the modest number that Coriolanus was content should accompany him on his errand of danger—*four hundred men, and their four officers*—Voilà tout. Soldiers would understand, if scholars cannot.

We are again on debatable ground in Act I, 9, 41-46, where Coriolanus in his usual incisive style is remonstrating with the army for sounding a salute in his honour:

> May these same instruments, which you profane,
> Never sound more! when drums and trumpets shall
> I' the field prove flatterers, let courts and cities be
> Made all of false-faced soothing!
> When steel grows soft as the parasite's silk,
> Let him be made an *overture for the wars!

---
*Ff

In the first two lines, where a wish is expressed that the drum and the trumpet may never sound more, it is of course implied, if they were to be prostituted to such unsoldier-like uses. A child may read here. But to whom, it has been asked, does *him* in the last line refer? I answer, to the person alluded to in the previous line—to steel grown soft—that is to say (for the abstract is used for the concrete) to the man who ought to be a steeled warrior, but who is no better than a silken parasite. A prose writer might have used the plural pronoun, the poet prefers the singular; under 'him' is probably comprehended the whole military body—*ex uno disce omnes*. To my mind, the difficulty does not consist in finding a word for 'him' to refer to, but in discovering a sense for 'overture,' suitable alike to the word and to the passage. How, then, is it used elsewhere in Shakespeare? There is no lack of examples,

> I bring no overture of war.
>> 'Twelfth Night,' Act I, 5, 225.

> I hear there is an overture of peace.
>> 'All's Well that Ends Well, Act IV, 3, 46.

> I could not answer in that course of honour
> As she had made the overture.
>> 'All's Well that Ends Well,' Act V, 3, 99.

> Without more overture.
>> 'Winter's Tale,' Act II, 1, 172.

> It was he
> That made the overture of thy treason to us.
>> 'King Lear,' Act III, 7, 89.

In all these passages (excepting the last, where it is somewhat differently applied, and seems to be almost synonymous with 'disclosure') the word means an offering of terms of some sort—whether amicable or hostile in character, depends upon the context. In a somewhat similar sense it is fair to suppose that 'overture' is used in 'Coriolanus.' The question, then, resolves itself to this, Can the word bear its ordinary meaning in this extraordinary connexion of it? I think it can. Just as, when a dispute arises between two nations, it is customary to try what can be done by an *overture* with the view of coming to an understanding, the ambassador holding in his hand both peace and war, so Coriolanus sarcastically recommends the Romans for their wars to see what could be done through such a one as he describes; let them make an '*overture*' of *him*; the ambiguous word well suited Coriolanus' purpose; the hearers might take it either way; as an overture of *peace*, or an overture of *war*; but none could doubt that, when such a body were put forward, a man of silk and not a man of steel, whose artillery was a cocoon rather than a cannon, the warlike sense was out of the question; the warlike solution was impossible; the word would be not 'treat,' but 'yield;' not equal terms such as freedom commands, but unconditional surrender fit only for crouching slaves. There is no more reason why a man should not be said to be *made* an *overture*, than a man is said to be *made* a sword; only the former is applied to the coward, the latter (as we have just seen) to Coriolanus. It is far too great a liberty to take with the text, to change '*overture*' to '*coverture*;' nor dare I assign to 'overture' a sense, which it may very well bear nowadays in musical literature, but which we have no proof that it ever bore in Shakespeare's time, nor is there a single example of its being used in that sense to be found in any one of his plays.

There is nothing now which calls for special comment, until we reach Act III, 1, 131, where we come across the very singular phrase, '*this bosom multiplied*,' which the critics convert—by what process I know not—to 'this bissom multitude!' The latter, being the harsher expression, is perhaps thought to accord better with Coriolanus' temper. As a matter of fact, however, for this particular passage the other phrase bears off the palm. It is not the blindness of the multitude that is here glanced at, but the dangerous knowledge bosomed up by them, and sure in time to be thoroughly digested, that they had wrung gratuities and concessions from a reluctant oligarchy. Multiply the bosom, and you augment the danger. 'Bissom multitude' is just the phrase that an unwary critic would catch at; and how triumphantly might he point to 'bissom conspectuities' in another part of the play! But 'bosom multiplied' is the phrase for the place, original, unique, strikingly apposite, bearing the stamp of discerning judgment and originating genius. It may be matched with the 'multitudinous tongue,' which occurs a little further down; only there *speech*, here *thought* is the dominant idea. By all means read, therefore,

> How shall this bosom multiplied digest
> The senate's courtesy?

A little question of punctuation, not altogether unimportant, in Act III, 1, 191, must next claim our attention. Menenius, who all along, in spite of his patrician sympathies, endeavours to maintain amicable relations with the commons, and to act as a sort of peacemaker between the two rival factions, and to be the candid friend of both, would surely not, when the populace were all a-fire, deliberately blow the flames, and incense the tribunes by crying out insultingly, 'You, tribunes to the people!' Rather does he do his utmost to check the conflagration, and prevent the flames from spreading, appealing to each one of the opposing parties in turn; admonishing first the tribunes, then Coriolanus; exhorting *them* to speak to, restrain, pacify the people; exhorting *him* to have patience. Such being the case, the passage should be stopped thus:

> What is about to be? I am out of breath;
> Confusion's near; I cannot speak. You, tribunes,
> To the people. Coriolanus, patience!
> Speak, good Sicinius.

To have upbraided the popular magistrates at such a critical juncture would have been as impolitic, as it would have been alien to the part which Menenius assumed. But perhaps I shall be told that the interpretation which I have given is the interpretation contemplated, *stops notwithstanding.*

What again is there awry in the line Act III, 2, 29,

> I have a heart as little apt as yours,

which has been banned by the Cambridge editors? Can it be that they object to 'apt'? In 'Timon,' Act I, 1, 132, we read, 'She is young and apt,' and in the same play, Act II, 2, 139-140, 'unaptness' and 'indisposition' are used convertibly. If there is a flaw here, all I can say is that I cannot perceive it.

I come now to a celebrated passage in Act III, 2, extending over several lines (52-80), where Volumnia endeavours to induce Coriolanus to disguise his real sentiments in order to pacify and conciliate the infuriated multitude. We must not expect to find in the language, which Shakespeare puts into the mouth of a Roman matron, the lofty morality of a purist, but we need not go the length of a certain expositor, who would *actually alter the text* to make Volumnia say that she would allow herself any amount of dissimulation, where her fortune and friends required it. Any amount of dissimulation was held lawful by Charles The Fifth and the leading celebrities of the sixteenth century, but the mother of Coriolanus professes to be guided by the code of 'honour,' which sets some bounds to dissimulation, even when fortune and friends are at stake. The chief difficulty of the passage is not one of ethics at all, but of syntax. How are we to construe the line—I punctuate it, as the 'Globe' Shakespeare editors do—

> Which often, thus, correcting thy stout heart?

Volumnia had just before told Coriolanus to 'wave his head,' which she instructs him to do 'often,' and she shows him how to do it—'thus'— and she adds the purpose—'correcting thy stout heart.' When expositors make such a fluster about the government of the relative 'which,' are they oblivious of the little verb '*do*,' and of its occasional ellipse, specially in conversation, supplemented too by gesticulation? I can only suppose that they shrink from this explanation because of the simplicity of it; but the simplicity of an explanation, if common sense go along with it, should recommend it rather than otherwise. With more reason it has been asked, what is the relation in which 'humble' stands to the rest of the sentence in the line,

> Now humble as the ripest mulberry?

Some connect it with 'head,' and some with 'heart,' and some think it a verb, and some an adjective, and some hold that it has no business here at all, but that it has usurped the place of some other more fitting word. But the word is right enough, and an adjective it is sure enough; and it refers neither to 'head,' nor to 'heart,' but, equally with 'bussing,' equally with 'waving,' to the subject of the main sentence, viz: to the pronoun 'thou,' which is understood. In fact 'now humble' is the last of a series of clauses, each one indicating a fresh attitude which the speaker would have Coriolanus assume; '*now humble*' is the *coup de grace*, the final pose to which all the others are but preludes; it marks the lowest level in the valley of humiliation; the limit beneath which humility itself could sink no further; 'now humble,' aye, now at last the very picture of humility, humble enough to satisfy even the most exacting tribunes; as soft, as sweet, as low-hanging, as ready to drop, as the ripest mulberry that will not bear the handling.

Having cleared the way here, I will next endeavour to remove a much more serious obstruction which occurs in another of Volumnia's speeches, the same Scene, the 126th and 127th lines:

>At thy choice, then ;
>To beg of thee, it is my more dishonour
>Than thou of them. Come all to ruin ; *let
>Thy mother rather feel thy pride than fear
>Thy dangerous stoutness,* for I mock at death
>With as big heart as thou.

The words that are printed in italics have been hidden from expositors, and, I must acknowledge, were equally so from myself, various shadows of interpretation having amused me from time to time, all alike illusory. If I have hit upon the right meaning now, it is due to a hint which I have received from a friendly critic. In the first place, let it be observed that almost in the same breath, that Volumnia avows a feeling of pride of some sort, *she disavows the pride which stiffened Coriolanus* (line 130), as not derived from her, nor appertaining to her, *but of his own begetting.* And secondly, it is evident that Coriolanus felt that his mother had *chidden him*, and had not come round to his view of her own free will, but rather because she felt that she could not do otherwise. Her surrender to her son, then, was not a cheerful and spontaneous, but a half-hearted and compulsory one. Thus much generally; and now to come to particulars: in what terms does Volumnia describe her own feelings? Certainly not as of one who *feared* the consequences; for (to use her own words) she mocked at death with as big heart as Coriolanus did. How then? As one who felt pride, but not exactly the pride which Coriolanus felt; but a rational pride akin to what we sometimes call self respect—a feeling that she had gone as far in entreating her son as a mother, or at least as Coriolanus' mother, should. *He* would be too proud to be continually suing, and continually denied; well then—*that* pride of his she too felt: she let it be as he willed; she passively permitted it, albeit it was contrary to her wish, her counsel, her best and highest judgment. I can almost fancy that Shakespeare had in his mind here that famous chapter in Israelitish history, when Jehovah, finding his people were determined to have a visible and temporal king, like all the nations around them, at length ceased to contend with them—let them have their will—allowing it rather than approving of it, conceding what was in reality repugnant to his commands and his counsel. Long was the ruin a-coming, but it came at last.

Twelve lines from the end of the third Scene of Act 3, there is not the least reason for substituting '*not*' for '*but*' in the line

> Making but reservation of yourselves,

though the change has been made by some editors. Coriolanus declares that the end and aim of the plebeian party is to drive from the city every one who is not of their way of thinking, *reserving none but themselves*—a suicidal policy; for the time would come, when their enemies would attack them, and then, having none among them who were possessed of military capacity—for, to use the words of Aufidius, 'their tribunes were no soldiers'—they would have to succumb without striking a blow, and would be carried away into a mean and miserable captivity.

I am now going to plead for a condemned word in Act IV, 3, 9,

> But your favour is well *appeared* by your tongue,

which Mr. Collier, following Steevens, changed to '*approved*.' The change is certainly specious; yet the Folios are all on the other side; it may be as well, therefore, to hear what is to be said for '*is appeared.*' It certainly would not be used in a novel or play of the nineteenth century, but it might have been familiar to the age of Shakespeare; numbers of words and phrases were then current, which have since fallen into disuse. We should hardly expect to hear any one say in conversation nowadays, 'His lordship *is walked forth*,' yet so says one of Shakespeare's characters. Stranger still, we have in the 'Comedy of Errors' Act V, 1, 388,

> And hereupon these errors *are arose.*

Examples like these bid us be cautious, ere we oust a word, because it jars upon modern ears. Had the expression been, 'His favour *is made apparent* by his tongue,' no one would have said a word against it. Is it not possible that, in Shakespeare's day, the participle may have been permitted to occupy the place of the adjective? 'Is entered'—'is arrived'—'is approached'—'is become'—'are ceased'—are all found in Shakespeare, used pretty much, if not exactly, like 'enters,' 'arrives,' 'approaches,' &c. Similarly 'is appeared' and 'appears' may both have been tolerated. There is an old smack about 'is appeared,' which, though some may not relish it, perhaps they must stomach. I am very much inclined to believe that it is the genuine reading, a relic of the English of olden times.

The dæmon of change has again seized the critics in the very beginning of the 6th Scene, where, though the reading of the copies is capable of being explained, it is altered, because it does not square with their notions of linguistic and grammatical propriety. What is easier than to construe the second line of the Scene thus,

> His remedies are tame, the present [is] peace and quietness of the people, which [that is, who] were before in wild hurry.

On the one hand, the substantive verb is dropped in the second sentence, because 'are' has been expressed in the first; on the other hand 'the present' is used as a noun substantive, of which there is no lack of examples. Thus in the 'Tempest,' Act I, 1, 57, the substantive verb is left to be understood, albeit it had not been previously expressed, as 'The king and prince at prayers;' and in the same play, Act I, 1, 24, we have 'to work the peace of *the present*.' Yet in this passage of 'Coriolanus' Theobald must needs interpolate 'i'' before 'the present,' and all break after him like a flock of sheep.

I now come to Aufidius' speech at the end of the 4th Act, which, it must be acknowledged, is as complicated a piece of work, as perhaps may be found in all Shakespeare. Before I glance at particular parts of it, I may as well state generally, that the sketch which Aufidius gives of Coriolanus' character, together with the statement that accompanies it that more depends on public opinion than on personal merit, *is subordinate to the prediction which he utters in the opening lines of his speech*, that

Coriolanus would be received with open arms by the people of Rome; while his reference to the instability of power, and to what I may call a great law of natural dynamics, is *preparatory to his second prediction*, that Coriolanus will fall, and be politically annihilated. A blaze, and then darkness—such, in a word, is Aufidius' prognostication of Coriolanus' future. Ominous forebodings, which, coming at the very end of the 4th Act, foreshadow the scenes of tumult and bloodshed, which disturb and stain the termination of the 5th! Such being the main drift, and such the general connexion of the various parts of the speech, we need not overmuch repine, if we cannot make sure of the precise meaning of every word and phrase in it. It may be a moot point, but it is not a matter of mighty moment, whether the sentence

<blockquote>
he has a merit
To choke it in the utterance
</blockquote>

means, as Mr. Aldis Wright takes it, 'to prevent the sentence being uttered,' or, as others, 'to prevent the fault being insisted on,' even if 'utterance' may not have to be considered a different word altogether—viz., the word which is used in 'Macbeth,' Act III, 1, 72, and in 'Cymbeline,' Act III, 1, 72,—in which case the meaning would rather be, 'he has a merit to choke the fault in the long run,' as we say, or 'when matters come to the uttermost extremity.' Nor will it make much odds, whether 'power unto itself most commendable' means 'power, which, if viewed objectively, in itself, independently of any other consideration, is worthy of commendation;' or, as others, 'power with a high opinion of itself;' or as another puts it, 'power of which the commendations are apt to be addressed to itself;' or, as another, 'power, which, kept to itself, not talked or boasted of, is most commendable or most commended.' As for the couplet

> Hath not a tomb so evident as a chair
> To extol what it hath done,

that can only mean that the *chair of office*, which silently proclaims a man's merit, is too often, if he could but foresee it, the very tomb of his power; his exaltation accelerates his precipitation; from the pinnacle to the pit is but a step.

Mr. Aldis Wright is of opinion that the reading of the Folios may be retained in the line

> Rights by rights *fouler*, strengths by strengths do fail ;

'Founder,' 'falter,' 'foiled are,' 'soiled are,' are some of the principal emendations which have been excogitated. If there is room for one more (and some one I really think we must choose, for I have not a word to say in defence of the reading of the copies *here*), I offer

> Rights by rights *fuller*, strengths by strengths do fail,

the adjective 'fuller' belonging to both clauses, though expressed only in the first, just as in 'Macbeth,' Act I, 2, 56, we have, according to the Folios,

> Point against point rebellious, arm 'gainst arm.

The word I have ventured to suggest does not far diverge from the *ductus literarum*.

We come now to the fifth Act, where it tasks the shrewdest cricital faculty to determine what the reading should be in the following lines—Act V, 1, 15-17—

> Why, so : you have made good work!
> A pair of tribunes that have *wrack'd* for Rome,
> To make coals cheap, a noble memory!

Let the reader be very sure that, whatever may be the word which happens to be printed in the particular edition of Shakespeare, which he has in his possession, '*wracked*' is the word which is set down in the Folios, and, inasmuch as our word '*wrecked*,' wherever it occurs, is almost invariably spelt in the original copies with an '*a*' and not with an '*e*,' the presumption is that '*wrecked*' is the word which is here authorized by the Folios. The meaning would be that the tribunes had (to borrow words from 'Macbeth') '*laboured in their country's wreck.*' The preposition '*for*,' coming after '*wreck*,' would be abnormal, but not necessarily un-Shakespearian. It might be illustrated by such expressions as the following,

> Revenge the heavens *for* old Andronicus!
> 'Titus Andronicus,' Act IV, 1, 129.

How unluckily it happened, that I should purchase the day before *for* a little part, and undo a great deal of honour!
'Timon,' Act III, 2, 52 ;

> Spare *for* no faggots.
> '1 Henry VI,' Act V, 4, 56.

This is the best account that I can give of 'wrecked for Rome.' Can more be said for the emendations which have been proposed?

'*Recked for*,' that is, cared for Rome, with the result that they had as good as brought it to the fire, and reduced it to ashes—this is one reading.

'*Racked for*,' that is, raised the price of it, with the result that it was only fit for fuel, so that coals would be cheap—this is another reading.

'*Wreaked for Rome*' may be mentioned as a third; they had wreaked their vengeance on Coriolanus by expatriating him under colour that it was for the public good; but what had they effected? They had cheapened coals! and cheap enough they would be, when the city was as it were the colliery to supply the fuel for its own conflagration; the allusion, of course, is to Coriolanus having refused to be called by any title,

    Till he had forged himself a name o' the fire
    Of burning Rome.

I can see no corruption, no obscurity, a little below in the 71st line, which is the last of the following passage;

    I kneel'd before him:
'Twas very faintly he said, 'Rise;' dismiss'd me
Thus, with his speechless hand: what he would do,
He sent in writing after me; what he would not,
Bound with an oath to yield to his conditions.

Coriolanus specified in his written despatch, what concessions he was willing to make, adding, as a proviso, that in everything else *Cominius* should bind himself by oath to submit to *his* (Coriolanus') conditions. In the last clause the subject is changed from Coriolanus to Cominius. The grammar may lack completeness, but it should be remembered that here we have a brief and hurried summary of a short and curt interview—a sort of running conversational comment: say there is a little looseness, there is no obscurity; the Romans who heard would not be slow to apprehend what was meant; their fears had already anticipated the sinister tidings. Brevity here is surely a merit. The passage continues,

> So that all hope is vain
> Unless his noble mother and his wife,
> Who, as I hear, mean to solicit him
> For mercy to his country.

Where, it has been asked, is the verb that should follow 'unless'? To which I reply, where is it in 'Richard II,' Act V, 3, 32?

> My tongue cleave to my roof within my mouth,
> *Unless a pardon* ere I rise or speak.

Where is it in 'All's Well That Ends Well,' Act IV, 1, 5?

> We must not seem to understand him, *unless some one* among us whom we must produce for an interpreter.

Where is it in 'Othello,' Act I, 1, 23-24?

> Nor the division of a battle knows
> More than a spinster, *unless the bookish theoric*,

It may be an open question with some, whether in the above passages 'unless' should be parsed as a conjunction, or should be held to partake rather of the nature of a preposition; but none can fail to be struck with the remarkableness of the coincidence, that in all the passages the same particle is found without a finite verb actually following it. For my own part, I hold that in the passage in 'Coriolanus' it is most certainly a conjunction, and that in all probability the verb that belongs to it, and that should be mentally supplied after it, is the verb that occurs in the *relative clause which follows*—yes, the same verb, but not used in exactly the same sense; for, whereas in the relative clause 'solicit' means 'to earnestly entreat,' in the principal clause, where we say that it is understood, it can only mean 'to prevail by entreaty,' one verb (as is not uncommon) serving for two clauses, which in its strict acceptation suits only one of them. There is surely no maze here to hinder us from treading out the way readily.

One passage more: the use of 'verify' in the sense of 'to truly represent,' and with a person for its object, is certainly not one with which we are familiar; yet such is the only meaning which it can bear in Act V, 2, 17,

> For I have ever *verified* my friends,
> Of whom he's chief, with all the size that verity
> Would without lapsing suffer.

We are not altogether surprised that 'verified' in this passage has been regarded as spurious. In the absence of examples, corroborating such an unusual signification of it, opinions will be divided as to its genuineness. That Shakespeare sometimes took an old word, and gave it a new meaning, is pretty well known to every one who has read his plays with ordinary attention. That he may have done so *here*, is quite within the bounds of possibility. The occurrence of 'verity' in the succeeding line seems to me to indicate that 'verify' was the verb used. From the same circumstance others may draw an inference the very reverse. But this I would say, we must not expect, as a matter of course, to find in Shakespeare duplicates of what I may call Shakespearian curiosities. Many of his strange and strangely used words occur but once, proving how careful he was not to adulterate with too liberal an admixture of alloy the pure gold of the English tongue. Perhaps it may not be irrelevant to add, that another verb of Latin origin, with similar termination and of like formation to 'verified'—I mean '*mortified*'—is used at times by Shakespeare in what seems to commentators a strange and exceptional signification. The reader has but to glance at a note of the Cambridge editors on 'Macbeth,' Act V, 3, 2, (Clarendon Press Series) and he will find that 'mortified' is as much a puzzle there as 'verified' is here. In the 'Tempest,' Act V, 1, 128, 'And *justify* you traitors,' can only mean 'justly represent,' and so 'prove' you traitors. For 'justly' substitute 'truly,' and have we not the meaning of 'verify' which is required here. It is true that this is not the ordinary signification of the word, but is it not one which may be fairly put upon it? It is Shakespeare with whom we are dealing, who with much originality of thought combined some originality of diction. That he did not abuse the power of language with which he was endowed, that he coined new words but rarely, and but rarely set a new and fancy value on old words, is proof alike of his moderation and his judgement. Upon the whole, then, we are more inclined in this passage to accuse the critics of intolerance, than the copyist of carelessness, or the great composer of licentious and unwarranted innovation.

TITUS ANDRONICUS.

The tragedy of 'Titus Andronicus' was published for the first time in Quarto, and published, we are told, with remarkable accuracy. There are certainly not many passages in it to exercise the ingenuity of the critic. Yet the editors of the 'Globe' Shakespeare must have thought that there is some inaccuracy in the line,

> And with that painted hope braves your mightiness,
> Act II, 3, 126,

as they have marked it as faulty, on the ground, I suppose, of metrical incompleteness. Perhaps the pronoun 'she' has been omitted before the verb 'braves'; perhaps the compound 'outbraves' originally stood, where the simple verb now stands; but it is quite as probable that the critics are too fidgety, and would enforce metrical uniformity at the expense of metrical variety. 'Braves,' emphasized in pronunciation into the time of two syllables, may be tantamount to a dissyllable, as is the case sometimes with 'safe,' and notably with 'fire,' 'hour,' 'near,' 'aches.' In 'The Taming of the Shrew' we have

> Pisa renown'd for grave citizens,
> Act I, 1, 10,

where 'grave' is so weighty, that it is equivalent to two syllables. There are not a few lines in Shakespeare which have the same curious peculiarity, and, as they cannot possibly be all author's oversights or transcriber's blunders, our best plan is to admit all of them as composed by Shakespeare, and not afterwards repented of, or rejected by him.

For a long time a cloud of doubt hung over the word 'castle' in Act III, 1, 170,

> Writing destruction on the enemy's castle,

but the cloud vanished the moment light fell upon it from 'Grose's Ancient Armour,' which revealed to us that 'castle' was a title given to a close kind of helmet. Immediately Theobald's 'casque' disappeared, and another critic's 'crest'; comes to the fore a passage from 'Troilus and Cressida,' Act V, 2, 187,

> and, Diomed,
> Stand fast, and wear a castle on thy head,

where, though the language may admit of being otherwise explained, there must be a partial reference to the head-piece of the hero. Compare also Clifford's threat to Warwick, '2 King Henry VI,' Act V, 1, 200,

> I am resolved to bear a greater storm
> Than any thou canst conjure up to-day;
> And that I'll *write upon thy burgonet,*
> Might I but know thee by thy household badge.

There is a difficulty in fixing the reading in the 282nd line of the same Act and Scene, where the

Quarto and the Folio differ as to the word with which the line should end, the former having

> Lavinia, thou shalt be employ'd in these *Armes*,

the latter 'in these *things*.' The Quarto, the prior publication, shall have the priority. 'Armes' was ousted, not because it was untenable, but because it was not understood; 'things' was put in its place, for want of a better word. I see no reason why 'arms' should not be taken here in its ordinary sense of 'hostilities,' but I much prefer to assign to it its more specific meaning of 'weapons,' or 'implements of war.' It is with the tone, and the air, and the terrible earnestness of a maniac, that Titus Andronicus, the conqueror in so many battles, rouses himself as it were for one more campaign of vengeance, not now against his country's foes, but against his domestic and personal enemies. Parodying the duties of his profession, he musters his strength, and flourishes his arms. Arms indeed! A stump of a hand! a pair of corpseless heads! Horrible mockery! nor less so, when, turning to Lavinia, a helpless, mutilated, hopelessly injured cripple, he exclaims triumphantly, that *she* shall be employed in the prosecution of that warfare, *or* in the management of those arms; and he enlists her in the service, and instructs her how to take her part. Were I seeking to alter rather than to explain, I should still take the word of the Quarto as the starting point, and say that the aspirate had been dropped, and that 'harms,' which is used in Shakespeare in the two-fold sense of injuries *inflicted* and injuries *received*, was in all likelihood the genuine original word.

In either case the accent of 'employ'd' will fall on the *first* rather than on the *last* syllable, which is surely not a Shakespearian impossibility. For is it not notorious that Shakespeare is variable—is sometimes eccentric—in his mode of accenting? In this very play 'ordained' is accentuated on the first syllable; and elsewhere we have 'cóngealed,' 'cúrtailed,' 'éxcuse' (the verb), 'ínfect,' 'óppose,' etc., etc. I take the line, then, as I find it; I offer what seems to be a reasonable explanation of the reading of the Quarto; all that I assume is an anomaly founded on Shakespearian analogy. Are those who would alter the text justified in doing so, merely on account of the exceptional accentuation of a single word?

And why change 'the' of the Quartos and Folios into 'ye' in Act IV, 1, 129,

> Revenge the heavens for old Andronicus.

The optative, for which there is no lack of precedent, is quite as admissible as the direct precatory form.

In Act IV, 2, 152, where all the Quartos and all the Folios have

> Not far one *Muliteus*, my countryman,
> His wife but yesternight was brought to bed,

editors, at a loss for a finite verb for the nominative

case 'Muliteus,' dock that word of its final syllable, and forge from the piece cut off the word which they think they require.

I shall broach the question, whether 'Muliteus' is a nominative case at all. There is an obsolete mode of forming the possessive or genitive case, by means of a noun followed by the possessive pronoun 'his' in lieu of the usual form of *s* preceded by an apostrophe. I will transcribe a few examples:

> Once, in a sea-fight, 'gainst *the count his galleys*
> 'Twelfth Night,' Act III, 3, 26 ;

> O, you, my lord? by *Mars his gauntlet*, thanks!
> 'Troilus and Cressida,' Act IV, 5, 177 ;

> Why, *the hot-blooded France*, that dowerless took
> Our youngest born, I could as well be brought
> To knee *his throne*.
> 'King Lear, Act II, 4, 215-217 ;

and perhaps

> *This misshapen knave*
> *His mother* was a witch.
> 'Tempest,' Act V, 1, 268.

Now is it not possible that we may have some such idiom as this in the passage which we are now considering? Whereas a modern author would have written 'One Muliteus, my countryman's, wife,' Shakespeare chose to write 'One Muliteus, my countryman, his wife.' The archaistic form of the genitive was more convenient, because the proper noun, which was intended for that case, stands in a different line, and consequently is somewhat *far removed from* the noun on which it depends, besides being cut off from it by an *intercalary appositional phrase*, so that there is a sort of compound complication. With regard to the name, it has been thought hardly possible that Shakespeare could have coined it, and consequently that orthographical or historical research might throw some light on the text here. I can only say that Muliteus is as appropriate for a Moorish slave, as Demetrius is for a Gothic prince. Were I obliged to find a *verb*, I am not sure that I should see in the termination '*teus*' the verb '*lives*,' which the Cambridge editors fancy; '*teus*' might here been miswritten for '*tents*,' Aaron's Moorish friend preferring the freedom of a tent to the confinement of a settled habitation, or Aaron, with more truth than he was aware of, might designate every house a tent.

At the same time that I suggest this mode of smoothing the difficulty, I can see another and simpler method, which does not interfere at all with the reading of the copies. Perhaps there was never meant to be a verb at all; the substantive verb is often dropped, is easily supplied, *e.g.*

<blockquote>My residence in Rome at one Philario's :
'Cymbeline' Act 1, 1, 97.</blockquote>

These loose constructions are common in the impromptu utterances of social life; they have additional fitness, where, as in the instance quoted, the conversation is hurried: *here* too there is a tickle business on foot which requires the utmost despatch; Aaron hits it off promptly and tells it quickly; rapid in his shifts—rapid in his speech—the expression suits the emergency. We need not here 'hedge aside from the direct forthright.'

Nor is there any reason to harbour suspicion of the 177th and 178th lines,

> I'll make you feed on berries and on roots,
> And feed on curds and whey, and suck the goat,

merely because the same verb happens to be twice repeated in two successive lines. The repetition is not intolerable. Such tiny specks may be noted; they should not be censured.

By the time that we have come to 'Titus Andronicus' we have become so familiar with the short lines that Shakespeare occasionally introduces, that we should cease to notice, or at least to comment on them, were it not that that they are stigmatized by the editors of the 'Globe' Shakespeare; but as touching Act V, 1, 132,

> Make poor men's cattle break their necks,

it may be sufficient to remark that the curtailment harmonizes with the catastrophe.

The same may be said of that line in 'The Taming of the Shrew'

> The match is made, and all is done.

In Act V, 3, 124, the words '*And as he is*' are unfairly accused, and would be badly altered to '*damn'd* as he is,' which one emendator conjectures. In the recapitulation of the events of the tragedy Marcus confines himself to a recital of that portion, in which Aaron bore a suspicious part;

> Behold this child:
> [*Pointing to the Child in the arms of an Attendant*]
> Of this was Tamora delivered;
> The issue of an irreligious Moor,
> Chief architect and plotter of these woes;
> The villain is alive in Titus' house,
> And *as he is*, to witness this is true.

Is it possible that '*he*' refers not to Aaron, but to the *child*, and that, when Marcus says, 'as he is,' he points a second time to the little one, intimating that such was the villain's hue, such were his features, leaving no doubt that *he* was the father? If, however, this position be accounted untenable, I will fall back upon a second line of defence, and contend that the phrase is a curt contemptuous mode of describing the physiognomy and character of Aaron. The affirmation or the adjuration of such a liar would hardly be accepted by any as evidence, but that there should be one alive in Titus' house, and that that one should have the coal-black hue that darkened the child, and the malignity of spirit capable of conceiving and executing such nefarious practices—that he should be alive, and be *as he was*—this might be considered by Marcus amply sufficient evidence to convince the Romans, that the tale that had been told was true. Compare

> Yet, as they are, here are they come to meet you.
> 'Taming of the Shrew,' Act IV, 1, 141.
> As we are ourselves, what things are we!
> 'All's Well That Ends Well,' Act IV, 3, 24.

TIMON OF ATHENS.

The first question that we have to ask in 'Timon of Athens' is, What is the force and significance of the last line of the following dialogue between Apemantus and Timon, which is found in Act I, 1, 236-241?

Apem.   Heavens, that I were a lord!
Tim. What wouldst do then, Apemantus?
Apem. E'en as Apemantus does now; hate a lord with my heart.
Tim. What, thyself?
Apem. Ay.
Tim. Wherefore?
Apem. That I had no angry wit to be a lord.

The last words are so extremely simple, that it would seem as if they must carry with them their own explanation, yet no commentator that I am aware of has yet succeeded in fixing their meaning, and many have confessed their inability by pronouncing them corrupt. We may safely start with the assumption that Apemantus' aim was to make Timon smart. How does he set about this? He begins by wishing that he himself were a lord.

Why this? To put himself as it were *en rapport* with Timon, to stand in Timon's place, to personate Timon, in order that every stone which he threw at himself might indirectly hit Timon. So far, then, as Apemantus' replies are concerned, we must regard him for the time being as in his own estimation *no longer himself, but a sort of quasi-Timon.* The question that would be next asked him he easily foresaw, 'What would he do then'? His answer was ready—'Hate himself? 'Wherefore? 'That he had no angry wit to be a lord'—that is to say, that he had not the sense and spirit to maintain his independence, vindicate his authority, dominate and frown away the flatterers who surrounded him, confounding them by his wit, scattering them in his wrath. Apemantus would be — that is, *Timon* should be — ashamed of himself, or (to use Apemantus' own expression) Apemantus would—that is, *Timon* should—hate himself for giving entertainment at all to such filthy hungry parasites, who hung upon him, and got complete mastery of him, and, under pretence of caressing him, would consume him away, till they had picked him clean and bare. *It is Timon's willing surrender of himself to the flatterers* that Apemantus here rails at. The words last-uttered by Apemantus before the dialogue commenced, viz., ' *He that loves to be flattered is worthy of the flatterers,*' is the key to pick the lock.

Our next difficulty consists of a word, which occurs in a line, which follows as a sort of rider to Apemantus' grace—Act I, 2, 73—

> Much good *dich* thy good heart, Apemantus!

In the glossary appended to the 'Globe' Shakespeare it is stated that 'dich' is the optative mood, contracted for 'do it'; and this is what Dr. Johnson says in his Dictionary, without, however, giving any other example of its use. It is worthy of observation that in two other passages of Shakespeare, viz., in the 'Merry Wives of Windsor,' Act I, 1, 83, where the very same words occur, and in 'The Taming of the Shrew,' where almost the same words do, '*do it*' is found, and not 'dich.' Some have supposed that 'dich' is merely a careless piece of copying, and should be ejected from the text for 'do it'; others have fancied that the final letter of 'good'—the word that immediately precedes 'dich'—has been repeated by mistake for *r*, the first letter of the verb 'rich,' the participle of which occurs in 'King Lear.' But I dismiss all these airy fancies, and the more readily, if, as has been whispered to me by a learned critic, '*dich*,' though not recognised by Dr. Johnson, nor familiar to the higher and more cultivated ranks of society, is notwithstanding a good old English word, used at times even now, though rarely—for such words have a tendency to die out, being succeeded by fitter which survive them—in the humbler walks of life: his face is '*diched*,' *i.e.*, covered, 'with dirt' —'the thighs of the bees are diched,' *i,e.*, laden, 'with honey'—such are expressions which are said to have been heard, and it is much to be wished that those, who have studied the English language, not merely as it is in books, but as it is spoken by the people themselves in outlying places, should give, if they can, confirmatory evidence. 'Dich' may have been common enough among poor folk in times gone by; Shakespeare may have heard it, and may have considered that a word, mumbled forth by some weird old crone, while munching her crust of bread in her miserable hovel, might not inappropriately be growled forth by the cynic—the brute, Apemantus, after he had howled forth his ungracious grace, and snarlingly gnawn his root. There are old words, ending in *ich*, such as '*mich*' and '*lich*,' which have fallen into disuse. 'Dich' may be another specimen of the tribe. For the present, then, I would retain it as at any rate good enough for Apemantus.

We may now read Scene after Scene without interruption, until we come to a part of the tragedy where

> Fortune in her shift and change of mood
> Spurns down her late beloved.

Timon is sliding down the hill, and, instead of being supported by troops of flatterers, is being pursued and sued by hosts of creditors, all eager that their claims should be instantly satisfied. Not a penny has Timon in hold, yet he cannot but believe that those, who tasted so largely of his bounty in the day of his affluence, would requite him now in the day of his indigence, or at least accommodate him with a *loan*; he sends forth his servants, therefore, to Lucullus for fifty talents; to Lucius for—the words actually attributed to the servant are 'so many talents'; but, if this is what he said, he must by some notation or other, by finger or by figure, graphically or pictorially, have made plain the sum that Timon required; from Lucius' reply I gather that it might have been 500, it might have been only 50 talents—the latter sum, perhaps, the more probable, as tallying with the amount that Lucullus was asked for. Not more taken aback was Lucius at the appeal thus made to him, than commentators appear to be at the answer which fell from Lucius' lips—Act III, 2, 43—

> He cannot want fifty five hundred talents.

I do not think that there has been any falsification of the amount. We may say of the difficulty *solvitur legendo*. The actor would annihilate it by a breath. It is simply a matter of how the line should be read— where the emphasis should be laid. By laying the stress on 500, if the sum asked for were 50, or on 50, if the sum asked for were 500, the amount is easily accounted for, Lucius affects to be incredulous; he cannot think that Timon can be in earnest. 'Fifty talents!'—he as good as cries—'Fifty talents! His lordship is merry with me: such a rich man as he cannot want'—that is, cannot be without, must have in his possession, and therefore can command—'fifty *five hundred* talents, if he needed them'; or, supposing the sum asked for were 500, on 50 be the emphasis laid. Does the explanation smack too much of the Multiplication Table? Is it not sufficiently poetical? Another mode of computation has been suggested to me by a critic whose judgment I value. After saying fifty, Lucius suddenly stops, and raises the sum to a much larger figure. Such are two modes of explaining the line; if either of them will stand, the charge of corruption falls to the ground.

Our next stopping-place is where Timon has assembled his false friends to a banquet such as they deserve; before the dishes are uncovered, he says a characteristic grace, in the course of which we come to the words—Act III, 6, 89,—

> The rest of your fees, O gods—the senators of Athens, together with the common lag of people—what is amiss in them, you gods, make suitable for destruction. For these my present friends, as they are to me nothing, so in nothing bless them, and to nothing are they welcome.

'Fees' is certainly not the word that we should have expected, but we are not so straitened as to be obliged to exchange it for Warburton's and Mason's obvious correction 'foes.' 'Fees' admits of being defended. It is true that it cannot be used in its ordinary sense of a pecuniary recompense, but may it not here bear the meaning that belongs to it in books of jurisprudence? Shakespeare was not averse to legal phraseology; this very word in its legal signification, either compounded or uncompounded, is found more than once in his plays; if, when speaking of the *evil* Deity, he could say, 'If the Devil have him not in fee-simple,' it is quite possible that, when addressing the good Gods, he might have used the simple word 'fees.' The fee includes all the interest in the property. 'Fees' would not be an inappropriate way of describing the great human estate belonging to the gods.

With regard to Act IV, 3, 134, if, as I think not improbable, *a bawd* is an error, it is just the error that a copyist might have committed, considering the particular class of persons, who were at the time the subject of Timon's denunciation; and if an error, we may be pretty sure it bears a rough resemblance both as to sound and as to lettering to the word set down in the original. Now it is stated that the power of gold is such as to make the unclean turn clean; with as much truth it might be said that it can make the clean unclean—make *whores*—the *number* of the noun is especially noteworthy—'abound.' Such, I conceive, is what Timon was meant to say in the second clause: '*a bound,*' illegibly and not continuously written, might not unnaturally in this place have been mistaken for '*a bawd.*' A similar sentiment is expressed in Act IV, 3, 386, of this play, where Timon says 'the blush of gold'

> doth thaw the consecrated snow
> That lies on Dian's lap,

and in 'Romeo and Juliet' gold is called 'saint-seducing,' and in 'Antony and Cleopatra' we are told that 'want will perjure the ne'er touch'd Vestal.' The remark would be anything but complimentary to Phryna and Timandra.

And now that we are about words, what is the epithet, and what is the force of the epithet, that should be applied to the trees in the 223rd line of this 3rd Scene, where the Folios have

> will these moyst [moist] trees,
> That have outlived the eagle, page thy heels,
> And skip where thou point'st out?

Is it the livery? or is it the age? or is it the vigour and strength that should give the finishing stroke to this splendid piece of composition? In other words, should we read 'moss'd' with Hanmer, and, I may add, with most editors? or should we adhere to 'moist,' the word of the Folios? The word of the Folios should have the precedence, which has been discounted perhaps somewhat too hastily and on insufficient grounds. For the contrast would be between Timon 'forwelked and fordwined,' and now after an ephemeral existence tottering on the brink of the grave, and these fine old giants of the forest, which, though they had already outlived the eagle, were yet 'moist,' that is, strong and vigorous, full of the juice and sap of life. So interpreted, the epithet 'moist' has a force and fitness, which can hardly be controverted. Admit this, and the critic will not be justified in displacing it even for Hanmer's happy hit, which is as poetical as it is plausible, and was in all likelihood suggested to him by a line in 'As You Like It,' Act IV, 2, 105,

<blockquote>Under an oak, whose boughs were moss'd with age.</blockquote>

I have defended the word of the Folios; I have admitted the possibility of Hanmer's conjecture; but, if conjectures are to be listened to, there is another which does as little violence as possible to the word of the copies, and on its own account deserves to be considered. Below in Act IV, 3, 422, we read, 'The oaks bear *mast*.' By writing the *o* and *i* closely together, instead of separately, '*mast*' and '*moist*' become one and the same. 'Will these mast-trees' would be a reading both strong and suitable. There *might* be an allusion not only to their kind and quality, but ambiguously—the play on the word would not shock Shakespeare's contemporaries—to their gigantic height as well; for their antiquity is sufficiently expressed in the relative clause that follows. I have now stated possibilities; probabilities I must leave to the critics.

There is nothing that I know of now, that calls for special comment, until we reach Act V, 2, 6-9, where the relative 'whom' certainly needs some explanation. It seems to hang loosely without anything to govern it, and, in fact, to be almost a superfluity; yet it has its part to perform in the sentence which it introduces, and must on no account be tampered with.

The duplication of the *preposition* for clearness' sake is an idiom of which we have perhaps a dozen examples in Shakespeare; for clearness' sake in the following passage,

> I met a courier, one mine ancient friend;
> Whom, though in general part we were opposed,
> Yet our old love made a particular force,
> And made us speak like friends,

the relative 'whom,' being a long way off from the verb which was intended to govern it, *no less than two sentences* intervening between it and the sentence of which it properly forms part, is virtually repeated— I say, virtually, because the actual repetition of the relative would be an impossibility; it is repeated, however, in its *equivalent*, and its equivalent, strictly speaking, would be the personal pronoun '*him;*' it is true that that pronoun is not found anywhere in the sentence to which the relative 'whom' belongs, but it undoubtedly would have been, had it not been for the disturbing influence of the pronoun '*me*,' which, as well as '*him*,' had to be supplied. But 'him and me' were more conveniently expressed by the pronoun '*us*,' and so '*us*' is inserted with as much boldness as briefness, and '*us*' is the word, in which the relative 'whom,' after performing its part as an introductory particle, is most certainly swallowed and lost. Had it not been for the complication caused by the necessity of expressing '*and me*,' the case would have been simple enough, and would have found an exact parallel in the following lines from the 'Tempest,' Act III, 3, 53-56:

> You are three men of sin, *whom* Destiny
> That hath to instrument this lower world
> And what is in't, the never surfeited sea
> Hath caused to belch up *you*.

Compare also 'Cymbeline,' Act V, 5, 464.

As an objective case, then, 'whom' is pleonastic; as a connecting particle, it could not be dispensed with. I will not anticipate that any objection will be raised to the repetition of the verb 'made' in two consecutive lines in the above passage; such repetitions are not unprecedented. Compare, *e.g.*, 'Titus Andronicus,' Act IV, 2, 177-178; 'Measure for Measure,' Act III, 2, 287-288; 'Merchant of Venice,' Act II, 8, 42, where the word 'love' is suspected, perhaps because it occurs again immediately after at the end of the 44th line; it will be sufficient to say of such repetitions, that, if they slipped from the author in the hurry of composition, he did not think so much amiss of them afterwards as to care to revise them.

I now come to—shall I call it a soldier's exclamation, or is it rather a sepulchral epitaph, in Act V, 3, 4, 5? At any rate it is a couplet, which has given a world of trouble to expositors, and perhaps will ever remain dark and inexplicable.

Sold. By all description this should be the place.

> Who's here? speak, ho! No answer! What is this?
> *Timon is dead, who hath outstretch'd his span:*
> *Some beast reade* [read] *this; there does not live a man.*
> Dead, sure; and this his grave. What's on this tomb
> I cannot read; the character I'll take with wax;
> Our captain hath in every figure skill,
> An aged interpreter, though young in days:
> Before proud Athens he's set down by this,
> Whose fall the mark of his ambition is.

The third and fourth lines of the above passage form the couplet disputed about. Theobald (Warburton) reads

> Some beast *rear'd* this; *here* does not live a man.

Mr Staunton regards the two lines printed in italics as the only part of the inscription which the soldier could read. The 'Globe' editors, though they read 'rear'd,' 'incline to think that the words were originally intended as an epitaph to be read by the soldier; but the author may have changed his mind, or forgotten to obliterate what was inconsistent with the sequel, or the text may have been tampered with.'

As I am about to offer a totally new solution of this old and exceedingly difficult problem, I must bespeak not a particle of indulgent favour, but some amount of patience from the critic, who perhaps will be suspicious and sceptical, when he hears me speak of novelties.

I conceive, then, that the soldier comes to what, from the description given him, he supposes must be the place of Timon's abode, and shouts out, 'Who's here? Speak, ho!' On receiving no answer, he says to himself, 'What is this? which may either be an expression of surprise at the silence of his reception—in which case it is equivalent to 'what is the meaning of this?' or an expression of wondering enquiry as to the *character of the place* which met his eye. I will take it in the *latter* of these two senses. In consequence of his eliciting no reply, he says,

> Timon is dead, who hath outstretch'd his span;

while in reference to his question, 'what is this?' he tells us what it is; he describes the character of the place—'some beast-tread,' or 'some beast-road this' (for so I read); 'here does not live a man?' This, he says, is rather fit to be a haunt of wild beasts, than to be a habitation for any of human kind. Suddenly he espies the tomb, and, concluding at once that his surmise was correct, 'Dead sure,' he repeats, 'and this his tomb.'

Thus without the addition—by the transposition only—of a single letter, I get rid of the necessity for supposing that there was a double epitaph, which appears to me extremely improbable, at the same time that I offer what I venture to think is a fair settlement of an exceedingly difficult question.

I foresee some objections, and I shall endeavour to meet them.

1. The interpretation, which I have given to the question, 'What is this?' has been suggested to me by a passage in 'Cymbeline,' Act III, 6, 17, where curiously enough the very same words have reference to a dreary wild:

> But what is this?
> Here is a path to't; 'tis some savage hold.

2. I acknowledge that I cannot give an example of the use of such a compound as 'beast-tread,' or 'beast-road,' but is it necessary? May not a word, compounded of two such simple English words as 'beast' and 'tread,' be suffered to pass, especially when we consider how freely and boldly Shakespeare at times links words together? If for every strange Shakespearian compound we must needs find a duplicate, we shall have to reject as spurious a number of words which Shakespeare undoubtedly compounded.

3. It cannot be fairly inferred that the couplet is an inscription which the soldier read, merely because the lines rhyme. The soldier concludes his speech with a rhyming couplet, and such couplets are repeatedly introduced by Shakespeare seemingly quite arbitrarily. There are examples enough in this very play, as, for instance, in Flavius' last speech in Act I, 2; and in Apemantus' in the same Act, beginning with 'Hoyday'; and elsewhere.

4. If it be thought that the relative clause, 'who hath outstretch'd his span,' sounds more like part of a sepulchral epitaph than a soldier's exclamation, what will be said of the relative clause

in the last line—'whose fall the mark of his ambition is?' The style is the same. There is not the least reason why the soldier, who spoke the one, might not have spoken the other also.

5. I cannot think that the soldier could have seen the grave, *before* he uttered the words, 'Dead sure, and this his grave'; nor that he could have read anything on the tomb, before he says, 'What's on this tomb, I cannot read.' The moment he saw the tomb, it were natural to suppose that he would have told us of it; he would not have approached leisurely, and tediously deciphered (for the soldier was no scholar) a couple of lines inscribed on it before coming to the conclusion that it was Timon's grave. Such slow processes are ill-suited to a soldier, whose object was not to read inscriptions, but to *find Timon*, and who would have known instantly what a grave in such a place meant. When he says 'Dead sure,' he clenches a belief which he had already avowed; he does not express his assent to an inscription which he had just read.

6. Those who would have us believe that the two lines are an epitaph are obliged to assume that there are two epitaphs, written in two different characters, one of which the soldier could read, the other he could not—a most improbable hypothesis.

Lastly, I remark that, in the epitaph which the soldier takes in wax, Timon speaks of himself in the *first* person, whereas in this couplet he speaks of himself in the *third*. *My* theory is that Timon spoke the one, the soldier the other. Besides, what object could Timon have in telling us two or three times over in six lines that he was dead? So far from increasing the length of the epitaph from four lines to *six*, I would rather reduce it from four to *two*, and regard two of the four, which are given as the epitaph at the end of the play, as an interpolation.

One passage more: in Act V, 4, 62, we read

> not a man
> Shall pass his quarter, or offend the stream
> Of regular justice in your city's bounds,
> But shall be *remedied* to your public laws
> At heaviest answer.

It is an unsound and hasty criticism, which has substituted here for 'remedied' either 'remitted' or 'rendered.' The prepositional phrase 'to your public laws' may either be construed with 'remedied,' in which case there is nothing more startling than what is commonly called *a prægnans locutio*, 'he shall be remedied to your public laws' being equivalent to 'he shall be surrendered to your public laws, and have a remedy applied to him at his heaviest responsibility;' *or* (and this is the method which I myself prefer, as it is eminently Shakespearian) 'to your public laws' grammatically follows 'at heaviest answer,' the usual order being 'inverted,' (of which I need not produce any examples here) so that we have the perfectly intelligible sentence, 'he shall be remedied at heaviest answer to your public laws.'

I have intimated that 'remedied' is authorized by the Folios; I may further remark that the noun 'remedy' is used by Shakespeare on one occasion where a certain one petitions for legal redress. In 'All's Well That Ends Well,' Act V, 3, 162-164, are the following lines,

> I am her mother, sir, whose age and honour
> Both suffer under this complaint we bring,
> And both shall cease, without your *remedy*,

'Rendered,' 'remitted,' would, no doubt, be more in harmony with modern phraseology, and more pleasing to popular taste, but they are inserted in defiance of Folio authority, and, what is more important still, in contravention of Shakespeare's known usage. Spurious importations they are with more glitter than gold. Such being the case, we have a right to insist that 'remedied'—apparently the worse, but really the better word—should be restored to the text.

JULIUS CÆSAR.

Although we are told that 'Julius Cæsar' was more correctly printed than any other play, and may perhaps have been printed from the original MS. of the author, yet there are not wanting passages in it, where we have to make up our minds, whether the reading of the copies requires to be emended, or only vindicated and explained. Take, for instance, the following passage from Act I, 2, lines 154, 155,

> When could they say till now, that talk'd of Rome,
> That her wide *walks* encompass'd but one man?

Here some commentators fancy that the printer's accuracy failed him, and that he set down 'walks,' when he should have set down 'walls,' the confusion having arisen from 'talk'd,' a word of similar cadence to 'walks,' occurring in the previous line. It is argued that the latter word is inappropriate, that a disagreeable assonance is produced by it, and that such a word as 'encompass' is a pretty clear proof that '*walls*' was the original reading. On a question of euphony, not every ear will hear alike. All I can say is, that, if these lines jar, there are scores of jarring lines to be found in Shakespeare. We will grant that 'walls' would in all probability have been preferred by a prose-writer; but '*walks*,' which is the rarer word, strikes me as of more exquisite fancy, more picturesque and poetical, true topographically, and even more appropriate here, because it admits of a more comprehensive span. For the walls of Rome did not include all the inhabitants of Rome; there were plenty of habitations outside, as well as inside, the old Servian ramparts; but the 'circuit of the walks,' (to introduce Milton's significant phrase, 'Paradise Lost,' 4, 586)—the outlying pleasure-grounds which environed the metropolis—the vast ring of groves and parks and gardens in which the citizens were wont to walk abroad and refresh themselves—these contained within their compass *all* the inhabitants of Rome, and to insinuate that but one man could be found within *them*, was monstrous, startling, invidious.

There is an allusion in this very play to a portion of these 'walks'—those which Cæsar bequeathed to the Roman people—Act III, 2, 252,

> Moreover, he hath left you all his walks,
> His private arbours and new-planted orchards,
> On this side Tiber; he hath left them you
> And to your heirs for ever, common pleasures,
> To walk abroad, and recreate yourselves.

It is a curious coincidence, though I have no wish to magnify its importance, that in 'Titus Andronicus,' where Aaron is speaking of a forest in the neighbourhood of Rome, we meet with the expression

<blockquote>The forest walks are wide and spacious.</blockquote>

'Walks' is entitled to the place on the ground that it is supported by the Folios, besides having distinct claims of its own to recommend it. 'Walls' reads to me poor and tame in comparison with it. Still less reason is there for tampering with the text in Act I, 3, 62-65:

<blockquote>
But if you would consider the true cause
Why all these fires, why all these gliding ghosts,
Why birds and beasts from quality and kind,
Why old men fools, and children calculate—
</blockquote>

Here we have a succession of sentences without any finite verb appearing—a loose easy offhanded mode of expression, which in poetry, in the drama, in conversation, more particularly in hurried and excited conversation, is extremely natural—the whole wound up with a regularly-formed complete sentence—'and children calculate.' There is nothing objectionable in this; there is nothing repugnant to Shakespeare's general style and manner; there is not the least occasion to drop the *s* of 'fools,' and make '*fool*' a verb, much less resort to an artifice, under cover of which 'old men, fools, and children,' is made to pass as a periphrasis for people of all capacities and ages. In the Folios a comma is found after old men; whether we omit or insert it, matters not one jot.

A little below in the 129th line there is room for diversity of opinion as to what the exact reading should be, though there can be no dissension as to the meaning. The first and second Folios have

> And the complexion of the element
> Is Fauors like the work we have in hand,

which in the third and fourth Folios is printed '*Is Favours.*' This some editors have changed to '*Is favour'd,*' others to '*In favour's*'—alterations which, though not considerable, are, in my opinion, both overdone and misdone. Anyhow I perceive another mode of mending the text, which is so extremely simple, so idiomatic and Shakespearian, and withal, besides being full of spirit, is so near the *ductus literarum*, that I marvel that it has not been broached by any of the commentators. Following closely, as I am bound to do, the track of the Folios, I retain 'is,' and 'favours' also; all that I assume is that *h* has been clipped, and that '*his*' was intended, where '*is*' has been inserted, and that 'favours' needs only the interposition of an apostrophe before its final *s*, in order that it may be, what I doubt not it was intended to be, equivalent to 'favour is.' The passage is now not only sound but strong. The construction admits of a twofold explanation. In the first place, 'his' may be regarded as a symbol of the old genitive, in which case the passage bears a close resemblance to one, to which I have already adverted in 'Titus Andronicus.' The end of the line was not altogether favourable to the ordinary form of the genitive, or, if it were, the metre of the following line was glad of an extra syllable; accordingly, at the end of the line the simple word 'element' stands, while at the commencement of the following line, by way of complement and compensation, stands the pronoun 'his; the ordinary and modern form of expression would have been 'the complexion of the element's favour,' instead of which we have the rarer and more archaic form 'the complexion of the element his favour,' which, odd as it may seem to some, was allowable, was convenient, and was not less forcible. Examples of this form of the genitive I have cited elsewhere; so I need not tire the reader by repeating them here. There is, however, another mode of explaining precisely the same words, which is even more forcible, and, I am inclined to think, more probable.

The point to which the speaker wished to draw attention is first stated in general terms and presented singly for contemplation,

And the complexion of the element—

Here there is a pause, and here I place a hyphen; next comes a more specific description of what was intended to be indicated,

His favour's like the work we have in hand,
Most bloody, fiery, and terrible.

Two subjects for one verb, the one introductory and

general, the other explanatory and particular. There is no little force in a construction of this sort. It is as if a person, who was about to throw a weight, were, after lifting it, and putting his arm in the proper attitude, to pause for a moment before discharging the projectile, in order to muster up his whole strength for the purpose of giving the heavy body the necessary impetus. A prose-writer might have said 'As for the complexion of the element, its appearance is like the work we have in hand'; but the poet, describing a startling and portentous phenomenon, preferred to use perhaps a startling construction, or at any rate a construction a little out of the common.

I have now to call attention to a passage in Act III, 1, 174, where a spiteful word, occurring in a speech addressed by Brutus to Antony, which was meant to be of a conciliatory character, is so impolitic and ill-timed that we eye it as we might a snake insidiously nestled in a bed of flowers.

> O Antony, beg not your death of us.
> ⎧ Though now we must appear bloody and cruel,
> ⎪ As, by our hands and this our present act,
> ⎨ You see we do, yet see you but our hands
> ⎩ And this the bleeding business they have done:
> ⎧ Our hearts you see not; they are pitiful;
> ⎨ And pity to the general wrong of Rome—
> ⎪ As fire drives out fire, so pity pity—
> ⎩ Hath done this deed on Cæsar. For your part,
> To you our swords have leaden points, Mark Antony:
> Our arms, in strength of malice, and our hearts
> Of brothers' temper, do receive you in
> With all kind love, good thoughts, and reverence.

Some more euphemistic word than 'malice' we certainly should have looked for on such an occasion; yet 'malice' is the plain undoubted word of the Folios, and we have no right to oust it, until we have exhausted every effort to give it an intelligible meaning. Now I have bracketed two sets of lines, containing four each, because I observe that Brutus' words,

> Our arms, in strength of malice, and our hearts
> Of brothers' temper,

which occur at the end of the speech, do but repeat in a short and summary way what had already been expressed more at length in the commencement of it, 'our arms in strength of malice' bearing a general resemblance to the first set in which the murderous look and bloody hands are described, 'our hearts of brothers' temper' being equivalent to what in the second set is stated, and being, in fact, almost identical with it. If this is so, the coincidence is too significant to be altogether overlooked.

They who offer to receive Antony in are the very persons who had just been described, and, if the same, then the combination of the *foul* and the *fair*, of 'arms in strength of *malice*' and 'hearts of *brothers*' temper,' are set in the scales to balance each other, and to substitute 'justice,' or 'amity,' or 'allies,' or aught else, for that ill-natured word 'malice,' would be to disturb the equipoise.

And here it may be well to remark that 'malice' is sometimes used in rather a peculiar sense by

Shakespeare, as I think may be seen from the following quotations,

'King John,' Act II, 1, 251-252,
> Our cannons' malice vainly shall be spent
> Against the invulnerable clouds of heaven.

'King John,' Act II, 1, 379-380,
> both conjointly bend
> Your sharpest deeds of malice on this town.

'Antony and Cleopatra,' Act III, 13, 178,
> I will be treble-sinewed, hearted, breathed,
> And fight maliciously.

In all these passages, although mischief is intended, the mischief is regarded with complacent satisfaction. Certainly Brutus was not dissatisfied with *their* deed of malice, nor yet with the strength, nor yet with the success of it. It is not at all impossible, then, that by the words 'in strength of malice' he was referring, as indeed some think he was, and as the context seems to indicate, *to the deed which they had just done;* he did not apologize for it, he avowed it, he gloried in it—he and all they who were with him; and, if by *such* Antony was willing to *be received in* (for they did not *require* his support), *such as they were,* they would receive him. As an equal, not as a suppliant, not as an apologist, the would-be liberator speaks. If, however, 'malice' does not bear this particular reference, I can only suppose that Brutus is making a sort of manifesto to Antony of the principles of his party; they had a strong arm for their foes, a warm heart for their friends; they could fight like devils, and at the same time love like brothers. Such was their motto. In offering to fraternize on these terms, Brutus would be speaking no strange language to Antony. Such principles were at the bottom of all the political clubs and associations of antiquity.

I pass on to the 206th line,

> Sign'd in thy spoil, and crimson'd in thy lethe,

where, if '*lethe*' were the word written by Shakespeare, it must bear the same relation to 'lethum,' that '*antres*,' a word used in another of his plays, does to 'antrum'; but it is such a stranger to us, and is so easily altered, that we can hardly wonder at Pope's wishing to strike it out, and put 'death' in its place. I am not ignorant that it was the practice of some writers to intersprinkle occasionally their native English with uncouth words of an antique and foreign tongue, and there is no lack of Latinisms in 'Julius Cæsar'; but I am prepared to account for, aye, and to justify, the use of this word here in another way. I believe it was used neither accidentally nor affectedly, but of set purpose, and as most pertinent. In a passage of high tragedy, of uncommon passion, full of grief and woe, where a colossal man is described as having fallen, not in a foreign land by the sword of a savage foe, but in the heart of his own city by the secret daggers of citizens and friends, the poet willed to use not the ordinary word applied to those who in the course of nature peacefully or painfully expire, but a distinct, an exceptional word—one, which, though strange and singular, is yet classic in its origin, and might have been used by a Roman poet when telling of a hero's— a patriot's murderous extinction—a word which closes the description with dignity, with feeling, and with force. The oftener I read it, the more I become reconciled to it, and I am not now in the least disposed to question the genuineness of

> Sign'd in thy spoil, and crimson'd in thy *lethe*.

And why, a little below in the 262nd line, should any take exception to the form of the curse?

> A curse shall light upon the *limbs* of men.

Such an imprecation, even when taken by itself, is not an impossible one, but, standing where it does, it is fitly placed, and, what is more, cannot be bettered. The curse is represented as a gradually progressive one; its progress is traced with undeviating precision. It begins with *a single man and a single member*—'the *hand* that shed this costly blood;'—and spreads to many men and *many members*; it next invades, with increasing energy, houses and cities, and finally possesses itself of the whole land. In 'King Richard III' Lady Anne invokes a curse on the hands, the heart, the blood of the murderer of her husband and of her husband's father. There is no reason whatever why the line should have been marked as corrupt. Take the curse as a whole from first to last, it was full enough, and deep enough, and diffusive and extensive enough to satisfy even an Antony.

I must now say a word on Act IV, 1, 36-39, where Antony, giving his opinion of Lepidus' character, says that he is

> One that feeds
> On objects, arts, and imitations,
> Which, out of use, and staled by other men,
> Begin his fashion.

'Objects, arts' has been condemned by many, and made to give way to Theobald's ingenious conjecture 'abject orts,' or to Mr. Staunton's variation of it, 'abjects, orts.' Notwithstanding its glitter, the new coin is not so good as the old. Such words as 'objects, arts' seem to me to be more naturally coupled with 'imitations,' than words bearing a totally different meaning. I am not sure, though possibly here I am hypercritical, that 'cast away and broken fragments'—I use the commentator's own words—that 'things which had been abandoned as useless' *could* properly be said to have been in use at all. It may be said that the relative clause does not refer to 'abject, orts,' but only to 'imitations.' Mr. Knight, however, thought otherwise, and on that very ground rested his defence of the reading of the copies. It has been asked, What is the meaning of 'objects, arts'? It may be answered that words like these admit of a great variety of meanings. What does Troilus mean, when he speaks of the Grecian youths 'flowing over with arts and exercise?' Or what is meant, when it is said—Ulysses is the speaker—Hector 'subscribes to tender objects?' Or what in 'Love's Labour's Lost,' when Holofernes says

This is a gift I have, simple, simple, a foolish extravagant spirit, full of forms, figures, shapes, *objects*, ideas, apprehensions?

For my part, I think that Shakespeare had large truths in his mind here, and distinguished two classes of politicians. Just as Bacon tells us that in philosophy there were some who thought that 'the dignity of the human mind was lowered by long and frequent intercourse with experiments and particulars, which are the *objects of sense and confined to matter*,' and in another place that '*reverence of antiquity and the authority of men* who have been esteemed great in philosophy, and *general unanimity, have retarded men from advancing*,' and yet again he speaks of those who 'seek nothing beyond that which is handed down to them as perfect,' so in policy there are two great divisions, sets, factions, parties—*these* depending a little too much on the sight of their eyes, on the material and visible; on arts, rules, methods, mechanical contrivances; on imitations, patterns, precedents—the *others*, men of original ideas, creative geniuses, brilliant in resource, always abreast of the revolutionary movement, and never suffering themselves to be outmatched by more cautious competitors—and the former class are despised by and are often made the tools and dupes of the latter. Now to the former class Lepidus belonged; to the latter Cæsar. Viewed in this light, 'objects,' 'arts,' are words full of significance, and would be ill exchanged for 'abjects,' 'orts,' ingenious as that conjecture is.

And here an admirable note of Professor Craik on Act IV, 2, quoted by Mr. Aldis Wright, is well worthy of insertion: 'It is strange that no one should have been struck with the absurdity of such an association as Lucius and Titinius for the guarding of the door. An officer of rank and a servant boy—the boy, too, being named first. The function of Lucius was to carry messages. As Cassius sends his servant Pindarus with a message to his division of the force, Brutus sends his servant Lucius with a similar message to his division.' The Professor, therefore, substitutes '*Lucius*' for '*Lucilius*' in the 49th line, and two lines below reads '*Lucilius*' for '*Let Lucius*'—a better sorting of the characters no doubt. Yet the Cambridge editors 'have not adopted' the alteration, 'because they are of opinion that the error, such as it is, is due to the author, and not to a transcriber.'

Before I conclude, I will briefly observe that in Act V, 1, 34-35, where a smart interchange of civilities passes between Cassius and Antony, Antony's retort admits of being presented either in an interrogative or in an affirmative form. The latter is the usual mode of arrangement: I incline to the former:

> *Cassius.* But for your words, they rob the Hybla bees,
> And leave them honeyless.
>
> *Antony.* Not stingless too?

And so I have since discovered that Delius punctuates.

MACBETH.

The editors of the 'Cambridge' Shakespeare inform us, that 'Macbeth' was one of the worst printed of all the plays. Possibly their knowledge of this circumstance may have made them a little over-suspicious in their examination of it. Anyhow, they have marked passages in it as corrupt, which, in my opinion, hardly deserve the stigma.

As early as in Act I, 2, 14, the scuffle between the critics commences. Should we read 'quarrel,' which is the word found in Holinshed's Chronicle, from which Shakespeare fetched much of his history, and sometimes also some of his phraseology? or should we rather read 'quarry,' which is set down in every impression of the Folio? The judges are divided; the scales of the balance are pretty evenly poised. 'Quarrel' being a word of frequent occurrence in Shakespeare, those who would force it into the text against the authority of the Folios may fairly be expected to show, that *elsewhere than here*, either in the Quartos or in the Folios, 'quarry' is at times printed, where 'quarrel' is undoubtedly intended. Till then, as 'quarry' admits of being explained, I prefer with Mr. Knight to retain the reading of the copies.

A little further on we come to the lines,

> For brave Macbeth—well he deserves that name—
> Disdaining fortune, with his brandish'd steel,
> Which smoked with bloody execution,
> Like valour's minion carved out his passage
> Till he faced the slave;
> Which ne'er shook hands, nor bade farewell to him,
> Till he unseam'd him from the nave to the chaps,
> And fix'd his head upon our battlements.

We are told that there is 'incurable corruption' here. I cannot for the life of me see it. A short line, beginning with an Anapæst, is surely not in Shakespeare a metrical impossibility. Such fragments of verse sometimes occur, where a crisis is reached in the action, and we pause for a moment, expecting the catastrophe. As for the second 'which,' it has been suggested that, if we could make it, like the first, refer to the 'brandished steel,' we should have a picturesque expression thoroughly Shakespearian; for my own part, I prefer to refer it to *Macbeth*, whose name heads the sentence, and whose prowess pervades it; that it does not refer to Macdonwald, I am as certain as that the two names begin with the same capital letter.

In the 49th line it has been asked why 'flout' and 'fan' are in the present, while the rest of the verbs are in the preterite tense; and in a roundabout way it has been attempted to show that the flouting fanning banners were not the haughty ensigns of a yet unconquered foe, but the captured standards of a beaten army, at that very moment flapping idly, and cooling the conquerors in the camp of Macbeth! Nothing is more improbable. 'Flout' and 'fan' are simply historic presents, just as in the 'Tempest,' Act I, 2, 201-205, Ariel mixes up present tenses with past, where he gives us his most vivid touches;

> Jove's lightnings, the precursors
> O' the dreadful thunder-claps, more momentary
> And sight-outrunning *were* not ; the fire and cracks
> Of sulphurous roaring the most mighty Neptune
> *Seem* to besiege.

Enobarbus does the same in 'Antony and Cleopatra,' Act II, 2, 210, where we have as it were in the present a panorama of the past. Cf. also 'Coriolanus,' Act III, 3, 126-27.

In the lines that follow, Duncan's brief exclamation, 'Great happiness,' hardly interrupts at all the continuity of Ross' narrative. With what propriety, then, is a full stop placed after 'victory fell on us,' and a capital letter given to 'That'? Yet, in spite of stops and capitals, it is hardly possible to mistake the meaning.

In the next Scene—Act I, 3, 95-98—where Ross; delivering the king's message to Macbeth, says

> He finds thee in the stout Norweyan ranks,
> Nothing afeard of what thyself didst make,
> Strange images of death. *As thick as tale*
> *Can post with post,*

there are some who are displeased with 'thick as tale,' the phrase of the Folios, because they cannot find any similar expression in any other part of Shakespeare. But how many words and phrases are they forced to tolerate in almost every play, of which no second example can be produced! Time and the fierce rays of a searching criticism will dissipate their 'hail'; 'thick as tale' will surely hold its ground; but whether it should be connected with the words that precede, or with the words that follow it—whether the images of death were too thick to be counted, or the posts were—that has been questioned. Rhythm and sense favour the latter; perhaps too the line from '2 Henry VI,' Act III, 1, 337,

> Faster than spring-time showers comes thought on thought,

and 'Antony and Cleopatra,' Act I, 5, 61-63,

> *Cleop.* Met'st thou my *posts*?
> *Alex.* Ay, madam, twenty several messengers;
> Why do you send so *thick?*

It has been assumed that 'can' was intended for 'came'; perhaps it was; yet 'ran' would be as near the original, and might not inaptly be applied to military couriers. We have authority for the latter word in '3 Henry VI,' Act II, 1, 109,

> Tidings, as swiftly as the posts could run.

The letter *c* not unfrequently usurps the place of the letter *r*.

I now come to a passage where we can with difficulty see our way for the volumes of smoke which issue forth from the workshops of the annotators. I refer to Act I, 5, 23-26,

> Thou'ldst have, great Glamis,
> That which cries 'Thus thou must do, if thou have it;
> And that which rather thou dost fear to do
> Than wishest should be undone.'

The inverted commas were first placed by Pope, and they are found in the 'Globe,' and in other editions of Shakespeare; nevertheless, Capell was right, when he printed in Italics *only* the words 'Thus thou must do, if thou have it.'

The passage is a very labyrinth of intricacies, yet so confident am I that I have the thread to guide me through it, that I implore the reader not to be deterred by my twistings and turnings from following me right through to the end.

Now observe: in Lady Macbeth's reflections on Macbeth's character we have a triplet of well-balanced antitheses: Macbeth's wish is represented as conflicting with Macbeth's wish. First in order comes

> What thou wouldst highly,
> That wouldst thou holily.

Next

> Wouldst not play false,
> And yet wouldst wrongly win.

Thirdly and lastly we shall certainly find mention of a similar contrast between two opposite desires, warring within him for supremacy, and pulling him in contrary directions. What, as a matter of fact, *have* we? First *this*,

> thou'ldst have, great Glamis,
> That which cries, 'Thus thou must do, if thou have it.'

What next, to counter-work this? We might *expect* some such statement as this,

> And thou wouldst have that which cries, 'This thou must leave undone,' or in other words, 'This thou must not do.'

But Shakespeare, instead of making Lady Macbeth continue her words in the *direct* form of speech, makes her rather continue in the *oblique* or *indirect* form (nor is the form otherwise than appropriate, where Macbeth's indirection is the theme); and, if she had expressed herself in this indirect form *simply*, by which I mean, *without any other idea crossing her mind*, she would have said,

> And thou wouldst have that which thou wouldst should be undone, *i.e.*, not done,

which would be tantamount to saying that Macbeth would fain grasp the prize without incurring the guilt and danger of getting it. But Lady Macbeth does *not* express herself thus simply and unreservedly, but, having a keen insight into her lord's character, she qualifies the statement by the bitter parenthetical reflection,

> That which [rather thou dost fear to do than] wishest should be undone.

She was not afraid that Macbeth lacked the *wish* to do the damned deed, she doubted and feared his *courage*. Exactly what she thought, she expressed. If her anatomical description of his character is dark, difficult, devious, it is because the character itself was so full of contrariety.

I pass on now to the second Act, in the first Scene of which, at the 25th line, where Macbeth says to Banquo,

> If you shall cleave to my consent, when 'tis,
> It shall make honour for you,

'consent,' though suffered to remain by editors, has been looked upon with suspicion and dislike. Capell, Malone, Grant White, conjecture severally 'ascent,' 'content,' 'consort'; yet, as there is no variation in the Folios, and as the very same word is used very similarly in '1 Henry VI,' Act I, 2, 44,

> By my consent, we'll even let them alone,

we may be pretty sure that 'consent' has a right to its place. I paraphrase the passage as follows: 'If you shall steadfastly pursue that line of conduct which has my sympathy and support, and to which I am a deliberately consenting party, *when, according to the prediction of the witches, I am king*'—for that, I take it, is what he means by his short significant '*it*'—'your having sided with me shall lead to your promotion and honour.' Others, however, refer '*it*' to the proposed interview.

A little further down there is another word—I mean '*sides*' in Act II, 1, 55—which has not merely been suspected, but has with singular unanimity been ousted from the text, although critics have not been able to agree among themselves as to the word that should take its place. 'Slides,' a verb, and 'strides,' a noun, have been nominated by rival parties. We may admit that 'sides' is not just the word that a modern dramatist would have thought of, or a modern critic expected; yet somehow or other it crops up in Shakespeare in places where we do not look for it, and in a manner which, to say the least, is at times peculiar. Nor is this the only passage, where its genuineness has been suspected, and efforts have been made to extrude it from the text. I will group together a few of the passages where it occurs, by way of accustoming the reader to it, and illustrating its use.

'Twelfth Night,' Act II, 4, 96,

> There is no woman's sides
> Can bide the beating of so strong a passion :

'King Henry VIII,' Act I, 2, 28,

> Language unmannerly, yea, such which breaks
> The sides of loyalty,

where Mr. Collier would have modernized the text by reading 'ties of loyalty':

'King Lear,' Act II, 4, 200,

> O sides, you are too tough ;

'Antony and Cleopatra,' Act II, 7, 118-119,

> The holding every man shall bear as loud
> As his strong sides can volley.

'Antony and Cleopatra' again, Act IV, 14, 39-41,

> O cleave, my sides!
> Heart, once be stronger than thy continent,
> Crack thy frail case!

and again

> The sides of nature
> Will not sustain it.

Now let it be distinctly understood that I do not cite these passages under the idea that any one of them is an exact exemplar of Tarquin's case, but merely for the purpose of illustrating Shakespeare's occasional use of the word. What I gather from them, however, is that 'sides' is frequently used where strong lusts and passions are referred to, which they are said to encase, contain, be beaten by, and the like. Now is it so very improbable that murder's 'sides' should be glanced at in 'Macbeth' in connexion with murder's monstrous lusts? His look, manner, movement are depicted by the epithet 'withered,' by the 'stealthy pace,' by the 'ghostlike move'; his outrageous desires, and his strength to execute those desires, may be implied in the phrase 'Tarquin's ravishing sides.' While portraying him, as he is seen outwardly, the poet forgets not to point also to his *heart*. I am strongly of opinion, then, that Shakespeare wrote,

> Wither'd murder,
> Alarum'd by his sentinel, the wolf,
> Whose howl's his watch, thus with his stealthy pace,
> With Tarquin's ravishing sides, towards his design
> Moves like a ghost.

We may now read on till we come to the lines—
Act III, 1, 128-131—

> Within this hour at most
> I will advise you where to plant yourselves,
> Acquaint you with the perfect spy o' the time,
> The moment on't.

The words I have italicized have occasioned some smart skirmishing, and, at the risk of bruises, I will fling myself into the fray. 'Spy' I take to be not a concrete, but an abstract noun; it is true that I cannot produce any instance of its being used in such a sense by Shakespeare, but is it, I again ask, either necessary or possible to find second examples of all that Shakespeare peculiarly uses? The nearest parallel that I can think of at this moment is the popular expression, 'let me have a spy at it,' and popular expressions may fairly be referred to, to corroborate dramatic phraseology. The phrase 'o' the time' I connect not, as do most, with 'spy,' but with the verb 'acquaint,' just as in 'The Winter's Tale,' Act II, 2, 48, we have

> Acquaint the queen of your most noble offer.

'Perfect' I believe to be a mistake for 'perfect'st,' having been docked of its last two letters from their so nearly resembling the first two letters of 'spy,' which immediately follows: the same word, superlative and all, occurs in another part of this same play.

Macbeth promises them that he will advise them as to the exact time and place after a thorough reconnaisance made.

Our next question is, how shall we understand—for that too is questioned—the compound pronoun 'ourselves' in Act III, 4, 32, where Macbeth says to the murderer,

> Get thee gone ; to-morrow
> We'll hear ourselves again.

A number of interpretations have been given, none of which seems to me to be right. I believe that 'ourselves' in this place is equivalent to 'by ourselves,' Macbeth naturally shrinking from conversing on such a subject, with such a man, when there were so many to see and hear them.

A little word occurs in Act III, 4, 105, too, in Macbeth's challenge to Banquo's ghost, which has caused no little difference of opinion. 'Be alive again,' says Macbeth,

> And dare me to the desert with thy sword ;
> If trembling I inhabit then, protest me
> The baby of a girl.

The emendations which have been proposed for this passage are as startling for their number, as they are amusing for their variety.

If trembling I inhibit,	If trembling I unknight me,
If trembling me inhibit,	If trembling I inherit :
If trembling I inhibit then ;	

Fantastic all of them! 'Inhabit' which is the word of the copies, we may be pretty sure, was the word also in Shakespeare's MS. It is used somewhat peculiarly at times in Shakespeare, though, of course, most poetically, *e.g.*, in

'King John,' Act IV, 2, 106-107,
>where is that blood
>That I have seen inhabit in those cheeks?

'King Richard III,' Act I, 4, 3,
>and in those holes
>Where eyes did once inhabit.

In both these passages the place of habitation is specified; but, though this is not the case in 'Macbeth,' there cannot be a doubt what the place of habitation is; it is the fleshly tabernacle in which the living individuality, the ' I ' dwells. And it seems to me that there is no little force in one, who is yet a sojourner in the flesh, using the term 'inhabit,' when accosting one who had ceased to tenant a house of clay. Macbeth trembles because he, a flesh-and-blood being, was, so to speak, too heavily handicapped to be matched against a shadowy antagonist; but let that shadowy spectre be circummured again by a fleshly habitation, and Macbeth will not then decline the *equal* encounter.

A little matter of punctuation, which I shall next mention, will only slightly affect the meaning of the passage I shall quote. If, as I am inclined to think, the words ' I will to morrow,' in Act III, 4, 132, are a reiteration by Macbeth of his determination to send, as indicated by him in the 130th line, rather than an expression of his determination to go to the weird sisters, as indicated in the line that follows, the passage will have to be pointed thus,

> I hear it by the way ; but I will send—
> There's not a one of them but in his house
> I keep a servant fee'd—I will to morrow ;
> And betimes I will to the weird sisters ;

or, instead of being placed between two hyphens, the words may be thrown into a parenthesis.

We now come to the 4th Act, in the 2nd Scene of which, beginning at the 18th line, we read,

> But cruel are the times, when we are traitors
> And do not know ourselves, when we hold rumour
> From what we fear, yet know not what we fear,
> But float upon a wild and violent sea
> Each way and move.

The last words have been twisted and turned in almost every imaginable way:

Each way and wave ;	And each way move ;
And move each way ;	Which way we move ;
Each way, and move ;	Each way and none ;

the last proposed with confidence, and charmingly ingenious. I will add one more to this heap of uncertainties ; 'each sway and move' shall take its chance with the rest, suggested to me by a passage in 'King John,' Act II, 1, 578, where occurs the expression 'This sway of motion.' But what am I about? Is it necessary that there should be any alteration at all ? 'Way' indicates the direction, 'move' the progress made in that direction. In whichever *direction* they go, to or back, this *way* or that,—however much or little they *move*—no rest, no peace, but like men they are who float on a wild and violent sea. Such seems a rational and sufficient explanation of a phrase, which has been a sea of trouble to expositors.

I should not have dreamt of making any comment on Act IV, 3, 15, if it had not been stated on high authority, 'there is certainly some corruption here;' and emendations have actually been contemplated, where no emendation should be so much as listened to.

> But something
> You may deserve of him though me, and wisdom
> To offer up a weak poor innocent lamb
> To appease an angry God.

I do not, of course, question here Theobald's emendation '*deserve*,' I merely refer to the isolation of 'wisdom,' which is observable, but should be no cause of offence. The substantive verb has to be supplied. Elsewhere Shakespeare uses the full expression, '*'tis* wisdom;' here the more laconic form was preferred by him, and such pithy off-hand utterances are permitted in common conversation, and consequently in the drama. Let those who doubt ponder such passages as 'Winter's Tale,' Act IV, 4, 417,

> *Reason* my son
> Should choose himself a wife, but as good *reason*
> The father . . . .
> . . . . should hold some counsel
> In such a business;

'Cymbeline,' Act I, 1, 60,

> To this hour *no guess* in knowledge
> Which way they went;

'Titus Andronicus,' Act II, 3, 81,

> And, being intercepted in your sport,
> *Great reason* that my noble lord be rated.

Shakespeare here is his own sufficient witness.

It is just possible that, up to this point of the play, I may upon the whole have carried the indulgent critic with me; at any rate, I have felt as one, who, in fording a stream, has been able to keep touch with the bottom; but I am now coming to a part, where I am not sure that I may not be out of my depth, and, though I shall try to swim, I may sink. There is a dark and profound passage in the latter part of one of Malcolm's speeches—Act IV, 3, 136-137—which runs as follows:

> Now we'll together, and let the chance of goodness
> Be like our warranted quarrel.

The Cambridge editors say 'The meaning seems to be, 'May the chance of success be as certain as the justice of our quarrel.' The sense of the word 'goodness' is limited by the preceding 'chance.' Without this, 'goodness' by itself could not have this meaning.' It seems to me that the sentence, 'the chance of goodness is like our warranted quarrel,' is one in which we have a notable example of *prægnans locutio*. There is much matter in small compass. The very conciseness of the expression hinders us from at once apprehending the meaning of it. Nor should we see it at all, unless we carried in our minds the substance and pith of the whole passage of which the words quoted form but a part. Malcolm had represented himself to Macduff as so irredeemably bad, that the latter was obliged to acknowledge that he could have nothing more to do with him. Upon this, Malcolm unsays the slander which he had uttered against himself, and avers that he is in reality as good as a moment before he had represented himself as bad. His concluding words I thus paraphrase: 'Now we'll together, and let the chance of my being—what in very truth I am—a well-doer, be as strong an inducement to our being friendly, as the chance of my being—had I been what I just now falsely represented myself as being—an evil-doer, would have led to our most justifiably quarrelling.' Or briefly, though somewhat freely, thus: 'Be as ready to be a friend to me now you know I am good, as you were prepared to be an enemy to me when you imagined that I was evil.' Here pausing, and not receiving from Macduff the assurance which he had expected, he asks, 'Why are you silent?' The latter replies

>Such welcome and unwelcome things at once
>'Tis hard to reconcile.

Here a doctor enters, and puts an end for the time to the conversation.

I have come at last to the fifth Act, in the 3rd Scene of which, in the 21st line, there is much uncertainty as to the reading. The first Folio has

> This push
> Will cheer me ever, or dis-eate me now.

The second Folio, instead of 'diseate,' has 'disease'; but, as the second Folio was merely copied from the first, this correction is merely a copyist's conjecture, and cannot be looked upon as in any sense authoritative; in fact, it has no more claim to be considered than any other emendation which may happen to be started. *It may be entitled to as much*, however, and we are bound to examine it on its merits. It has been objected that it supplies too feeble an antithesis to 'cheer.' The validity of this objection will depend on the sense or senses which it was capable of bearing. There cannot be a question that 'disease' had formerly a fuller and more comprehensive signification than it is wont to have now: it meant discomfort and inconvenience in general, and not merely bodily disorder. In both senses Shakespeare uses it. To illustrate the former meaning of it, I may cite '1 Henry VI,' Act II, 5, 44,

> And, in that case, I'll tell thee my disease.

Here Richard, who is the speaker, is going to explain the reason why he was so downhearted and disconsolate. Some one had cast it in his teeth, that his father had been beheaded. Such a taunt must have touched him to the quick. To use an expressive colloquialism, it must have quite upset him. We should not have supposed that in reference to such a cause of disquietude Shakespeare would have put into his mouth a word of *feeble* import; yet, whether feeble or not, '*disease*' is the word.

The next passage that I shall quote for illustration's sake is from 'Coriolanus,' where Volumnia says,

> She will but *disease* our better mirth.

I will not say that '*disease*' is used here in a very strong sense; what, however, is noticeable and pertinent, is, that *it stands in contradistinction to mirth*.

The third passage, which I shall bring forward, is chiefly remarkable, because an effort has been made in it to substitute some other word for '*disease*,' on the very ground that '*disease*' has not a sufficiently strong meaning. Mr. Aldis Wright in his note on 'King Lear,' Act I, 1, 160, tells us, that, where the first and second Quartos read '*diseases*,' the Folios have the stronger word '*disasters*.' Now it is not at all probable that the copyist introduced '*diseases*' into the Quartos; it is much more likely that he found it in the author's MS. '*Disasters*' was in all likelihood afterwards inserted in the Folios, under the mistaken notion that the word of the Quartos was not sufficiently strong. Upon the whole, then, we are warranted in saying that '*disease*,' as it was understood in Shakespeare's day, was strong enough to be opposed to such words as '*ease*,' '*mirth*,' '*cheer*.'

If, however, it be admitted that, according to Shakespearian usage, 'cheer' and 'disease' may stand in contradistinction to each other, but that 'cheer' does not more forcibly represent the favourable, than 'disease' does the unfavourable contingency—in fact, that *neither* word seems equal to the occasion, for argument's sake I will not dispute it, and, in order to meet this new mode of attack, I will fall back upon what are called euphemistic expressions, which are not wanting in this play; thus, 'taking off' is equivalent to 'killing,' 'going off' to 'dying'; and similarly 'cheer' may be a modest way of expressing victory and sovereignty, 'disease' expressing defeat, disgrace, and death.

Capell proposed

> Will cheer me ever, or *disseat* me now ;

Dyce adopted Bishop Percy's clever conjecture,

> Well *chair* me ever, or *disseat* me now.

I will add one of my own, for the value of which I will not vouch,

> Will cheer me ever, or *disheart* me now.

'Unheart' is used in 'Coriolanus.' 'Disheart'! cries a critic jocularly; 'disembowel' would be more to the purpose. But the heart gone, the bowels would soon follow. Macbeth would be more likely to understate than to overstate the dread alternative.

I have now reached my last station, where, however, we shall have to be detained for a while;

impatiently we ask, what's the matter, and we learn that the 11th line of Act V, 4,

> For where there is advantage to be given,
> Both more and less have given him the revolt,

is out of order, and must needs be repaired. The authorities are in a fluster; no one seems to know what had best be done. It is not the meaning which causes this disquietude; it is the phraseology which they consider unsound and untrustworthy. The most objectionable word seems to be 'given,' for which it has been proposed to put 'gone,' 'got,' 'gotten,' 'taken,' 'ta'en'; yet the Cambridge editors appear to be under the impression that the weak part of the line is in the phrase 'is to be'; for they suggest that perhaps the first line should stand thus,

> For where there is advantage given to flee,

or

> For where there is advantage to 'em given.

They commence their note, however, with the remark that the passage, as it stands, is not capable of any satisfactory explanation. Let me take it to pieces, and see whether there is really anything amiss with it. I presume that no one will question that 'advantage' may be used in the sense of an 'advantageous opening,' 'a favourable opportunity,' 'a good chance,' to use a common but expressive phrase. Thus we have in 'Othello,' Act I, 3, 298,

> And bring them after in the best advantage;

'Othello' again, Act II, 1, 247,

A slipper and subtle knave, a finder of *occasions*, that has an eye can stamp and counterfeit advantages, though *true advantage never present itself*;

'2 Henry VI,' Act I, 1, 242,

And, when I spy advantage, claim the crown;

'King Lear,' Act II, 1, 24,

You have now the good advantage of the night;

'Troilus and Cressida,' Act III, 3, 2,

The advantage of the time prompts me aloud
To call for recompense.

Well now, cannot the phrase 'is to be given' mean 'is capable of being given,' or, 'can possibly be given'? Undoubtedly it can. Here are examples:

'Othello,' Act I, 2, 45,

When, being not at your lodging to be found;

'Winter's Tale,' Act V, 1, 101,

She had not been,
Nor was not to be equall'd,

But this use of the Gerundive participle will hardly be disputed.

May we not write, then, 'an advantage is given' in the sense of 'a favourable occasion is offered'? In the passage above quoted from 'Othello' we have the words 'the advantage *presents itself*,' which, passively expressed, would be '*is presented*.' And what difference between 'an advantage *is presented*,' and 'an advantage *is given?*' Given by whom? am I asked. Given by a favouring fortune; given by negligent guards; given by the nature of the place. If now 'an advantage *is given*' is admissible, 'an advantage *is to be given*' is equally so, and the meaning of the lines will be 'where there is a possibility of a favourable opportunity [of deserting] being presented or given, men of all ranks revolt from him.' Call it what English you like, old English, or colloquial English, or Shakespearian English, good sound English I am positive that it is.

And now, Sirs, we have come to our journey's end.

HAMLET.

I shall not undertake.—I do not profess to be able —to deal with all the doubtful and difficult passages in 'Hamlet,' which yet require elucidation; I shall confine myself to the more modest and feasible task of throwing a few rays of light on three or four dark corners, which others, aiming at a more diffusive illumination, have in my opinion left in comparative obscurity. There is a passage, for instance, beginning at the 113th line of Act I, Scene 1, the main drift of which is clear enough, and the several parts taken separately are perfectly intelligible; but the construction of the sentence as a whole seems loose and disjointed, and the connecting particles are irregular, and to all appearances inadequate. We must acknowledge that there is some ground here for the suspicion entertained by commentators, that the text has suffered mutilation, or even that a line has fallen out. Yet I cannot consent to abandon the vantage-ground of the copies until I have satisfied myself that it is quite untenable. I will examine, therefore, the parts which are alleged to be weak and defenceless, and try whether they may not be explained, if not in accordance with the general rules of grammar, yet agreeably to those occasional deviations from them, with which scholars are perfectly familiar.

The circumstances may be thus briefly stated: the sight of the ghost of the murdered king leads Horatio to remark that such spectral apparitions usually foreshadow political and social disturbance. An eminent example of this he cites from a page of Roman history:

> In the most high and palmy state of Rome,
> A little ere the mightiest Julius fell,
> The graves stood tenantless and the sheeted dead
> Did squeak and gibber in the Roman streets.

To put a comma at the end of these lines, as if the speaker had something more to say on the particular subject of the *ghost-parallel,* or to leave a vacant space, and fill it up with a number of asterisks as an indication that something has been probably omitted, is not only not necessary, it is objectionable—it is wrong. The parallel, which is commenced in the above lines, is also completed and concluded by them. A full stop, or at least a colon, should mark the termination of a period. There is a pause, and the pause heightens the effect of an exceedingly striking picture. But, after drawing a comparison between the Cæsarean age and his own *in respect of the particular phenomenon of the ghostly apparition,* Horatio pursues the train of thought, and carries the parallel further still, showing that there was also a *general resemblance* between the two periods *in respect of other signs and wonders*; it was not merely that the earth had cast forth her dead, but the heavens also spoke a language ominous and fearful. There were warnings celestial as well as warnings terrestrial.

'As in the time gone by there were'—but the poet omits the finite verb, which a prose-writer would be careful to express—'stars with trains of fire and dews of blood; as there were disasters in the sun,'—here again the finite verb is wanting—'and as the moon was sick almost to doomsday with eclipse, even so'—but for this conventional conjunction the poet substitutes, perhaps has a reason for substituting the less usual, unlooked for, and even startling combination *'and even'*—'even so not the earth only, but heaven, as well as earth, has demonstrated to our climate and countrymen the coming on of fearful changes.'

There is no doubt some confusion here—confusion, not corruption. It is even possible that Shakespeare intended, by the chaotic sentence with its finite verb suppressed and its heterogeneous conjunction introduced, to impress the confusion of the times, or perhaps rather the mental agitation of the speaker. But even if it be objected that, with the exception of these two lines, there seems nothing chaotic in the passage, nor does the speaker seem much agitated, still I contend that such literary irregularities need not be incredible—are quite tolerable. In classical literature they are called anacolutha; but call them what you will, they now and then may be found lying in our way, without really and seriously obstructing our progress; they arrest the attention without baffling the understanding; there is a good deal of rough vigour about them; they are as it were extemporaneous effusions; left in their natural state, and not worked up afterwards and polished; if they are not a master's way of portraying, as only a master can, the terror felt and the confusion apprehended.

On the principle that we should always stick to the reading of the Quarto or the Folio, wherever we can do so consistently with the idiom of the English language, or with Shakespearian usage, I will venture now to offer a suggestion even for Act I, 3, 74, where Polonius is represented as saying,

> For the apparel oft proclaims the man,
> And they in France of the best rank and station
> *Are of a most select and generous chief in that.

The phraseology here is certainly peculiar, and the prolongation of the metre has tempted some to cut the knot by simply omitting 'of a.' But this heroic method of dealing with a difficulty should be resorted to only in an extreme emergency. *An article and an adjective*, often in the superlative

---

* The second and the third Quartos have 'or.'

degree, but *without any substantive with which to connect them*, is not an unprecedented Shakespearian combination. We come across such phrases as 'does not talk after the wisest,' 'the ordinary of nature's sale work,' 'a fever of the mad,' 'in the smallest,' 'with your speediest bring us what she says,' 'I advise you to the best,' to which add 'my false o'erweighs your true'—all occurring in Shakespeare, and all undoubtedly genuine: as genuine, perhaps, may be the somewhat similar phrase '*of a most select and generous*'; only here the indefinite, and not the definite, article precedes the adjective A comma, which stands after 'generous' in the Quarto, seems to indicate that the copyist regarded 'chief' as an adverb, and not a noun.

There is even another explanation possible: as the nouns 'rank and station' follow the superlative adjective in the preceding line, *it is left to the reader to supply a noun adapted to the superlative* in the line that follows. The nouns of the one line might *suggest* a noun for the other.

It may be the merest accident, but it is not a little singular, that, in the next passage which we have to consider, the very same little words, viz., 'of a,' again form the subject of controversy—with this difference, however, that, whereas in *that* passage they were deemed superfluous, in *this* they are looked upon as corrupt substitutes for some other word which should take their place; *there* the wish was to get rid of them altogether; *here* the endeavour is not to excise them but to effect a favourable exchange. And, if I remember rightly, these are not the only two places, where the same two little words have discomfited the critics. Let us look at them once again in their new connexion in Act I, 4, 36-38,

> the dram of eale
> Doth all the noble substance of a doubt
> To his own scandal :

That 'eale' is the old form of 'evil' is as certain as that 'deale' is frequently found in the Quartos and Folios for 'devil.' As, then, in the latter case editors do not scruple to introduce the modern form into the text, so neither should they in the former.

But in the prepositional phrase 'of a doubt' we have no mere ghost of a difficulty, but a real and substantial one. What are we to make of it?

Had the expression been 'doth it all of a doubt,' or 'makes it all of a doubt,' we should have thought no more amiss of it, than we do of the well-known conversational phrase, 'I am all of a tremble'; or had it been 'doth all the noble substance doubt,' we might have found ample warrant for it in the parallel expressions,

> To do you rest,
> Do him disparagement,
> Do you wrong,
> Doing me disgrace,
> Thou hast done good feature shame,

all quotations from Shakespeare ; but such a phrase as 'doth it of a doubt' can hardly be grouped with these, but stands as it were in a corner by itself.

I have thought it possible that Shakespeare, in order to intensify the slur sought to be cast on the character, may have purposely used, instead of the more direct decided and downright phrase 'doth it *doubt*,' the partitive limited and more dubitative and insinuative one 'doth it *of a doubt*'; for we know that the suggestion of a little bit of doubt, a whisper, a breath, will often do ten times more to blast and damn the character, than a plainer, fuller, and more sonorous censure.

Nor ought we, in weighing possibilities, to leave out of the balance the item, that Shakespeare is in the habit of inserting prepositions, where we should not think of admitting them. Take as a specimen a portion of a line in 'As You Like It,' Act V, 4, 56,

> I desire you of the like.

There are two other instances, where the noun 'doubt,' preceded by an article and a preposition, concludes a line ; one occurs in 'The Merchant of Venice,' Act III, 2, 145,

> still gazing in a doubt ;

the other in '3 King Henry VI,' Act IV, 7, 27,

> Why stand you in a doubt ?

Thus much, then, in favour of the reading of the Quartos ; if the probabilities are still against that reading ; if we *must* pronounce the phrase, as it stands, to be manifestly corrupt, then decidedly the simplest plan would be to suppose that 'of' has been docked of its final letter, and is a slip of the pen for 'oft': in favour of this view I may note by the way that in the 23rd line, and again in the 28th, 'oft' is introduced as a modifying adverb; this would give us the thoroughly Shakespearian line,

> Doth all the noble substance oft a doubt.

Other emendations which have been broached the reader may find elsewhere; some of the most plausible are 'overdoubt,' 'overcloud,' 'oft adoubt,' 'often dout,' 'oft weigh down,' the last an ingenious conjecture of Bailey's, suggested probably by a line in 'Timon,' Act V, 1, 154,

> Than their offence can *weigh down* by the *dram.*

But I have said enough of this passage, and I will pass on to Act III, 4, 169, where a gap occurs in the text:

> And either . . . the devil, or throw him out
> With wondrous potency.

Now I do not pretend to be able to guess what the exact word was which originally filled the vacancy. There are many which would serve the turn. 'Resist' would have Apostolic, 'renounce' Patristic authority to back it; 'rebuke' would not be without precedent. If, however, we can light upon a verb *used by Shakespeare himself, albeit elsewhere, in the same connexion*, it would come to us with a sort of recommendation from the author. Now in 'Twelfth Night,' Act III, 4, 108, Sir Toby says to Malvolio, 'What, man! *defy* the devil.' In 'Merry Wives of Windsor' we have 'Now shall the devil be *shamed*.' The former word would fit in with the metre (for I need scarcely say that 'either' is frequently treated as a monosyllable), and would give the sense required, or at least a tolerable sense. There would be no harm in introducing *defy*—italicized, if you like—into the text. But no doubt the original word might have been a totally different one with more force and point. Perhaps we should give the preference to 'master,' the word found in the 4th, 5th, and 6th Quartos.

In my next piece of criticism I can hardly hope to command the suffrages and support of a majority of the critics; yet almost all will agree that some other word, than that which we have at present, was in all probability in Shakespeare's MS. In that famous Scene, where two clowns in a churchyard rub their rough wits against each other right sparklingly, who will say much for

<blockquote>Go, get thee to Yaughan?</blockquote>

I do not doubt that 'Yaughan' very fairly represents the sound that proceeded from the gravedigger's lips; but I feel pretty sure that the actual words were either '*the tavern*,' or '*the inn*'—probably the former—where the stoup of liquor he wanted only waited for a fetcher.

I shall be expected to say something on Act V, 2, 39-42, and I shall commence with Singer's apt exclamation, 'Think of peace standing as a comma!'

We must admit that such a comparison, even when we look at it by itself apart from the context, is in the highest degree improbable; when, however, we view it in connexion with a passage, which is adorned with a succession of grand images grandly expressed—when we read it in sequence to such beautiful lines as

> As England was his faithful tributary,
> As love between them like the palm might flourish,
> As peace should still her wheaten garland wear,

the improbability, it is hardly too much to say, waxes into an impossibility. It is a step from the sublime to the ridiculous—a fall from a firmament powdered with stars to a realm of mist and Tartarean gloom. 'Comma' is not the legitimate issue of Shakespeare's genius, but a bastard slip of a copyist, whose eye deceived him, but whose intellectual faculty was not strong enough to correct him. Fortunately in this instance we have not much difficulty in discovering with—I had almost said, *certainty* the actual word which Shakespeare inserted. Let it be granted—no very extravagant concession—that *lu* may be somewhat indistinctly written, so as to differ not very much from an *m*—let it be granted that an *n* may easily melt into and be confused with *a*, and then there is positively no difference whatever between *column* and *comma*, in respect of form, though in respect of meaning and suitableness to the present passage there is a vast immeasurable distance.

'Peace' and 'column' are a natural couple, linked together over and over again by historic associations. The column, or pillar, was set up as a witness that peace had been formally concluded; the names of the parties, the terms of the agreement were graven upon it; it stood as a monument and testimony of amicable relations in the past, and a pledge of continued amity in the future.

A figure of peace, then, wearing a garland of wheat, standing columnar-like (these are all but the very words of the text) between two friendly powers, if it had not in some part of the world been seen by the author as an architectural or pictorial reality, is at any rate an artistic possibility, and quite worthy to figure in a great poet's airy creation.

I commend, therefore, to the cold calm severe scrutinizing eye of the impartial critic, how far 'column' and 'comma' resemble—how far they differ from each other. The result of that scrutiny, unless I am too sanguine, will be to get rid of such rubbish as 'comma,' to set up again the 'column' that has been displaced, and to restore 'peace,' if not to the members of the Shakespeare Societies, at any rate to the ghost of Shakespeare and to the text.

I conclude, as I commenced, with Singer's words, but slightly varied, 'Think of peace standing as a column'!

Eloquar an sileam? Should I stop here, or may I venture to speak once more? There is a passage in Act V, 2, 118, the depths of which no critic's plumb-line has yet sounded, nor perhaps ever will. It is where Osric, sent by the King to Hamlet on an insidious and sinister errand, approaches him with strained courtesy, and in language with more sound than sense proceeds to pass an extravagant eulogium on Laertes. Hamlet, perceiving his evil purpose, mimics his bombastic nonsense:

> Sir, his definement suffers no perdition in you; though, I know, to divide him inventorially would dizzy the arithmetic of memory, and yet but yaw neither, in respect of his quick sail.

Mr. Aldis Wright, who is entitled to be listened to, especially when we want to know the meaning of a word, tells us that ' to yaw' is a nautical phrase, used of a ship which moves unsteadily, and does not answer her helm; but neither he, nor any one else, can apply the meaning to the passage without making other alterations which may not be tolerated. On the presumption that any solution will be listened to, where none has yet been forthcoming, I will hazard an explanation, which, be its worth what it may, shall at least give sense and consistency to the passage.

I conceive that the actual words, which Hamlet uttered, were 'and yet *bout you* neither,' or possibly, as 'yet' and 'not' are sometimes confused, 'and *not* boot you neither'; but that, as Hamlet took off Osric's affected tone and manner, 'boot' he minced to 'but,' and 'you' he drawlingly pronounced 'yaw': what the actor, to sustain the part, did on the platform, the shorthand writer, consciously or unconsciously, might have done on his paper: the transcriber and the printer followed suit. Thus we have the tone of the speaker rather than the terms of his speech. The words, as I have given them, explain themselves. Hamlet tells Osric that to divide Laertes inventorially would dizzy the arithmetic of his memory, and yet be of no advantage to him, in respect of Laertes' 'quick sail,' that is to say, because of his shifting Protean-like character. Elsewhere editors have not hesitated to read '*boat*,' where the reading of the Folios is unquestionably '*butt*'—'*but*.'

But I may be asked, 'Whence comes 'yaw,' and what authority is there for making it the ground of a conjecture'? I answer that 'yaw' is the reading of the Quarto which was printed in 1604, and it has been thought peculiarly deserving of consideration, because that was the edition in which the tragedy appeared for the first time as it has come down to us. The other editions in Quarto, and the Folios, have 'raw.'

KING LEAR.

'King Lear' is one of those plays, of which we have both a Quarto and a Folio edition, and the text of the Folio, we are told, was not printed from the Quarto, but from an independent MS. When, therefore, the Quarto and the Folio agree, we may reasonably conclude that we have a faithful reproduction of Shakespeare's original; at any rate, in such a case it would be highly imprudent to meddle with the text, unless it were glaringly corrupt, and there were no possibility of making anything of it. Ingenious conjectures, imaginary improvements, are out of place as against the silent testimony of two independently-printed copies, both pointing without variation in the self-same direction. With this fresh in our minds, let us proceed to examine the following passage which occurs in Act I, 2, 17-22,

> Our father's love is to the bastard Edmund
> As to the legitimate : fine word,—legitimate !
> Well, my legitimate, if this letter speed,
> And my invention thrive, Edmund the base
> Shall to the legitimate. I grow : I prosper :
> Now, gods, stand up for bastards.

'Shall to' th' legitimate' is the reading of the Folio; 'shall tooth' legitimate' is the reading of the Quarto. That these readings, though slightly discrepant verbally, are the same virtually, I hold to be certain from the fact that, elsewhere in Shakespeare, where the words 'to the' unquestionably are intended, 'to the' and 'too th'' are at times written indifferently. We have no reason, then,—no strong compelling reason—to dispute the integrity of the text. There is no scent of corruption, there is merely an ellipse of the verb—an idiom which occurs too frequently in Shakespeare to excite suspicion or surprise.

The words are susceptible of more meanings than one:

1. Edmund the base shall stretch himself to the height of, shall reach unto, and put himself on a level with, the legitimate.

2. Edmund the base shall hie to him, to do upon him that foul deed, which we may well suppose he was already ruminating in the dark chambers of his wicked heart.

3. Edmund the base shall to the legitimate, shall attain unto legitimacy, shall work out his own legitimation.

I suggest these explanations, but I do not wish to lay particular stress on any one of them. To explain is to weaken. The aposiopesis was probably intended. The bastard's sudden concealment of his exact purpose, just at the moment, too, that he seemed about to reveal it—his broken utterance, accompanied perhaps with a wink of the eye, a wave of the hand, or a nod of the head, and this even in a soliloquy—are far more ominously expressive than the most distinct articulation, or the most direct enunciation.

How is it, then, that critics, so acute and learned as the editors of the Cambridge Shakespeare, forgetting the strictly ascetic principles which they proposed to themselves in their Preface, have introduced into the 'Globe' edition Capell's fanciful conjecture 'shall top the legitimate,' which is founded on no authority, and is negatived point blank by two independent impressions? And can Mr. Aldis Wright imagine that he is furnishing us with corroborative evidence, when he quotes a passage from 'Macbeth,' and a passage from another part of this play, to show that Shakespeare uses the word 'top,' of which fact we have no doubt whatever? I take my stand here on the Folio and on the Quarto, and maintain that 'top' is the bastard word, and 'to the' is legitimate.

A little further on there is some little misapprehension as to the exact meaning of Act I, 3, 18-20,

> Now, by my life,
> Old fools are babes again; and must be used
> With checks as flatteries—when they are seen abused.

The usual explanation is that given by Tyrwhitt, who says—I copy from Mr. Wright's note—'old men must be used with checks, as well as flatteries, when they,' *i.e.*, the *flatteries*, 'are seen abused.' He should rather have said, 'when they,' *i.e.*, the *old men*, 'are seen abused.' A passage in 'Pericles,'—Act I, 2, 37-43—where *kings* are said to be *abused* by the flatteries addressed to them, confirms me in the opinion, that here too the subject of the verb is not the flattery offered, but the persons to whom it is offered.

> Peace, peace, and give experience tongue.
> *They do abuse the king* that flatter him :
> For flattery is the bellows blows up sin ;
> The thing the which is flatter'd, but a spark,
> To which that blast gives heat and stronger glowing :
> Whereas *reproof*, obedient and in order,
> *Fits kings*, as they are men, for they may err.

A cry has been raised as to the soundness of the text in Act II, 2, 175-177, where Kent says that Cordelia

> shall find time
> From this enormous state seeking to give
> Losses their remedies.

For my part, I can see no justification of any suspicion of unsoundness here. The phrase 'shall find time' is used absolutely, as it is in 'Julius Cæsar,' Act V, 3, 103,

> I shall find time, Cassius, I shall find time.

A comma, therefore, had perhaps better part it off from the words that follow ; as for *them*, they may be a little out of their natural order ; they may express in rather an uncommon way a not uncommon sentiment, but neither of these peculiarities is repugnant to Shakespeare's style. If there is obscurity, it arises from the inversion, and partly also from the condensation. I understand Kent to say—it has been suggested that he may be reading his letter by snatches for want of light—that Cordelia would find the opportunity she was looking for, in her endeavour to gain for King Lear his lost independence and rule, and would remedy the abnormal state of things which then prevailed.

I must not pass over unnoticed an extraordinary interpretation, which Mr. Aldis Wright has set down for the 165th line of Act II, 4, where King Lear, calling down curses on Goneril for her unnatural conduct, exclaims,

>   Strike her young bones,
> You taking airs, with lameness!
> You nimble lightnings, dart your blinding flames
> Into her scornful eyes! Infect her beauty,
> You fen-suck'd fogs, drawn by the powerful sun,
> To fall and blast her pride!

To understand 'her young bones' as 'her unborn infant,' because in the 'Chronicle of King Lear' we have

> Alas, not I; poor soule, she breeds yong bones,
> And that it is makes her so tutchy sure,

seems to me to be a '*non sequitur*.' The context is fatal to such an interpretation. King Lear, after denouncing Goneril in general terms, proceeds to frame against her a three-fold curse: her *bones* are young; lame them: her *eyes* are scornful; blind them:

her *beauty* carries her away; blast it. The last two refer to Goneril personally, to Goneril personally it were reasonable to suppose that the first does also. In the 'Tempest' we read, 'my *old* bones ache'; as well in 'King Lear' may 'her *young* bones' be used in their natural sense. Moreover, there is a special fitness in her father's cursing her *young* bones, as she had taunted him with being *old*. Nor is it likely that the king, after he had petitioned the gods to carry into her womb sterility, would assume that there was an unborn infant to strike with lameness. This is an instance in which I cannot but think that the much book-learning of the Cambridge annotator has led him astray.

What again is it which has caused such perturbation among commentators in Act II, 4, 273-274, where King Lear cries

> But, for true need,—
> You heavens, give me that patience, patience I need?

It cannot be the *meaning*; for the meaning is as clear as the heavens. 'As for true need, need in the strictest barest sense of the word, give me, (says the old king), power to endure *that*; power to endure I need.' Is it, then, the *repetition of the word* 'patience' that offends? But therein consists the force, and beauty, and pathos of the passage. The old man harps on that, which he knows too well he has not, but which he knows too well is the one only thing which it is absolutely necessary for him now to have. Or is it the *scansion* that jars upon the ear? But what greater licence here than a superfluous syllable in the middle pause of the verse, so common in Shakespeare, as, for instance, in 'King Richard III,' Act I, 1, 116,

> G. Meantime have *patience*. C. I must perforce. Farewell.

though there would be no difficulty in citing examples, where there is no change of speaker. Or, lastly, is it the *difference of accentuation*, occurring in the same word in the same line? But neither is that anything to be startled at. We have in '3 King Henry VI,' Act I, 1, 228,

> Pardon me, Margaret ; pardon me, sweet son ;

'Twelfth Night,' Act V, 1, 101,

> But for thee, fellow ; fellow, thy words are madness ;

'King Henry VIII,' Act V, 1, 133,

> Might corrupt minds procure knaves as corrupt.

If there had not been a note on this passage, we certainly should not have asked for one.

I must say a word, too, in passing, in vindication of the reading of the Quartos in Act IV, 1, 71,

> Let the superfluous and lust-dieted man,
> That *stands* your ordinance, that will not see
> Because he doth not feel, feel your power quickly.

'Stands' here may be good for the compound 'withstands,' the prefix being frequently omitted in

Shakespeare, where the exigency of the metre requires it. Thus we have

'nointed	vice	anointed.	'long	vice	belongs.
'raged	,,	enraged.	'rested	,,	arrested.
'xcuse	,,	excuse.	'leges	,,	alleges.
'scape	,,	escape.	'pointed	,,	appointed.
'filed	,,	defiled.	'cerns	,,	concerns.
'braid	,,	upbraid.	'stroyed	,,	destroyed.

An example of this use of 'stand' actually occurs in 'The Taming of the Shrew,' Act I, 2, 112,

I'll tell you what, sir, an she stands him but a little, he will throw a figure in her face.

It is not, however, very easy to certify what Shakespeare wrote in Act IV, 2, 57, where the Quartos have

France spreads his banners in our noiseless land,
With plumed helm thy slayer begin threats;
 slaier begins threats;

while the reading of the corrected copies of the earliest impression is, 'thy state begins thereat,' on which is based Eccles' conjecture, which for lack of a better has been accepted by many editors, 'thy state begins to threat.'

I had at one time thought that the original line might have been

With plumed helm thy standard 'gins to threat,

that is, France, by which is meant, of course, the king of France, begins to threaten Albany's standard. So serious a deviation, however, from the text of the

Quartos would hardly be listened to by the critics, and does not quite satisfy myself. I offer, therefore, another conjecture, which differs from the Quarto version by but a single letter,

> With plumed helm, thy slayer, big in threats.

A contrast would thus be drawn between France and Albany: the former already on the march; the latter—the critic will now please to read with care the line that follows—'sitting still': the former, full of menace; the latter, so far from meeting threat with threat, crying, 'Alack, why does he so'? In a word, on the one side alacrity and stout defiance; on the other inactivity and pusillanimous complaining. The weights in the two opposite scales are nicely adjusted. The phrase 'big in clamour,' I may add, is used a little further on in the play.

I need not make any apology for commenting on the lines—Act IV, 3, 20-21—

> you have seen
> Sunshine and rain at once; her smiles and tears
> Were like a better way,

because there seems to be a general consent among commentators that the passage is not now as Shakespeare wrote it. '*Better way*' has been puzzled over—has been found fault with; in lieu of it several emendations, none of them satisfactory, have been proposed. Boaden, however, held to the reading of the copies, which he explained to mean 'in a more beautiful fashion'—an explanation, which, though pointing in the right direction, is yet wanting in definiteness and clearness. The use of 'way,' however, in the sense suggested by him is not uncommon in Shakespeare. Compare

Sonnet XVI,
> But wherefore do not you a mightier way
> Make war upon this bloody tyrant, Time ?

'Cymbeline,' Act I, 1, 137,
> Past hope, and in despair ; that way, past grace.

'Cymbeline,' Act I, 4, 101,
> A that way accomplished courtier.

Now what did the gentleman, when describing the effect produced on Cordelia by certain letters which he had delivered to her, mean, when he said that her smiles and tears were like sunshine and rain at once, but like after a better fashion? He meant that, though that beautiful phenomenon was the best comparison that he could think of to convey some idea of the expression of Cordelia's countenance, *it did not adequately represent it*; her smiles and tears were like it, but in a better fashion; what that better fashion was, Shakespeare himself, if we will accept his explanation, proceeds at once to reveal to us;

> those happy smilets
> That play'd on her ripe lip, *seem'd not to know*
> *What guests were in her eyes* ?

This, then, was the peculiarity in Cordelia's case— her smiles and tears were simultaneous, but they were not intermingled, as in the natural phenomenon; though the tear wetted her eye, the smile on her lip knew it not; there was no cloud, no shade, no dampness in her beautiful sunshine; it was unique; it was incomparable; it was *most* like sunshine and rain at once, but sunshine and rain at once did not express it, and did not equal it.

A dozen lines further down, the same gentleman, having been asked by Kent, whether she made verbal answer, replies that she uttered, almost in spite of herself, sundry ejaculations,

> 'Faith, once or twice she heaved the name of 'father'
> Pantingly forth, as if it press'd her heart;
> Cried, 'Sisters! sisters! Shame of ladies! sisters!
> Kent! father! sisters! What, i' the storm? i' the night?
> Let pity not be believed' There she shook
> The holy water from her heavenly eyes,
> And clamour moisten'd: then away she started
> To deal with grief alone.

The words 'And clamour moisten'd' have given rise to a great deal of learned wrangling, some disputants insisting that they are corrupt, others who try to defend them making a mess both of the construction and the meaning. I myself was at one time tempted to cast about for some emendation, and I felt almost positive that 'moisten'd' had crept into the line by mistake for *maister'd*, *master'd*, the noun 'clamour' being, of course, the *object*, and not the subject of the verb: first, *she ceased weeping*, or, as it is beautifully expressed,

> She shook the holy water from her heavenly eyes;

and, secondly, *she ceased crying out*—'she mastered clamour'; but on further reflection I perceived that I had been endeavouring to plaster Shakespeare's magnificent granite with poor untempered mortar. A critic friend asking me whether there were not a fine poetic fancy in moistening clamour with tears, I threw aside my idol with scorn and contempt, and clung to the poet's image with assurance and satisfaction. She shook off the tears, and moistened clamour with them. That this was in Shakespeare's mind—in Shakespeare's MS.—it is hardly too much to say that we have Shakespeare's own testimony, when we read such lines as

'2 King Henry IV,' Act IV, 5, 139-140,

But for my tears,
The moist impediments unto my speech ;

'King Henry VIII,' Act V, I, 158,

He has *strangled*
His language in his tears ;

'As you Like it,' Act IV, 2, 141,

Tears *our recountments had most kindly bathed.*

add too '3 King Henry VI,' Act V, 4, 74-75,

For every word I speak
Ye see I drink the water of my eyes.

With regard to the next passage to which I shall advert,—Act V, 3, 129-130—it is not so easy to say what Shakespeare wrote, as that he certainly could not have written what is ascribed to him either in the Quarto or in the Folio. The reading of the former is

> Behold it is the priviledge of my tongue ;

of the latter

> Behold it is my priviledge, the priviledge of mine honours.

By judicious blending, Pope compounded a line, which has found a place, I believe, in most editions. Yet for all that I shall not be deterred from offering a new arrangement of an old difficulty. I put a colon after 'my privilege,' and blot out 'the priviledge' which follows, which I believe to have been a clerical or typographical error, the noun 'priviledge' having been carelessly repeated, and possibly the definite article having been prefixed to it under the idea that the phrase 'of my honours' depended upon it. Such, however, is not the case. 'Of my honours'—we may either drop the plural termination as a mistake, or suppose that Shakespeare here used the plural, as he often does, where we should permit only the singular—in common with 'my oath and my profession' is a solemn asseveration, the preposition 'of' being not unfrequently used in such forms of speech, where we should rather use the preposition 'on.' The passage, then, will stand thus:

> Behold it is my privilege ; of mine honours,
> My oath, and my profession, I protest
> . . . .
> . . . . thou art a traitor.

I pass on now to somewhere about the 200th line,

where, after Edgar had told his brief tale, and Edmund had interposed a few words, Albany says,

> If there be more, more woeful, hold it in ;
> For I am almost ready to dissolve,
> Hearing of this ;

whereupon Edgar resumes—line 204—

> This would have seem'd a period
> To such as love not sorrow ; but another,
> To amplify too much, would make much more,
> And top extremity.

Opinions are divided as to what, or whom, 'another' refers to.

Some take it to mean 'another person,' others 'another calamity,' both person and calamity alike indefinite. I am strongly of opinion that it refers to the person who is definitely and distinctly delineated in the verses which follow. 'But' is a conjunction, not an adverb; it coordinates two clauses, the several parts of which are without a doubt antithetical to each other. The particular clause introduced by it, which commences with 'another' and ends with 'extremity,' is merely an introduction to, and a brief summary of, what follows. It is, in fact, the heading of that new chapter of horrors which is about to be described. Who was the man who would not suffer a period to woe, but would make much more, and top extremity? The answer is given in the lines that follow ;

> Whilst I was big in clamour came there in a *man*,
> Who, having seen me, &c.

That man was Kent—

> Kent, Sir, the banish'd Kent ; who in disguise
> Follow'd his enemy king, and did him service
> Improper for a slave.

He it was who

> bellow'd out
> As he'ld burst heaven ; threw him on my father ;
> Told the most piteous tale of Lear and him
> That ever ear received : which in recounting
> His grief grew puissant, and the strings of life
> Began to crack :

This is the amplification, this the much made more, the topping of extremity. To Kent, then, 'another' refers—an interpretation, which, although it has not been surmised, or at least not suggested, by any previous expositor, I hold to be not only possible, but extremely probable, though I may not flatter myself that I shall be able all at once to turn the tide of opinion which has run for so long, and with such persistence, in two totally different directions.

ANTONY AND CLEOPATRA.

It is not until we come to 'Antony and Cleopatra,' Act I, 5, 28, where we meet with the lines,

> Think on me,
> That am with Phœbus' amorous pinches black,
> And wrinkled deep in time,

that we can vouch for the correctness of those beautiful lines in 'The Two Gentlemen of Verona,' Act IV, 4, 160,

> The air hath starved the roses in her cheeks,
> And pinch'd the lily-tincture of her face,
> That now she is become as black as I,

where efforts have been made to expunge 'pinch'd,' and substitute I know not what in its place. The identity of expression in the two passages forbids us to suppose that there is error in either. If 'pinching' may be attributed to the scorching sun, it may be also to the freezing air, the part pinched, be it of animal or vegetable, becoming black in consequence.

But what are we to say of 'arm-gaunt' in Act I, 5, 48,

> So he nodded,
> And soberly did mount an *arm-gaunt steed,
> Who neigh'd so high, that what I would have spoke
> Was beastly dumb'd by him?

We can only guess at the meaning of the word, if it is genuine, or guess at the word, or words, of which it is a hideous disfigurement, if it is counterfeit. The only meaning that I can imagine for it is either that the steed was gaunt to look at from the armour that he wore, or that he was gaunt as a veteran charger who had been used to the service of arms. I acknowledge that I have no great faith in either of these interpretations, nor indeed in the word itself, which I will liken to one of those nondescript monsters of antiquity, which shadow forth some historical fact or legend, but what, we can hardly make out. 'Arm-gaunt'—I give it as my opinion, I cannot substantiate it by any proof—is a miserable and grotesque bit of bad spelling, worthy to be shovelled into the same gulf of oblivion as '*my rackles*' (miracles), '*burbolt*' (birdbolt), '*unsistered*' (unscissored), '*foretel*' (fertile), '*pannelled*' (spaniel'd), *et hoc genus omne*. Indistinctly and possibly confusedly written in the original, in the transcript it became further defeatured, and frightfully and undistinguishably mutilated. Will

---

* Arme-gaunt Ff.

the reader have patience with me, while I turn
about this lump of a word a little, in the hope of
beating it again into what I conceive may have been
its pristine shape? I start with the assumption
that an epithet, which Shakespeare assigns to the
lion, would not be too *mean* to apply to such a
noble domesticated animal as the horse—such a
horse as Cleopatra would like to hear that Antony
had mounted. The 'ramping lion' and 'rampant
bear' of former plays have suggested to me '*a
rampant steed*' for this. Wherein can we trace any
sign of resemblance? I will suppose that the line
originally stood thus,

> And soberly did mount on a rampant steed.

The first thing that I shall do is to throw the
last words into confusion, and present them dis-
guisedly thus, '*on arampaunt steed.*' Now it is well-
known that *p* is often so formed as to bear a close
resemblance to *g*, with which, as a matter of fact,
it is sometimes confused. We have only to
suppose, then, that *arampaunt* was so written as to
look like *aramgaunt*, and we have the genealogy of
this Centaurean production, which may be set down
thus, *arampaunt, aramgaunt, armgaunt*. There can be
no valid objection to the preposition 'on' following
the verb 'mount'; 'to mount on a steed' is a
possible 'pregnant locution' for mounting, and
sitting, as a rider, on a steed. Even were the
preposition superfluous, prepositional superfluities

abound in Shakespeare. And as regards the rhythm, the line may be matched with the following one from 'All's Well That End's Well,'

> The well lost life of mine on his grace's cure;

while, as for the meaning, 'rampant' pictures to us the pawing rearing restlessness of the high-neighing charger, which strikingly contrasts with, if it does not to a certain extent account for, Antony's *soberly* mounting.

Such, then, is the explanation, which with some misgiving I offer of this commentator's puzzle, until some one arise, endowed with the gift of clairvoyance, to tell us what it was which Shakespeare really wrote; for I dismiss such emendations as 'an argent steed,' 'a roan gelt steed,' 'an ungelt steed,' as mere illusions of the fancy, bearing but a faint resemblance to the word of the Folios.

And now I am going to take editors to task for thrusting a negative particle into the text in Act II, 2, 53, where there is neither authority for doing so, nor yet absolute necessity. Undoubtedly Shakespeare might have written

> If you'll patch a quarrel,
> As matter whole you have *not* to make it with,
> It must not be with this;

but as undoubtedly he might have written, what he is represented in the Folios as having written,

> If you'll patch a quarrel,
> As matter whole you *have* to make it with,
> It must not be with this.

In the former case 'as' is a conjunction meaning 'inasmuch as'; in the latter it is a particle used in the sense of 'as being,' 'as if it were.' Either reading being possible, which should have the precedence? Unquestionably that which has Folio warrant. The passage may be thus paraphrased, 'If you are bent on patching a quarrel, you must not make it with *this*, under the idea that, or as considering that, *this* were whole matter you have to make it with; it should be something less flimsy than *this* that should serve as material for a quarrel between Cæsar and Antony.'

What the true reading is in Act III, 10, 10—whether Antony calls Cleopatra a 'Nag,' or a 'hag,' or, as some would have it, a 'rag,' and what 'ribaudred' is, and what it means—'ribald crows' occurs in 'Troilus and Cressida'—I confess that I have a very indistinct idea; but in Act III, 11, 47,

> Most noble sir, arise; the queen approaches:
> Her head's declined, and death will *cease* her, but
> Your comfort makes the rescue,

I will not without a strong protest permit '*seize*' to be put into the place of '*cease*.' At first sight, the alteration may seem not only unobjectionable but indispensable. Yet transcribers do not usually write a less common and less familiar word for a trite and hackneyed one. In favour of 'cease,' it may be urged that it is authorized by the Folio; that, even if there were no examples of its having been used thus transitively by any of Shakespeare's predecessors or contemporaries, there is no reason why he should not have so used it just once and away, as indeed he has done, in reference both to persons and to things, *e.g.*, in 'Cymbeline,' Act V, 5, 255,

> A certain stuff, which, being ta'en, would cease
> The present power of life ;

and in 'Timon,'

> Be not ceased
> With slight denials.

Moreover I contend that 'cease,' used as it is here, is a high word, a poetical word, and, I have authority for adding, a *royal* word; for have we not in 'Hamlet,' the phrase '*the cease of majesty*'? In spite, therefore, of 'rescue' which follows, and which has no doubt led many to an opposite conclusion, I prefer to read 'cease,' as having a sound and genuine ring, as an antique rare and precious, and above all as thoroughly Shakespearian.

With regard to 'mered,' or 'meered,' in Act III, 13-10, it is not surprising that doubts have been entertained of its genuineness; we can only regard it now as a sort of fossilized participle; yet that it was once a living portion of the English language can hardly be questioned. Such a word, authentic, though possibly at the time at which it was written becoming antiquated, could not have been set down by a copyist accidentally. He must have seen it before him in black and white. We may be *positive* that Shakespeare *knew* the word; though we can find no second example of it in any other portion of his writings, we may *believe* that he *used* it; its poetic fitness is vouched for by Spenser; and the meaning of 'divided,' which it is said to bear, is one which suits the context well enough. There is certainly no *palmaria emendatio* to take its place.

I next come to a passage in Act V, 1, 15, where the phrase 'the *round* world' has had a stigma attached to it, perhaps because it is thought too poor and tame, considering who was the speaker, and what the passion and power of his speech; anyhow, being strictly a monosyllable, it may be arraigned on the charge of leaving the line short of a syllable. In its place '*ruined*' might stand, which, pronounced by some 'ru-und,' sounds almost exactly as 'round' would do, were it mouthed into a dissyllable, which might account for 'round' having crept into the text. And this word 'ruined' meets the requirements of the metre, gives additional terror to a scene of confusion, and might have been suggested by more than one passage in ancient classical literature. No wonder, then, that it occurs to almost every one who reads the passage, as it did long ago to myself, and that long ago it has been conjectured. Yet the wary critic will pause ere he parts with 'round.' The verse of the Psalmist, 'He hath made the round world so sure that it cannot be moved,' induces us to ask whether the shape of the world may not be suggestive of the world's steadfastness. 'Round' and 'safe' are closely connected in 'Pericles,' Act I, 3, 122,

> But in our orbs we'll live so round and safe.

If, then, roundness implies perfection of make, structural strength, solidity, steadfastness, irremoveability, at least so far as the world is concerned, then 'round,' so far from being a colourless epithet, to be castigated by every chiding critic, has a complexion and character which give it a right to its place. That the world should be shaped so strongly, and yet should be shaken so violently! Such may have been Cæsar's way of putting the portent that he says he should have expected when Antony fell. As for the metrical difficulty, it may easily be disposed of by supposing that 'round' here is *tantamount* to a dissyllable—a licence which Shakespeare would not have hesitated to take. I write, therefore,

> The breaking of so great a thing should make
> A greater crack; the round world
> Should have shook lions into civil streets,
> And citizens to their dens.

Before I pass from this splendid tragedy, I will hazard a conjecture on one more passage, if at least conjecture be needed. The question has been mooted, whether '*caves* of Nile' can be right in Act V, 2, 355,

> This is an aspic's trail: and these fig-leaves
> Have slime upon them, such as the aspic leaves
> Upon the caves of Nile.

'Canes,' and 'caves,' have been conjectured as more appropriate and probable. The exact word of the Folios is '*caues.*' Now I believe that I am not incorrect in saying that in one other passage in Shakespeare, where '*caues*' appears in the copies, there is a strong probability that '*course*' is the word intended. It may have been intended here. It certainly bears a strong phonetic resemblance to '*caues,*' and, if it be not too poor a word, it yields a sense which no one can quarrel with. Where the Nile had flowed with its swollen waters, there, after it had ebbed, was a muddy deposit, over which the aspic might be tracked by the slime which he left.

CYMBELINE.

The first passage which I shall notice in 'Cymbeline' is in the 3rd Scene of the 3rd Act, where Belarius, contrasting the rough freedom of a mountain life with the polished servitude of the court, exclaims,

> O, this life
> Is nobler than attending for a check,
> Richer than doing nothing for a babe,
> Prouder than rustling in unpaid-for silk :
> Such gain the cap of him that makes 'em fine,
> Yet keeps his book uncross'd : no life to ours.

Suspicion here has fallen upon 'babe,' which, though found in every impression of the Folio, neither suits the context, nor satisfies the critic; if it is correct, it must be used to mark the degradation of the courtier who had to lackey an imbecile monarch; but in all probability it has been set down by mistake for some other word which it more or less resembles. What can that word be? The editors of the 'Globe' Shakespeare are confident that it was 'bauble'; others guess that it was 'bribe'; others that it was 'brabe'. I know not by whom 'bribe' was first conjectured, but I think it not at all improbable that it was the true original word: my reasons I will proceed to state.

The proper meaning of 'bribe,' as given by Tyrwhitt in his Glossary to Chaucer, is 'that which is given to a beggar,' and this meaning matches the passage admirably. The old refugee of the mountains estimates life's value, according as it ennobles, according as it enriches, according as it fosters a manly and honourable independence. How is it with the courtier? For nobleness he has rebuffs; for riches a portion which, like a beggar, he receives for doing nothing; his pride is to rustle in unpaid for silk.

A similar sentiment, though differently applied, occurs in the 91st Sonnet;

>   Thy love is better than high birth to me,
>   *Richer than wealth,* prouder than garments' cost.

Between this couplet and the passage in 'Cymbeline' there is plainly a partial resemblance, 'high birth' and 'garments' cost' in the one corresponding to 'nobility' and 'unpaid for silk' in the other; the resemblance would be complete, if 'bribe' in 'Cymbeline' were to correspond to 'wealth' in the Sonnet.

But how could 'babe' have found its way into the Folio, if 'bribe' had been set down in the author's MS.? Easily enough. *Bri* may have been so written as to have been hardly distinguishable from *ba*; or 'bribe,' pronounced by one who could not sound his *rs*, would have been almost homophonous with 'babe'; a short-hand writer in the theatre, a clerk or compositor writing or printing from dictation, would have been at the mercy of such a one, and would not have been able to help himself.

A singular expression occurs in Act III, 4, 52, which has puzzled many:

> Some jay of Italy
> Whose mother was her painting, hath betray'd him.

The Cambridge editors say, 'If the text be right, the meaning probably is, 'whose mother aided and abetted her daughter in her trade of seduction,' adding that it suits the character of Imogen that she should conceive a circumstance to account for, and in some measure palliate, her husband's fault. I had taken my stand on Dr. Johnson's exposition of the passage, without, however, being aware that I had such a doughty champion to back me. 'Some foreign beauty,' says Imogen, 'some bird with borrowed plumage, a woman who gat her face from artist's pigments and not from mother nature, some painted virago, has betrayed him'? A somewhat analogous expression is found in 'All's Well That Ends Well,' Act I, 2, 62, where mention is made of 'younger spirits,'

> whose judgements are
> Mere fathers of their garments;

and in the same play—Act II, 5, 48—we read,

> The soul of this man is his clothes;

Compare also 'Cymbeline,'

> No, nor thy tailor, rascal,
> Who is thy grandfather; he made those clothes,
> Which, as it seems, make thee.

Bold figures of speech, but not too bold for a Shakespeare!

It is not surprising, however, that a mark of corruption has been set against the 135th line of this same Act and Scene, where Imogen is represented as saying,

> No court, no father; nor no more ado
> With that harsh, noble, simple nothing,
> That Cloten;

for, unless 'noble' is used with the bitterest irony, the epithet is neither proper nor applicable. It is true that Cloten, speaking of himself, says, 'I had rather not be so noble as I am,' and in another place he talks of his 'noble and natural person'; but others describe him as a 'thing too bad for bad report,' and Imogen invariably speaks of him in terms of deserved contempt. Is it likely that she would call him 'noble' in the same breath that she calls him 'harsh' and 'simple nothing'? The passage would lose none of its pathos, the metre of the line would actually be made good, if we suppose that Shakespeare wrote,

> No court, no father; nor no more ado
> With that harsh—no, no noble—simple nothing.

The accumulation of negatives would be in Shakespeare's manner; such an arrangement of them is actually found in 'As You Like It,' Act II, 3, 19,

> Your brother—no, no brother, yet the son.

But, be this as it may, there is no reason why the critics should be uneasy about the 150th line—I am still in Act III, Scene 4—where Pisanio, speaking to Imogen, says,

> If you could wear a mind
> Dark as your fortune is, and but disguise
> That which, to appear itself, must not yet be
> But by self danger, you should tread a course
> Pretty and full of view; yea, haply near
> The residence of Posthumus.

A 'pretty course' is a course which is right and proper—one which would not be derogatory to her sex, while it would give her an opportunity of seeing and perhaps might be even near the residence of Posthumus. In 'Romeo and Juliet' Lady Capulet says to the nurse,

> Thou know'st my daughter's of a pretty age,

i.e. of just the age to be married. A 'pretty act,' and 'pretty behaviour,' are phrases in common use which are understood by every one.

But does no critic start at the phrase ' so citizen a wanton' in Act IV, 2, 7-9, where Imogen's words are thus given,

> So sick I am not, yet I am not well;
> But not so citizen a wanton as
> To seem to die ere sick?

A very phœnix we have here! Could any other than Shakespeare have created it? Yet, if we allow that the substantive noun is used adjectively—that 'citizen' stands for 'citizen-like'—the order of the words ceases to be singular. What, however, it may be asked, is the meaning and force of 'citizen'? Was it characteristic of citizens to feel or feign to die sooner than other folk? I can only suppose that 'citizen' must be referred to a period when the name passed for a corrupt enervated spiritless die-away creature, very different from that hardy type which resisted feudal encroachment and wrung concessions from kings. I may not place a conjecture on the same high level as the *litera scripta* of a Folio, yet I can conceive it possible that Shakespeare, with his usual fondness for a *jeu de mots*, may have written,

> But not so sickening a wanton as
> To seem to die ere sick.

There is sufficient community of sound between 'citizen' and 'sickening' to have rendered the confusion not improbable. For the sentiment we may quote 'King Richard II,' Act III, 3, 163,

> Or shall we play the wantons with our woes?

Further on, the 16th and 17th lines need, I think, to be slightly differently punctuated. Guiderius states concerning his love first the quantity, then the weight; in its quantity and in its weight, it was equal to the love which he had for his father:

> I love thee; I have spoke it;
> How much the quantity, the weight, as much
> As I do love my father.

For the comma after 'weight' I only am responsible.

We next come to a passage in Act V, 1, 14-15, where Posthumus enunciates the measures adopted by the divine governours of the world for the prevention of crime and the reformation of offenders.

> You snatch some hence for little faults ; that's love,
> To have them fall no more : you some permit
> To second ills with ills, each elder worse,
> And make them dread it, to the doers' thrift.

I at one time thought, as Singer also seems to have done, that 'elder' must be a mistake for 'alder'; but, as there is no example of that old genitive being used with an adjective not in the superlative degree, I have repudiated that heresy, and I am now prepared to show that the text has been unfairly accused, and would be wrongfully altered.

The difficulty has arisen from a mistaken notion that 'each elder worse' must be grammatically connected with 'ills,' whereas in point of fact it is grammatically independent of it, being used absolutely, and having reference to the *ill-doer*, and not to the *ill done*. The gods permit some to add sin to sin; the older a man grows, the heavier the debt which stands to his account, until at last the sum becomes so enormous, as to have a chance of causing uneasiness and apprehension even to the most inveterate transgressors, leading them at times to repentance and amendment of life: this mode of dealing with evil doers is said to be 'thrift,' that is, advantage to them. For this signification of 'thrift' we may quote 'The Merchant of Venice,' Act I, 1, 175,

> I have a mind presages me such thrift
> That I should questionless be fortunate;

'Twelfth Night, Act II, 2, 40.

> thriftless sighs;

'Winter's Tale,' Act I, 2, 311,

> Their own particular thrifts.

No need, then, to substitute 'shrift' for 'thrift,' as some would have done.

Before I conclude, I must needs say a few words on Act V, 5, 92-96, which is not altogether free from difficulty: the passage runs thus,

> I have surely seen him:
> His favour is familiar to me. Boy,
> Thou hast look'd thyself into my grace,
> And art mine own. I know not why, wherefore,
> To say, 'live, boy'; ne'er thank thy master; live.

The obelus prefixed to the last line but one by the Cambridge editors, the singular form of the expression, the halting disconnected construction, led me at one time to believe that some emendation here was imperatively necessary. Accordingly I struck out the full stop after 'mine own'; threw the sentence 'I know not why, wherefore' into a parenthesis; and made the infinitive 'to live' a continuation of, and dependent on, the sentence which my parenthesis had interrupted; the passage then stood thus,

> And art mine own, (I know not why, wherefore),
> To say, 'live, boy';

but time and reflection have convinced me that the alteration was an unnecessary one: the full stop after 'mine own' is right; the omission of a connecting particle between 'why' and 'wherefore,' so far from being censurable, is worthy of admiration, and, I can hardly doubt, was purposed by the author. It just gives that broken character to the king's utterances which was natural to him under the circumstances; he stuttered and stammered, while trying to recollect where and on what occasion he had seen the lad. The actor, too, would affect the same perplexity, and 'why,—wherefore,' stammered out by him, would be acknowledged by every one to be happily disconnected. If there were any doubt about the possibility of the infinitive 'to live' depending on the words which immediately precede it, the doubt would vanish after reading in the 49th Sonnet the line,

> Since why to love I can allege no cause.

The accentuation of 'wherefore' on the last syllable is a licence which Shakespeare did not hesitate to take; for the close proximity of 'why' and 'wherefore' we may refer to 'The Comedy of Errors,' Act II, 2, 43-50, where, however a conjunction unites them, because *there* there is no dramatic reason for its omission :

Ant. S.   Shall I tell you why ?
Dro. S.   Ay, sir, and wherefore ; for they say every why hath a wherefore.
Ant. S.   Why, first,—for flouting me ; and then, wherefore,— For urging it the second time to me.
Dro. S.   Was there ever any man thus beaten out of season, When in the why and the wherefore is neither rhyme nor reason ?

It has been remarked that Cymbeline does not know what it is which attracts him to 'the seeming boy'; it is, of course, *La fuerza de sangre,* as one of Cervantes' stories is called—the unknown relationship.

PERICLES.

What was the word that Shakespeare probably wrote in 'Pericles,' Act I, 1, 17, where the first and the second Quartos have '*racte*,' and the third Quarto '*racket*'? The editors of the 'Globe' Shakespeare read 'razed,' which, it must be admitted, agrees with the metaphor of a book to which the princess' face is compared, and may be thought to derive a sort of sanction from the fact that it is found in a similar connexion in the 25th Sonnet:

> The painful warrior famoused for fight,
> After a thousand victories once foiled,
> Is from the book of honour razed quite.

Yet 'razed' bears but a slight resemblance to the word of the copies, and we may reasonably ask whether there is any necessity here for supposing that there has been error at all. In the beginning of this my last paper on Shakespeare's plays I must protest against learned men introducing unnecessarily their own conjectures into the text to the exclusion of a word, which is authorized, which is explicable, and which it is not at all impossible that Shakespeare wrote. Be it that the metaphor of a book is not sustained, but neither is it in the *second* of the two dependent adverbial clauses;

and testy wrath
Could never be her mild companion.

How then may we interpret this word 'racket'? In the first place, there is a participle 'racked' (to adopt modern spelling), which is used in the sense of drawing off liquor from a hogshead, and might possibly be applied to the drawing off the humour of sorrow from the headpiece of the daughter of Antiochus. This is one word, but this is not the word of my choice; there is another, a far superior one in my estimation, and eminently suitable. In '3 Henry VI' we have the phrase *'racking clouds.'* Now the sense given in that passage to 'rack,' as it is explained in the glossary appended to the 'Globe' Shakespeare, is to *'drive as a cloud.'* What is sorrow but a cloud on the face? and the face from which sorrow is *'racked'* is the face from which sorrow is *driven*; and this, I have no doubt, was the word which the poet used, and which is set down, spelt in an old fashioned way, in the Quartos.

For a long time I had considerable doubt as to what in all likelihood was the true reading in Act I, 2, 1-5; but here too, after much pondering, I have come to the conclusion that we need none of the somewhat free emendations which have been offered by the critics, but should adhere pretty closely to the reading of the Quartos, save only in the matter of punctuation; I write thus:

> Let none disturb us.—Why should this change of thoughts?
> The sad companion, dull-eyed melancholy,
> By me ['s] so used a guest, as not an hour
> In the day's glorious walk, or peaceful night,
> The tomb where grief should sleep, can breed me quiet.

I have put a note of interrogation at the end of the first line, where the Quartos have a comma, and consequently I have no need, two lines further down, of Dyce's conjecture, which has been adopted by some editors, '*Be my* so used a guest' in lieu of '*By me* so used a guest.' I believe with Malone that the substantive verb has fallen out before 'so,' and I have written accordingly. What, then, is my explanation of the interrogatory sentence, 'Why should this change of thoughts'? I answer that the grammatical complement of the auxiliary verb 'should' is the verb 'disturb,' which Pericles had just used, which he *mentally repeats*, and which we have to supply; or, if it be thought that 'disturb' is not the most suitable verb to be supplied, 'disturb' must suggest the verb that should be supplied. The king can silence or command away every visible corporeal creature, but he cannot command, he cannot silence, he cannot secure himself from the intrusion and interruption of those invisible agencies, which crowd into the heart, and lord, and riot there. 'How is it' he asks. To his courtiers he can say, 'Let none disturb us'; why, then, should his *thoughts disturb*? He proceeds to describe his state a little more particularly, and then with some metaphysical subtlety sums up his conclusion. To commence a new sentence with the line,

> The sad companion, dull-eyed melancholy,

seems to me a better arrangement, and more in harmony with Shakespeare's style, than, by placing a comma after 'thoughts,' to continue the interrogation to the end of the 5th line. There is a passage in 'Othello,' where Iago urges Roderigo to 'throw some changes on Othello's joy, that it may lose some colour': the colour of Pericles' thoughts had undergone a 'change,' when the black goddess became his companion: 'change,' therefore, may well hold its place.

There is nothing more startling in Act I, 2, 74, than an ellipse of the relative—a somewhat harsher ellipse than we come across ordinarily, but not more so than occurs, I will not say, in other plays of Shakespeare, but in other portions of the play:

> I went to Antioch,
> Where, as thou know'st, against the face of death,
> I sought the purchase of a glorious beauty,
> From whence an issue I might propagate,
> Are arms to princes, and bring joys to subjects.

The plural verb 'are' is used, because the noun 'issue,' which is the antecedent of the relative 'which' which has to be mentally supplied, is, as the grammarians express it, plural in sense, though singular in form: the following examples will serve, if any are considered necessary:

'Winter's Tale,' Act IV, 2, 29,

> Kings are no less unhappy, their issue not being gracious, than they are in losing *them* when they have approved their virtues.

'King Henry VIII,' Act II, 4, 191,

> for her male issue
> Or died where *they* were made, or shortly after
> This world had air'd *them*.

It was, I am inclined to think, this plural verb coming after a singular noun, together with the further complication of a very bold ellipse of the relative, which made the doctors shake their heads, and pronounce the case beyond remedy.

But how are we to mend the metre, how make good the sense, in Act I, 3, 38, where Thaliard says,

> But since he's gone, the king's seas must please?

If the words of this ragged line are to remain as they are at present, the only account that I can give of it is that "'s" is used here, as it is very commonly even in passages which are not colloquial and familiar, for 'his,' and that Thaliard says that, since Pericles is gone, 'his,' that is, '*the king's*' seas must please 'the king,' to wit, by drowning Pericles—a consummation which is hinted at in the line which follows.

> He 'scaped the land, to perish at the sea;

but I confess that I have my misgivings as to the possibility, and certainly as to the general acceptability of this exegesis, and I must needs admit that some emendation is much to be desired; yet the only emendation which I can think of is one, which, as being a total stranger to the critics, will, I fear, please none of them. I will take the responsibility, however, of giving it an introduction. I ask, then, that '\'s' may be allowed to represent 'this,' or 'these,' and that 'seas'—there are the same number of letters in each word, two of which are for me, and two against me—may be considered a mistake for, or a malformation of, 'news': the lines then will stand thus,

> But since he's gone, the king this news must please,
> He 'scaped the land to perish at the sea,

or, if any think it probable that the couplet was a rhyming one, he may, if he will, write 'seas.'

In Act II, 1, 56-60, where Pericles says,

> Peace be at your labour, honest fishermen,

and the second Fisherman replies,

> Honest! good fellow, what's that? If it be a day fits you, search out of the calendar, and nobody look after it,

the Cambridge editors remark, 'Perhaps, as Malone suggested, Pericles had said, ' Peace be at your labour, honest fishermen! Good day!' and the fisherman replies, 'Honest! Good! Fellow, what's that?' I cannot agree with them. I have no objection to point the passage as I have transcribed it, but in other respects it may remain precisely as we find it. The word 'honest,' which Pericles had applied to the fishermen, they for some reason or other are loth to accept, either because they knew that they were not great sticklers for honesty, when it did not seem to square with their interests, or because they did not care to be thus flatteringly accosted by a stranger. Accordingly, the fisherman replies, 'Honest! good fellow, what's that'? The force of the words which follow will be better understood, if I first call the reader's attention to the following dialogue, which takes place in 'Timon of Athens,' Act I, 1, 265;

> *First Lord.* What time o' day is't, Apemantus?
> *Apem.* Time to be honest.
> *First Lord.* That time serves still.

'Time to be honest serves still,' was no doubt a popular proverb; was known to the sailors; is alluded to by the one who spoke to Pericles; shows us the connection between 'Honest!' and 'If it be a *day* fits you.' 'No need'—he as good as says—'to trouble yourself about honesty, for which any time will serve; but, if it be the case that a day fits you, without consulting the calendar or worrying yourself after for not having done so, use the time, seize the opportunity, do what it suits your convenience to do.' The day, however, which had been a very rough and tempestuous one, and had caused the sea to give Pericles a good ducking, had been anything but fitting to *him*; he, therefore, naturally enough rejoins,

> May see the sea hath cast upon your coast,

as much as to say, that, seeing that he had been shipwrecked, they must know very well that the day had not been a fitting one to *him*.

This seems to me to be the meaning of the passage, which Malone would alter in the most extraordinary fashion without making it a jot clearer.

My next passage is in Act III, 1, 51, where the first Quarto reads—I pay no regard to obsolete spelling—

> 1. Pardon us, sir; with us at sea it hath been still observed.
> And we are strong in easterne, therefore briefly yield her,
>
> *Per.* As you think meet; for she must overboard straight: most wretched Queen.

'Malone was the first who read the whole passage as 'prose, and transferred the words, 'for she must 'overboard straight,' to the sailor's speech.

'For '*easterne*' Steevens first adopted Mason's 'conjecture 'earnest,' and Singer first adopted Bos-'well's conjecture 'custom.' Steevens himself had 'guessed 'credence.'

'Mr. Knight, adopting Jackson's conjecture, reads ''And we are strong in astern,' *i.e.*, 'we are driving 'strongly in shore astern.' Malone, who retained ''eastern,' supposed the words to mean, 'There is a 'strong easterly wind'.'

Such is the critical history of this much-vexed passage, gathered from the Notes appended to 'Pericles' in the 'Cambridge Shakespeare.' We may safely say that the reading is anything but certain, that not one of the conjectures is altogether satisfactory.

It is on this ground alone that I venture to ask the reader's attention to a new and totally different reading of the passage, at the risk of causing something very much like a feeling of sea-sickness to the perhaps already unsettled stomachs of the critics.

In the first place, then, I think it important to observe that, in the lines immediately preceding, the reason given by the sailor for wishing to cast the corpse overboard was the high working of the sea, and the loudness of the wind; the wind will not lie till the ship be cleared of the dead. In all probability *the same reference to the state of the weather* underlies the words, however they should be written, 'we are strong in easterne,' as immediately after the sailor *reasserts the necessity of casting the dead corpse into the sea.*

Is it possible that the original word was written 'eestreme' (extreme), which was mistaken for 'easterne,' and that the sailor insists on the great extremity to which they were reduced; they were 'strong,' *i.e.*, 'strongly,' *i.e.*, 'exceedingly in extreme,' or 'in extremity,' they were hard put to it, they were seriously jeopardized. Some such meaning as this would well suit the context, provided the phraseology be passable, and for Shakespeare possible. It is certain that there are numerous phrases to be found in almost every play, which strike the ear of a modern hearer as unusual, and at times even questionable.

Briefly remarking by the way that the 55th line of Act III, 2,

> It is a good constraint of fortune that belches upon us,

admirably expresses both by its metre and its rhythm the undulatory movement of the sea vomiting up again the chest which it had swallowed, I proceed to Scene 3, 36, where we should be losers rather than gainers, were Sydney Walker's conjecture 'moist' to be substituted for Shakespeare's 'masked' as an epithet of Neptune. When Coriolanus' face was seen covered with blood, it was said of him that he was 'masked with blood;' and similarly the sea-god is represented as 'masked' with the broad waters with which he is covered. To describe the ocean as Neptune's mask is a pretty enough poetical conceit.

The next passage that I must notice is in Act IV, 1, 11, where the Cambridge editors make Dionyza say of Marina,

> Here she comes weeping for her only *mistress' death*,

though the Quartos have '*onely Mistresse death*' followed by a comma; the third Folio '*onely Mistresse death*' followed by a colon; and the fourth Folio '*only Mistress death*' also followed by a colon. Singer, however, accepts Dr. Percy's reading 'her old nurse's death,' on the ground that Lycorida could not have been her only mistress to teach her so many accomplishments. But it is quite possible that Dionyza may have called her her only mistress for all that. Dionyza would not probably care to speak as correctly as Dr. Percy would have her, nor, I may add, as *kindly*. More of a demon than a woman was this would-be murderess, full of jealousy and hatred, gall and bitterness. Her *sarcastic* designation of Lycorida as Marina's '*mistress*' needs surprise, needs deceive no one. A misnomer it would be beyond all question, but it would be purposed, and it would be *like Dionyza*. 'Her *only* mistress' would mean 'a very paragon of a mistress,' 'a very non-such'—a sense in which 'only' is used in 'Much Ado About Nothing,' Act III, 1, 92, in the phrase, 'He is the only man in Italy.'

But what ails all the editors that they are so shy here of the reading of the copies? It can hardly be because that reading does not admit of being explained; it must be because it does not accord with their preconceived notions of what Dionyza ought to have said. But a woman like Dionyza might have said anything—the more malignant and diabolical, the more suitable to her character. She sees Marina coming weeping for her nurse's death; she knew very well for whom she was weeping; but it suited her Satanic spirit to say, sardonically smiling the while, that she is weeping for that *fate*, which she has already, she fancies, assured for her; she is weeping for one who will best take care of her, and best *manage* her—her best and only *nurse*—her best and only *mistress*—'She is weeping for her only mistress *death*.' **Depend upon** it, a woman like Dionyza was quite capable of giving expression to such an unfeeling sentiment. It will be remembered that in 'Antony and Cleopatra' death is called the 'beggar's nurse and Cæsar's.'

In the last Act there is a minute, but not unimportant, change which I should make in the punctuation of the last line but one of old Gower's Prologue. I understand him to say that, what is done on board of Pericles' ship, he must leave to those who act the play to report, or, as it is expressed elsewhere, 'action's self shall be tongue to.'

> Think this his bark :
> Where what is done, in action more, if might,
> Shall be discovered ; please you, sit and hark.

Compare Gower's Prologue, Act III, 53-56,

> And what ensues in this fell storm
> Shall for itself itself perform,
> I nill relate, *action* may
> Conveniently the rest convey;
> *Which might not*, what by me is told.

I have not yet done with the stops. In Act V, 1, 172-175, we read,

> The king my father did in Tarsus leave me,
> Till cruel Cleon, with his wicked wife,
> Did seek to murder me : and having woo'd
> A villain to attempt it, who having drawn to do 't,
> A crew of pirates came and rescued me.

Now I will not go so far as to say that these lines, which will seem to many utterly confused and anacoluthic, may not be printed and punctuated, just as I have transcribed them, consistently with the idiom of the English language, and with Shakespearian usage. Undoubtedly the conjunction 'and,' which precedes 'having woo'd,' may be used here, as I have shown in my notes on the 'Tempest,' that it is used in other parts of Shakespeare, in order to indicate some additional circumstance, generally of considerable importance, which the narrator wishes to emphasize and impress. But it would be to the full as consistent with Shakespearian usage, and as consistent with the idiom of the English language, and it would add to the clearness without taking from the force of the passage, if the participle 'having,' which precedes 'woo'd,' were parted off by a couple of commas from 'woo'd' on the one hand, and from the 'and' which precedes on the other, so as to stand by itself, and be treated as an absolute participle, equivalent to the adverbial clause, 'after he had sought to murder me.' This mode of pointing and construing the passage I greatly prefer, and I venture to press it upon the consideration of editors. A passage in 'Antony and Cleopatra,' Act III, 6, 27-29, may serve both as an illustration and a parallel:

> lastly he frets
> That Lepidus of the triumvirate
> Should be deposed, and, *being*, we detain
> All his revenue.

Here, even if commas had not been effectually made use of by the editors of the Globe Shakespeare to isolate 'being,' no one could have failed to understand that it was a laconic way of saying, 'now that he is deposed.'

As touching Act V, 1, 206-210, the Cambridge editors tell us that the first Quarto, followed substantially by the rest, reads thus,

> I
> Am Pericles of Tyre : but tell me now
> My drown'd queen's name, as in the rest you said
> Thou hast been god-like perfect, the heir of kingdoms
> And another like to Pericles thy father.

After filling more than a page of their Notes with the various versions of various emendators and editors, they say in conclusion that 'the passage is so corrupt that it cannot be corrected with any approach to certainty by conjecture, and accordingly they have left it as it stands in the Quartos and Folios.'

But *so* surely it may stand, and, *so* standing, it very well admits of being explained.

The prince says that in the rest which she had said she had been god-like perfect, *i.e.*, she had thoroughly shown herself his very and true daughter, so that he recognized her not only as the heiress of all his dominions, but as the very counterpart of himself, 'another like'—why should any mislike the expression?— a second 'I,' to be his successor and representative, when he should be no more.

One passage more: in Act V, 1, 234, the first three Quartos read

> *Ly.* Musicke my Lord ? I heare.

Mr. Dyce first suggested that 'music' should be printed as a stage-direction. The Cambridge editors say that no music is mentioned in Wilkins' Novel, and any music of earth would be likely to jar with that music of the spheres which was already lulling Pericles to sleep. They add that perhaps the passage might be arranged thus,

>   *Ly.* Music, my lord?
>   *Per.* I hear most heavenly music.

Why not thus?

>   Rarest sounds. Do ye not hear music?
>   *Ly.* My lord!
>   *Per.* I hear
>   Most heavenly music.

The music heard by Pericles was heard by none but by Pericles. The surprise which it caused him is evinced by the persistence with which he mentions it—'what *music*?'—'The *music* of the spheres!'—'Do ye not hear *music*?'—'I hear most heavenly *music*.'

Lysimachus, though he counsels the rest not to cross, but to give way to Pericles, would not feign that he heard, what, as a matter of fact, he did not; his exclamation 'My lord!' was neither a 'yes,' nor a 'no,' but left it happily ambiguous whether he had heard or not.

'Do ye not hear music?' and 'I hear most heavenly music' might well have proceeded, both of them, from Pericles.

INDEX.

I. PASSAGES NEWLY CORRECTED:

(a) where the suggested emendations are apparently certain.

Tempest	Act I. 2. 386.
Measure for Measure	Act I. 3. 20.
Comedy of Errors	Act IV. 3. 13.
Midsummer-Night's Dream	Act II. 1. 54.
Taming of the Shrew	Induction. Sc. 1. 17; Act I. 2. 7.
Twelfth Night	Act III. 3. 15.
1 Henry IV.	Act IV. 1. 31.
2 Henry IV.	Act I. 3. 36-37.
1 Henry VI.	Act IV. 6. 45.
2 Henry VI.	Act IV. 10. 56.
Richard III.	Act V. 5. 27-28.
Coriolanus	Act III. 1. 190.
Timon	Act IV. 3. 134.
Julius Cæsar	Act I. 3. 129.
Hamlet	Act 3. 2. 42.
Pericles	Act I. 2. 1-5; Act V. Prologue. 23; Act V. 1. 174.

(b) where the suggested emendations are not improbable.

Two Gentlemen of Verona	Act II. 5. 2; Act V. 4. 129.
Measure for Measure	Act I. 2. 126.
Comedy of Errors	Act IV. 1. 98.
Midsummer-Night's Dream	Act III. 2. 14; Act IV. 1. 150; Act V. 1. 59.
Merchant of Venice	Act II. 2. 166; Act III. 3. 26-29.
As You Like It	Act I. 1. 1-5.
Taming of the Shrew	Prologue. Sc. 1. 64; Act I. 2. 29.
All's Well that Ends Well	Act IV. 1. 17-21; Act IV. 4. 31; Act V. 3. 6. 216.
Twelfth Night	Act III. 4. 86-91.

INDEX.

Winter's Tale.	Act I. 2. 273-76, 325 ; Act IV. 4. 250, 592.
King John	Act III. 1. 259 ; Act V. 7. 16.
Richard II.	Act III. 2. 175-77.
1 Henry IV.	Act V. 2. 8.
2 Henry IV.	Act II. 4. 409.
Henry V.	Act I. 2. 126.
1 Henry VI.	Act I. 1. 56, 62 ; Act V. 3. 192.
Richard III.	Act I. 2. 64, 101 ; Act I. 3. 113, 188.
Henry VIII.	Act I. 1. 205 ; Act II. 2. 94 ; Act III. 2. 64, 383 ; Act V. 3. 1-2, 108, 130.
Coriolanus	Act I. 3. 46 ; Act I. 4. 31.
Timon	Act V. 3. 4.
Julius Cæsar.	Act V. 1. 35.
Macbeth.	Act I. 2. 58 ; Act I. 3. 98 ; Act III. 1. 130 ; Act III. 4. 130-133 ; Act IV. 2. 22.
Hamlet	Act III. 4. 169 ; Act V. 1. 68 ; Act V. 2. 118.
King Lear	Act IV. 2. 57 ; Act V. 3. 129-30.
Antony and Cleopatra.	Act I. 5. 48 ; Act V. 2. 355.
Cymbeline	Act III. 3. 23 ; Act III. 4. 135 ; Act IV. 2. 8, 17.
Pericles.	Act I. 3. 28 ; Act III. 1. 53.

II. Passages needlessly corrected in the 'Globe' Shakespeare.

Tempest.	Act I. 1. 68-70 ; Act I. 2. 173.
Comedy of Errors.	Act V. 1. 406.
Merchant of Venice	Act II. 7. 69 ; Act IV. 1. 51.
As You Like It	Act II. 4. 1 ; Act II. 7. 55.
Taming of the Shrew.	Act III. 2. 16.
All's Well that Ends Well.	Act II. 1. 176 ; Act V. 3. 66.
Winter's Tale.	Act V. 1. 56-60.
King John	Act V. 6. 12.
Richard II.	Act I. 2. 70 ; Act I. 3. 128 ; Act II. 2. 39-40 ; 110 ; Act V. 1. 25.
Henry V.	Act II. 2. 139 ; Act III. 3. 35.
Richard III.	Act I. 3. 69.
Coriolanus	Act I. 9. 46 ; Act III. 1. 131 ; Act III. 3. 130 ; Act IV. 3. 9 ; Act IV. 6. 2 ; Act V. 1. 16.
Titus Andronicus.	Act III. 1. 282 ; Act IV. 1. 129 ; Act IV. 2. 152.
Timon	Act V. 4. 37, 62.

Julius Cæsar	Act I. 2. 155 ; Act I. 3. 65 ; Act IV. 1. 37.
Macbeth	Act I. 2. 14 . Act I. 3. 97 ; Act II. 1. 55.
King Lear	Act I. 2. 21 ; Act IV. 1. 71.
Antony and Cleopatra	Act II. 2. 53 ; Act III. 11. 47.
Pericles	Act I. 1. 17 ; Act II. 1. 56-60.

III. PASSAGES NEEDLESSLY SUSPECTED.

Tempest	Act I. 2. 29, 307, 488 ; Act II. 1. 130-31 ; Act II. 2. 15.
Two Gentlemen of Verona .	Act III. 1. 81 ; Act V. 4. 82-83.
Measure for Measure	Act I. 1. 8 ; Act 1. 3. 42 , Act I. 4. 30 ; Act II. 1. 39 ; Act III. 2. 275-96.
Comedy of Errors	Act I. 1. 39 ; Act I. 2. 38 ; Act II. 1. 103-115.
Midsummer-Night's Dream	Act IV. 1. 162-163 ; Act V. 1. 92.
Merchant of Venice	Act I. 1. 35 ; Act III. 2. 99, 160-67 ; Act III. 5. 82.
As You Like It	Act II. 7. 73 ; Act III. 5. 7. 23 ; Act V. 4. 4.
Taming of the Shrew	Act IV. 2. 61.
All's Well that Ends Well..	Act I. 1. 179. 237, 238. 241 ; Act I. 2. 31-45 ; Act I. 3. 141 ; Act II. 5. 52.
Twelfth Night	Act II. 5. 71 ; Act IV. 1. 14-15.
Winter's Tale	Act I. 2. 457-60 ; Act II. 1. 133-36 ; Act III. 2. 60-62.
King John	Act III. 3. 39.
Richard II.	Act II. 1. 246-48.
1 Henry IV.	Act I. 1. 5.
2 Henry IV.	Act IV. 1. 50.
Henry V.	Act I. 2. 91-95, 274 ; Act IV. 1. 262.
1 Henry VI.	Act V. 3. 71.
2 Henry VI.	Act I. 3. 153 ; Act II. 1. 26.
Richard III.	Act V. 3. 173.
Henry VIII.	Act I. 1. 80, 224-26 ; Act V. 3. 11-12.
Coriolanus	Act I. 1. 262 ; Act I. 6. 76 ; Act III. 2. 29, 52-80 ; Act V. 1. 69-71 ; Act V. 2. 17.
Titus Andronicus	Act II. 3. 126 ; Act III. 1. 170 ; Act IV. 2. 178 ; Act V. 1. 132 ; Act V. 3. 124.
Timon	Act I. 1. 241 ; Act III. 2. 43 ; Act III. 6. 90 ; Act IV. 3. 223 ; Act V. 2. 8.
Julius Cæsar	Act III. 1. 206, 262.
Macbeth	Act I. 2. 21, 49 ; Act II. 1. 25 ; Act III. 4. 32, 105 ; Act IV. 3. 15 ; Act V. 4. 11.

Hamlet	Act I. 1. 117.
King Lear	Act II. 4. 274 ; Act IV. 3. 21. 33.
Antony and Cleopatra.	Act III. 13. 10 ; Act V. 1. 15.
Cymbeline	Act III. 4. 52, 150 ; Act V. 1. 14 ; Act V. 5. 95.
Pericles	Act I. 2. 74 ; Act III. 2. 55 ; Act IV. 1. 11 ; Act 5. 1. 209.

IV. PASSAGES REQUIRING ELUCIDATION NOT EMENDATION.

Tempest.	Act IV. 1. 61.
Merchant of Venice	Act IV. 1. 380.
As You Like It	Act III. 2. 207.
All's Well that Ends Well.	Act II. 1. 3.
Winter's Tale	Act II. 1. 143.
1 Henry IV.	Act V. 2. 77-79.
2 Henry IV.	Act IV. 1. 88-96.
Richard III.	Act III. 3. 23.
Henry VIII.	Act II. 3. 46 ; Act III. 2. 192.
Coriolanus	Act III. 2. 126-27 ; Act IV. 7. 28-55.
Macbeth.	Act I. 5. 23-26 ; Act IV. 3. 136-37.
King Lear	Act I. 3. 20 ; Act II. 2. 176.

V. PASSAGES MORE OR LESS DOUBTFUL.

Tempest.	Act III. 1. 15.
Measure for Measure.	Act III. 1. 126-128.
All's Well that Ends Well.	Act IV. 2. 38.
Winter's Tale	Act IV. 3. 98 ; Act IV. 4. 760.
King John	Act II. 1. 183-190 ; Act III. 1. 279-285 ; Act IV. 2. 40-43.
3 Henry VI.	Act I. 4. 152-53.
Timon	Act I. 2. 73.
Julius Cæsar.	Act III. 1. 174.
Macbeth.	Act V. 3. 21.
Hamlet.	Act I. 3. 74 ; Act I. 4. 37.
King Lear	Act 5. 3. 205.

THE END.

T. J. RAWLINGS, STEAM PRINTER, CHERTSEY.

February 1885.

A CATALOGUE OF
WORKS IN GENERAL LITERATURE & SCIENCE
PUBLISHED BY
MESSRS. LONGMANS, GREEN, & CO.
39 PATERNOSTER ROW, LONDON, E.C.

Classified Index.

AGRICULTURE, HORSES, DOGS, and CATTLE.

Dog (The), by Stonehenge	21
Fitzwygram's Horses and Stables	10
Greyhound (The), by Stonehenge	11
Horses and Roads, by Free-Lance	12
London's Encyclopædia of Agriculture	14
Lloyd's The Science of Agriculture	14
Miles' (W. H.) Works on Horses and Stables	17
Neville's Farms and Farming	18
——— Horses and Riding	18
Scott's Farm-Valuer	20
Steel's Diseases of the Ox	21
Ville's Artificial Manures	23
Youatt on the Dog	24
——— Horse	24

ANATOMY and PHYSIOLOGY.

Ashby's Notes on Physiology	5
Buckton's Health in the House	7
Cooke's Tablets of Anatomy and Physiology	8
Gray's Anatomy, Descriptive and Surgical	11
Macalister's Vertebrate Animals	15
Owen's Comparative Anatomy and Physiology	18
Quain's Elements of Anatomy	20
Smith's Operative Surgery on the Dead Body	21

ASTRONOMY.

Ball's Elements of Astronomy	22
Herschel's Outlines of Astronomy	12
'Knowledge' Library (The)	20
Proctor's (R. A.) Works	19
Nelson's The Moon	15
Webb's Celestial Objects for Common Telescopes	23

BIOGRAPHY, REMINISCENCES, LETTERS, &c.

Bacon's Life and Works	5
Bagehot's Biographical Studies	5
Bray's Phases of Opinion	7
Carlyle's (T.) Life, by James A. Froude	7
——— Reminiscences	7
——— (Mrs.) Letters and Memorials	7
Cates Dictionary of General Biography	7
Cox's Lives of Greek Statesmen	8
D'Eon de Beaumont's Life, by Telfer	8
Fox's (C. J.), Early History of, by G. O. Trevelyan	10
Grimston's (Hon. R.) Life, by Gale	11
Hamilton's (Sir W. R.) Life, by R. P. Graves	11
Havelock's Memoirs, by J. C. Marshman	11
Macaulay's Life and Letters, by G. O. Trevelyan	15
Malmesbury's Memoirs	16
Maunder's Biographical Treasury	16
Mendelssohn's Letters	17
Mill (James), a Biography, by A. Bain	16
Mill (John Stuart), a Criticism, by A. Bain	16
Mill's (J. S.) Autobiography	17
Mozley's Reminiscences of Oriel College, &c.	18
——— Towns, Villages, &c.	18
Müller's (Max) Biographical Essays	16
Newman's Apologia pro Vitâ Suâ	18
Pasolini's Memoir	19
Pasteur's Life and Labours	19
Shakespeare's Life, by J. O. Halliwell-Phillipps	21
Southey's Correspondence with Caroline Bowles	21
Stephen's Ecclesiastical Biography	21
Wellington's Life, by G. R. Gleig	23

BOTANY and GARDENING.

Allen's Flowers and their Pedigrees	4
De Caisne & Le Maout's Botany	8
Lindley's Treasury of Botany	14

BOTANY and GARDENING—*continued.*

London's Encyclopædia of Gardening	14
——— Encyclopædia of Plants	14
Rivers' Orchard-House	20
——— Rose Amateur's Guide	20
Thomé's Botany	22

CHEMISTRY.

Armstrong's Organic Chemistry	22
Kolbe's Inorganic Chemistry	13
Miller's Elements of Chemistry	17
——— Inorganic Chemistry	17
Payen's Industrial Chemistry	18
Thorpe & Muir's Qualitative Analysis	22
———'s Quantitative Analysis	22
Tilden's Chemical Philosophy	22
Watts' Dictionary of Chemistry	23

CLASSICAL LANGUAGES, LITERATURE, and ANTIQUITIES.

Aristophanes' The Acharnians, translated	5
Aristotle's Works	5
Becker's Charicles	6
——— Gallus	6
Cicero's Correspondence, by Tyrrell	7
Homer's Iliad, translated by Cayley	12
——— Green	12
Hort's The New Pantheon	12
Mahaffy's Classical Greek Literature	16
Perry's Greek and Roman Sculpture	19
Plato's Parmenides, by Maguire	19
Rich's Dictionary of Antiquities	20
Simcox's History of Latin Literature	21
Sophocles' Works	21
Virgil's Æneid, translated by Conington	8
——— Poems	8
——— Works, with Notes by Kennedy	23
Witt's Myths of Hellas	24
——— The Trojan War	24
——— The Wanderings of Ulysses	24

COOKERY, DOMESTIC ECONOMY, &c.

Acton's Modern Cookery	4
Buckton's Food and Home Cookery	7
Reeve's Cookery and Housekeeping	20

ENCYCLOPÆDIAS, DICTIONARIES, and BOOKS of REFERENCE.

Ayre's Bible Treasury	5
Blackley's German Dictionary	6
Brande's Dict. of Science, Literature, and Art	6
Cabinet Lawyer (The)	7
Cates Dictionary of Biography	7
Contanseau's French Dictionaries	8
Cresy's Encyclopædia of Civil Engineering	8
Gwilt's Encyclopædia of Architecture	11
Johnston's General Dictionary of Geography	13
Latham's English Dictionaries	14
Lindley & Moore's Treasury of Botany	14
Longman's German Dictionary	14
London's Encyclopædia of Agriculture	14
——— ——— Gardening	14
——— ——— Plants	14
M'Culloch's Dictionary of Commerce	15
Maunder's Treasuries	16
Quain's Dictionary of Medicine	20
Rich's Dictionary of Antiquities	20
Roget's English Thesaurus	20
Ure's Dictionary of Arts, Manufactures, &c.	23
White's Latin Dictionaries	23
Willich's Popular Tables	23
Yonge's English-Greek Dictionary	24

ENGINEERING, MECHANICS, MANUFACTURES, &c.

Anderson's Strength of Materials	22
Barry & Bramwell's Railways, &c	6
———'s Railway Appliances	22
Black's Treatise on Brewing	6
Bourne's Works on the Steam Engine	6
Cresy's Encyclopædia of Civil Engineering	8
Culley's Handbook of Practical Telegraphy	8
Edwards' Our Seamarks	9
Fairbairn's Mills and Millwork	10
——— Useful Information for Engineers	10
Goodeve's Elements of Mechanism	11
——— Principles of Mechanics	11
Gore's Electro-Metallurgy	22
Gwilt's Encyclopædia of Architecture	11
Mitchell's Practical Assaying	17
Northcott's Lathes and Turning	18
Piesse's Art of Perfumery	19
Preece & Sivewright's Telegraphy	22
Sennett's Marine Steam Engine	21
Shelley's Workshop Appliances	22
Swinton's Electric Lighting	22
Unwin's Machine Design	22
Ure's Dictionary of Arts, Manufactures, & Mines	23

ENGLISH LANGUAGE and LITERATURE.

Arnold's English Poetry and Prose	5
——— Manual of English Literature	5
Latham's English Dictionaries	14
——— Handbook of English Language	14
Roget's English Thesaurus	20
Whately's English Synonyms	23

HISTORY, POLITICS, HISTORICAL MEMOIRS, and CRITICISM.

Abbey & Overton's Eng. Church in 18th Century	4
Amos' Fifty Years of the English Constitution	4
——— Primer of the English Constitution	4
Arnold's Lectures on Modern History	5
Beaconsfield's Selected Speeches	6
Boultbee's History of the Church of England	6
Bramston & Leroy's Historic Winchester	6
Buckle's History of Civilisation	7
Chesney's Waterloo Lectures	7
Cox's General History of Greece	8
——— Lives of Greek Statesmen	8
Creighton's History of the Papacy	8
De Witt's (John) Life, by Pontalis	8
De Tocqueville's Democracy in America	8
Doyle's The English in America	9
Epochs of Ancient History	9
——— Modern History	9
Freeman's Historical Geography of Europe	10
Froude's History of England	10
——— Short Studies	10
——— The English in Ireland	10
Gardiner's History of England, 1603-42	10
——— Outline of English History	11
Grant's University of Edinburgh	11
Greville's Journal	11
Hickson's Ireland in the 17th Century	12
Lecky's History of England	14
——— European Morals	14
——— Rationalism in Europe	14
——— Leaders of Public Opinion in Ireland	14
Lewes' History of Philosophy	14
Longman's (W.) Lectures on History of England	14
——— Life and Times of Edward III.	14
——— (F. W.) Frederick the Great	14
Macaulay's Complete Works	15
——— Critical and Historical Essays	15
——— History of England	15
——— Speeches	15
Maunder's Historical Treasury	16
Maxwell's Don John of Austria	16
May's Constitutional Hist. of Eng. 1760-1870	16
——— Democracy in Europe	16
Merivale's Fall of the Roman Republic	17
——— General History of Rome	17
——— Romans under the Empire	17
——— The Roman Triumvirates	17
Rawlinson's Seventh Great Oriental Monarchy	20
Seebohm's The Oxford Reformers	20
——— The Protestant Revolution	20

HISTORY, POLITICS, HISTORICAL MEMOIRS and CRITICISM—*cont.*

Short's History of the Church of England	21
Smith's Carthage and the Carthaginians	21
Taylor's History of India	22
Walpole's History of England, 1815-41	23
Wylie's England under Henry IV.	24

ILLUSTRATED BOOKS and BOOKS on ART.

Dresser's Japan; its Architecture, &c.	9
Eastlake's Five Great Painters	9
——— Hints on Household Taste	9
——— Notes on Foreign Picture Galleries	9
Jameson's (Mrs.) Works	13
Lang's (A.) Princess Nobody, illus. by R. Doyle	14
Macaulay's (Lord) Lays, illustrated by Scharf	15
——— illustrated by Weguelin	15
Moore's Irish Melodies, illustrated by Maclise	18
——— Lalla Rookh, illustrated by Tenniel	18
New Testament (The), illustrated	18
Perry's Greek and Roman Sculpture	19

MEDICINE and SURGERY.

Bull's Hints to Mothers	7
——— Maternal Management of Children	7
Coats' Manual of Pathology	7
Dickinson On Renal and Urinary Affections	10
Erichsen's Concussion of the Spine	10
——— Science and Art of Surgery	10
Garrod's Materia Medica	10
——— Treatise on Gout	10
Howard's Orthopaedic Surgery	12
Hewitt's Diseases of Women	12
——— Mechanic. System of Uterine Pathology	12
Holmes' System of Surgery	12
Husband's Questions in Anatomy	12
Jones' The Health of the Senses	13
Little's In-Knee Distortion	14
Liveing's Works on Skin Diseases	14
Longmore's Gunshot Injuries	14
Mackenzie's Use of the Laryngoscope	15
Macnamara's Diseases of Himalayan Districts	16
Morehead's Disease in India	18
Murchison's Continued Fevers of Great Britain	18
——— Diseases of the Liver	18
Paget's Clinical Lectures and Essays	18
——— Lectures on Surgical Pathology	18
Pereira's Materia Medica	18
Quain's Dictionary of Medicine	20
Richardson's The Asclepaid	20
Salter's Dental Pathology and Surgery	20
Smith's Handbook for Midwives	21
Thomson's Conspectus, by Birkett	22
Watson's Principles and Practice of Physic	23
West's Diseases of Infancy and Childhood	23

MENTAL and POLITICAL PHILOSOPHY, FINANCE, &c.

Abbott's Elements of Logic	4
Amos' Science of Jurisprudence	4
Aristotle's Works	5
Bacon's Essays, with Notes, by Abbott	5
——— by Hunter	5
——— by Whately	5
——— Letters, Life, and Occasional Works	5
——— Promus of Formularies	5
——— Works	5
Bagehot's Economic Studies	5
Bain's (Prof.) Philosophical Works	6
De Tocqueville's Democracy in America	8
Dowell's History of Taxes	9
Hume's Philosophical Works	13
Jefferies' The Story of My Heart	13
Justinian's Institutes, by T. Sandars	13
Kant's Critique of Practical Reason	13
Lang's Custom and Myth	13
Lewis' Authority in Matters of Opinion	14
Lubbock's Origin of Civilisation	14
Macleod's (H. D.) Works	16
Mill's (James) Phenomena of the Human Mind	16
Mill's (J. S.) Logic, Killick's Handbook to	13
——— Works	17
Miller's Social Economy	17
Monck's Introduction to Logic	18
Morell's Handbook of Logic	17
Seebohm's English Village Community	20

LONGMANS & CO.'S LIST OF GENERAL AND SCIENTIFIC BOOKS. 3

MENTAL and POLITICAL PHILOSOPHY, FINANCE, &c.—*continued.*

Sully's Outlines of Psychology	22
Swinburne's Picture Logic	22
Thompson's A System of Psychology	22
Thomson's Laws of Thought	22
Twiss on the Rights and Duties of Nations	22
Webb's The Veil of Isis	23
Whately's Elements of Logic	23
—— Elements of Rhetoric	23
Wylie's Labour, Leisure, and Luxury	24
Zeller's Works on Greek Philosophy	24

MISCELLANEOUS WORKS.

Arnold's (Dr.) Miscellaneous Works	5
A. K. H. B., Essays and Contributions of	4
Bagehot's Literary Studies	5
Beaconsfield Birthday Book (The)	6
Beaconsfield's Wit and Wisdom	6
Evans' Bronze Implements of Great Britain	10
Farrar's Language and Languages	10
French's Drink in England	10
Hassell's Adulteration of Food	12
Johnson's Patentee's Manual	13
Longman's Magazine	14
Macaulay's (Lord) Works, Selections from	15
Müller's (Max) Works	18
Peel's A Highland Gathering	19
Smith's (Sydney) Wit and Wisdom	21

NATURAL HISTORY (POPULAR).

Dixon's Rural Bird Life	9
Hartwig's (Dr. G.) Works	11
Maunder's Treasury of Natural History	16
Stanley's Familiar History of Birds	21
Wood's (Rev. J. G.) Works	24

POETICAL WORKS.

Bailey's Festus	5
Dante's Divine Comedy, translated by Minchin	8
Goethe's Faust, translated by Birds	11
—— translated by Webb	11
—— with Notes by Selss	11
Homer's Iliad, translated by Cayley	12
—— translated by Green	12
Ingelow's Poetical Works	13
Macaulay's (Lord) Lays of Ancient Rome	15
Macdonald's A Book of Strife	15
Pennell's 'From Grave to Gay'	19
Reader's Voices from Flower-Land	20
Shakespeare, Bowdler's Family Edition	21
—— Hamlet, by George Macdonald	15
Southey's Poetical Works	21
Stevenson's Child's Garden of Poems	21
Virgil's Æneid, translated by Conington	23
—— Poems, translated by Conington	23

SPORTS and PASTIMES.

Dead Shot (The), by Marksman	8
Francis' Book on Angling	10
Jefferies' Red Deer	13
Longman's Chess Openings	14
Pole's The Modern Game of Whist	19
Ronalds' Fly-Fisher's Entomology	20
Verney's Chess Eccentricities	23
Walker's The Correct Card	23
Wilcocks' The Sea-Fisherman	24

SCIENTIFIC WORKS (General).

Arnott's Elements of Physics	5
Bauerman's Descriptive Mineralogy	22
—— Systematic Mineralogy	22
Brande's Dictionary of Science &c.	6
Ganot's Natural Philosophy	10
—— Physics	10
Grove's Correlation of Physical Forces	11
Haughton's Lectures on Physical Geography	11
Helmholtz Scientific Lectures	12
—— On the Sensation of Tone	12
Hullah's History of Modern Music	12
—— Transition Period of Musical History	12
Keller's Lake Dwellings of Switzerland	13
Kerl's Treatise on Metallurgy	13
'Knowledge' Library (The)	20
Lloyd's Treatise on Magnetism	14
Macfarren's Lectures on Harmony	15
Maunder's Scientific Treasury	16
Proctor's (R. A.) Works	19
Rutley's The Study of Rocks	22

SCIENTIFIC WORKS (General)—*cont.*

Smith's Air and Rain	21
Text-books of Science	22
Tyndall's (Prof.) Works	22, 23

THEOLOGY and RELIGION.

Arnold's (Dr.) Sermons	5
Ayre's Treasury of Bible Knowledge	5
Boultbee's Commentary on the 39 Articles	6
Browne's Exposition of the 39 Articles	7
Calvert's Wife's Manual	7
Colenso's Pentateuch and Book of Joshua	7
Conder's Handbook to the Bible	7
Conybeare and Howson's St. Paul	8
Davidson's Introduction to the New Testament	8
Lewes' Life and Letters of St. Paul	9
Edersheim's Jesus the Messiah	9
—— Warburton Lectures	9
Ellicott's Commentary on St. Paul's Epistles	9
—— Lectures on the Life of Our Lord	9
Ewald's Antiquities of Israel	10
—— History of Israel	10
Hobart's Medical Language of St. Luke	12
Hopkins' Christ the Consoler	12
Jukes' (Rev. A.) Works	13
Kalisch's Bible Studies	13
—— Commentary on the Old Testament	13
Lyra Germanica	15
Macdonald's Unspoken Sermons (second series)	15
Manning's Temporal Mission of the Holy Ghost	16
Martineau's Endeavours after the Christian Life	16
—— Hours of Thought	16
Monsell's Spiritual Songs	18
Müller's (Max) Origin and Growth of Religion	18
—— Science of Religion	18
Paley's Christian Evidences, &c., by Potts	18
Psalms (The) of David, translated by Seymour	21
Rogers' Defence of the Eclipse of Faith	20
—— The Eclipse of Faith	20
Sewell's Night Lessons from Scripture	21
—— Passing Thoughts on Religion	21
—— Preparation for Holy Communion	21
Smith's Shipwreck of St. Paul	21
Supernatural Religion	22
Taylor's (Jeremy) Entire Works	22

TRAVELS, ADVENTURES, GUIDE BOOKS, &c.

Aldridge's Ranch Notes	4
Alpine Club (The) Map of Switzerland	4
Baker's Eight Years in Ceylon	5
—— Rifle and Hound in Ceylon	5
Ball's Alpine Guide	4
Brassey's (Lady) Works	7
Crawford's Across the Pampas and the Andes	8
Dent's Above the Snow Line	8
Freeman's United States	10
Hassall's San Remo	12
Howitt's Visits to Remarkable Places	12
Johnston's Dictionary of Geography	13
Maritime Alps (The)	16
Maunder's Treasury of Geography	16
Melville's In the Lena Delta	16
Miller's Wintering in the Riviera	17
Three in Norway	22

WORKS of FICTION.

Anstey's The Black Poodle, &c.	5
Antinous, by George Taylor	5
Atelier du Lys (The)	17
Atherstone Priory	17
Beaconsfield's (Lord) Novels and Tales	6
Burgomaster's Family (The)	17
Elsa and her Vulture	17
Harte's (Bret) In the Carquinez Woods	17
—— On the Frontier	17
In the Olden Time	13
Mademoiselle Mori	17
Modern Novelist's Library (The)	17
Oliphant's (Mrs.) In Trust	17
—— Madam	18
Payn's Thicker than Water	17
Sewell's (Miss) Stories and Tales	17
Six Sisters of the Valleys (The)	17
Sturgis' My Friends and I	22
Trollope's (Anthony) Barchester Towers	17
—— The Warden	17
Unawares	17
Whyte-Melville's (Major) Novels	17

A CATALOGUE

OF

WORKS IN GENERAL LITERATURE & SCIENCE

PUBLISHED BY

MESSRS. LONGMANS, GREEN & CO.

39 PATERNOSTER ROW, LONDON, E.C.

ABBEY and OVERTON.—*THE ENGLISH CHURCH IN THE EIGHTEENTH CENTURY*. By the Rev. C. J. ABBEY and the Rev. J. H. OVERTON. 2 vols. 8vo. 36s.

ABBOTT. — *THE ELEMENTS OF LOGIC*. By T. K. ABBOTT, B.D. 12mo. 2s. 6d. sewed, or 3s. cloth.

ACTON. — *MODERN COOKERY FOR PRIVATE FAMILIES*, reduced to a System of Easy Practice in a Series of carefully tested Receipts. By ELIZA ACTON. With upwards of 150 Woodcuts. Fcp. 8vo. 4s. 6d.

A. K. H. B.—*THE ESSAYS AND CONTRIBUTIONS OF A. K. H. B.*—Uniform Cabinet Editions in crown 8vo.

Autumn Holidays, 3s. 6d.
Changed Aspects of Unchanged Truths, 3s. 6d.
Commonplace Philosopher, 3s. 6d.
Counsel and Comfort, 3s. 6d.
Critical Essays, 3s. 6d.
Graver Thoughts of a Country Parson. Three Series, 3s. 6d. each.
Landscapes, Churches, and Moralities, 3s. 6d.
Leisure Hours in Town, 3s. 6d.
Lessons of Middle Age, 3s. 6d.
Our Little Life. Two Series, 3s. 6d. each.
Present Day Thoughts, 3s. 6d.
Recreations of a Country Parson. Three Series, 3s. 6d. each.
Seaside Musings, 3s. 6d.
Sunday Afternoons, 3s. 6d.

ALDRIDGE. — *RANCH NOTES IN KANSAS, COLORADO, THE INDIAN TERRITORY AND NORTHERN TEXAS*. By REGINALD ALDRIDGE. Crown 8vo. with 4 Illustrations engraved on Wood by G. Pearson, 5s.

ALLEN.—*FLOWERS AND THEIR PEDIGREES*. By GRANT ALLEN. With 50 Illustrations engraved on Wood. Crown 8vo. 7s. 6d.

ALPINE CLUB (The).—*GUIDES AND MAPS*.

THE ALPINE GUIDE. By JOHN BALL, M.R.I.A. Post 8vo. with Maps and other Illustrations :—

THE EASTERN ALPS, 10s. 6d.

CENTRAL ALPS, including all the Oberland District, 7s. 6d.

WESTERN ALPS, including Mont Blanc, Monte Rosa, Zermatt, &c. 6s. 6d.

THE ALPINE CLUB MAP OF SWITZERLAND, on the Scale of Four Miles to an Inch. Edited by R. C. NICHOLS, F.R.G.S. 4 Sheets in Portfolio, 42s. coloured, or 34s. uncoloured.

ENLARGED ALPINE CLUB MAP OF THE SWISS AND ITALIAN ALPS, on the Scale of Three English Statute Miles to One Inch, in 8 Sheets, price 1s. 6d. each.

ON ALPINE TRAVELLING AND THE GEOLOGY OF THE ALPS. Price 1s. Either of the Three Volumes or Parts of the 'Alpine Guide' may be had with this Introduction prefixed, 1s. extra.

AMOS.—*WORKS BY SHELDON AMOS, M.A.*

A PRIMER OF THE ENGLISH CONSTITUTION AND GOVERNMENT. Crown 8vo. 6s.

A SYSTEMATIC VIEW OF THE SCIENCE OF JURISPRUDENCE. 8vo. 18s.

FIFTY YEARS OF THE ENGLISH CONSTITUTION, 1830-1880. Crown 8vo. 10s. 6d.

ANSTEY.—*The Black Poodle*, and other Stories. By F. ANSTEY, Author of 'Vice Versâ.' With Frontispiece by G. Du Maurier and Initial Letters by the Author. Crown 8vo. 6s.

ANTINOUS.—An Historical Romance of the Roman Empire. By GEORGE TAYLOR (Professor HAUSRATH). Translated from the German by J. D. M. Crown 8vo. 6s.

ARISTOPHANES. — *The Acharnians of Aristophanes*. Translated into English Verse by ROBERT YELVERTON TYRRELL, M.A. Dublin. Crown 8vo. 2s. 6d.

ARISTOTLE.—*The Works of*.

The Politics, G. Bekker's Greek Text of Books I. III. IV. (VII.) with an English Translation by W. E. BOLLAND, M.A.; and short Introductory Essays by A. LANG, M.A. Crown 8vo. 7s. 6d.

The Ethics; Greek Text, illustrated with Essays and Notes. By Sir ALEXANDER GRANT, Bart. M.A. LL.D. 2 vols. 8vo. 32s.

The Nicomachean Ethics, Newly Translated into English. By ROBERT WILLIAMS, Barrister-at-Law. Crown 8vo. 7s. 6d.

ARNOLD. — *Works by Thomas Arnold, D.D. Late Head-master of Rugby School.*

Introductory Lectures on Modern History, delivered in 1841 and 1842. 8vo. 7s. 6d.

Sermons Preached Mostly in the Chapel of Rugby School. 6 vols. crown 8vo. 30s. or separately, 5s. each.

Miscellaneous Works. 8vo. 7s. 6d.

ARNOLD. — *Works by Thomas Arnold, M.A.*

A Manual of English Literature, Historical and Critical. By THOMAS ARNOLD, M.A. Crown 8vo. 7s. 6d.

English Poetry and Prose: a Collection of Illustrative Passages from the Writings of English Authors, from the Anglo-Saxon Period to the Present Time. Crown 8vo. 6s.

ARNOTT.—*The Elements of Physics or Natural Philosophy*. By NEIL ARNOTT, M.D. Edited by A. BAIN, LL.D. and A. S. TAYLOR, M.D. F.R.S. Woodcuts. Crown 8vo. 12s. 6d.

ASHBY. — *Notes on Physiology for the Use of Students Preparing for Examination*. With 120 Woodcuts. By HENRY ASHBY, M.D. Lond., Physician to the General Hospital for Sick Children, Manchester. Fcp. 8vo. 5s.

AYRE. —*The Treasury of Bible Knowledge*; being a Dictionary of the Books, Persons, Places, Events, and other matters of which mention is made in Holy Scripture. By the Rev. J. AYRE, M.A. With 5 Maps, 15 Plates, and 300 Woodcuts. Fcp. 8vo. 6s.

BACON.—*The Works and Life of*.

Complete Works. Collected and Edited by R. L. ELLIS, M.A. J. SPEDDING, M.A. and D. D. HEATH. 7 vols. 8vo. £3. 13s. 6d.

Letters and Life, including all his Occasional Works. Collected and Edited, with a Commentary, by J. SPEDDING. 7 vols. 8vo. £4. 4s.

The Essays; with Annotations. By RICHARD WHATELY, D.D., sometime Archbishop of Dublin. 8vo. 10s. 6d.

The Essays; with Introduction, Notes, and Index. By E. A. ABBOTT, D.D. 2 vols. fcp. 8vo. price 6s. The Text and Index only, without Introduction and Notes, in 1 vol. fcp. 8vo. price 2s. 6d.

The Essays; with Critical and Illustrative Notes, and other Aids for Students. By the Rev. JOHN HUNTER, M.A. Crown 8vo. 3s. 6d.

The Promus of Formularies and Elegancies, illustrated by Passages from SHAKESPEARE. By Mrs. H. POTT. Preface by E. A. ABBOTT, D.D. 8vo. 16s.

BAGEHOT. — *Works by Walter Bagehot, M.A.*

Biographical Studies. 8vo. 12s.

Economic Studies. 8vo. 10s. 6d.

Literary Studies. 2 vols. 8vo. Portrait. 28s.

BAILEY. — *Festus, a Poem*. By PHILIP JAMES BAILEY. Crown 8vo. 12s. 6d.

BAKER.—*Works by Sir Samuel W. Baker, M.A.*

Eight Years in Ceylon. Crown 8vo. Woodcuts. 5s.

The Rifle and the Hound in Ceylon. Crown 8vo. Woodcuts. 5s.

6   LONGMANS & CO.'S LIST OF GENERAL AND SCIENTIFIC BOOKS.

BAIN. — *Works by Alexander Bain, LL.D.*
Mental and Moral Science; a Compendium of Psychology and Ethics. Crown 8vo. 10s. 6d.
The Senses and the Intellect. 8vo. 15s.
The Emotions and the Will. 8vo. 15s.
Practical Essays. Crown 8vo. 4s. 6d.
Logic, Deductive and Inductive. PART I. *Deduction,* 4s. PART II. *Induction,* 6s. 6d.
James Mill; a Biography. Crown 8vo. 5s.
John Stuart Mill; a Criticism, with Personal Recollections. Crown 8vo. 2s. 6d.

BARRY & BRAMWELL. — *Railways and Locomotives:* a Series of Lectures delivered at the School of Military Engineering, Chatham. *Railways,* by J. W. BARRY, M. Inst. C.E. *Locomotives,* by Sir F. J. BRAMWELL, F.R.S., M. Inst. C.E. With 228 Wood Engravings. 8vo. 21s.

BEACONSFIELD. — *Works by the Earl of Beaconsfield, K.G.*
Novels and Tales. The Cabinet Edition. 11 vols. Crown 8vo. 6s. each.
Endymion.
Lothair.
Coningsby.
Sybil.
Tancred.
Venetia.
Henrietta Temple.
Contarini Fleming, &c.
Alroy, Ixion, &c.
The Young Duke, &c.
Vivian Grey, &c.
Novels and Tales. The Hughenden Edition. With 2 Portraits and 11 Vignettes. 11 vols. Crown 8vo. 42s.
Novels and Tales. Modern Novelist's Library Edition, complete in 11 vols. Crown 8vo. 22s. boards, or 27s. 6d. cloth.
Selected Speeches. With Introduction and Notes, by T. E. KEBBEL, M.A. 2 vols. 8vo. Portrait, 32s.
The Wit and Wisdom of Benjamin Disraeli, Earl of Beaconsfield. Crown 8vo. 3s. 6d.
The Beaconsfield Birthday-Book: Selected from the Writings and Speeches of the Right Hon. the Earl of Beaconsfield, K.G. With 2 Portraits and 11 Views of Hughenden Manor and its Surroundings. 18mo. 2s. 6d. cloth, gilt; 4s. 6d. bound.

BECKER. — *Works by Professor Becker, translated from the German by the Rev. F. Metcalf.*
Gallus; or, Roman Scenes in the Time of Augustus. Post 8vo. 7s. 6d.
Charicles; or, Illustrations of the Private Life of the Ancient Greeks. Post 8vo. 7s. 6d.

BLACK. — *Practical Treatise on Brewing;* with Formulæ for Public Brewers and Instructions for Private Families. By W. Black. 8vo. 10s. 6d.

BLACKLEY & FRIEDLÄNDER. — *A Practical Dictionary of the German and English Languages:* containing New Words in General Use not found in other Dictionaries. By the Rev. W. L. BLACKLEY, M.A. and C. M. FRIEDLÄNDER, Ph.D. Post 8vo. 3s. 6d.

BOULTBEE. — *Works by the Rev. T. P. Boultbee, LL.D.*
A Commentary on the 39 Articles, forming an introduction to the Theology of the Church of England. Crown 8vo. 6s.
A History of the Church of England; Pre-Reformation Period. 8vo. 15s.

BOURNE. — *Works by John Bourne, C.E.*
A Treatise on the Steam Engine, in its application to Mines, Mills, Steam Navigation, Railways, and Agriculture. With 37 Plates and 546 Woodcuts. 4to. 42s.
Catechism of the Steam Engine, in its various Applications to Mines, Mills, Steam Navigation, Railways, and Agriculture. With 89 Woodcuts. Crown 8vo. 7s. 6d.
Handbook of the Steam Engine; a Key to the Author's Catechism of the Steam Engine. With 67 Woodcuts. Fcp. 8vo. 9s.
Recent Improvements in the Steam Engine. With 124 Woodcuts. Fcp. 8vo. 6s.
Examples of Steam and Gas Engines of the most recent Approved Types. With 54 Plates and 356 Woodcuts. 4to. 70s.

BRAMSTON & LEROY. — *Historic Winchester;* England's First Capital. By A. R. BRAMSTON and A. C. LEROY. Cr. 8vo. 6s.

BRANDE'S *Dictionary of Science, Literature, and Art.* Re-edited by the Rev. Sir G. W. Cox, Bart., M.A. 3 vols. medium 8vo. 63s.

BRASSEY. — *WORKS BY LADY BRASSEY.*

A VOYAGE IN THE 'SUNBEAM,' OUR HOME ON THE OCEAN FOR ELEVEN MONTHS. By Lady BRASSEY. With Map and 65 Wood Engravings. Library Edition, 8vo. 21s. Cabinet Edition, crown 8vo. 7s. 6d. School Edition, fcp. 2s. Popular Edition, 4to. 6d.

SUNSHINE AND STORM IN THE EAST; or, Cruises to Cyprus and Constantinople. With 2 Maps and 114 Illustrations engraved on Wood. Library Edition, 8vo. 21s. Cabinet Edition, cr. 8vo. 7s. 6d.

IN THE TRADES, THE TROPICS, AND THE 'ROARING FORTIES'; or, Fourteen Thousand Miles in the *Sunbeam* in 1883. By Lady BRASSEY. With 292 Illustrations engraved on Wood from drawings by R. T. Pritchett, and Eight Maps and Charts. Edition de Luxe, imperial 8vo. £3. 13s. 6d. Library Edition, 8vo. 21s.

BRAY. — *PHASES OF OPINION AND EXPERIENCE DURING A LONG LIFE:* an Autobiography. By CHARLES BRAY, Author of 'The Philosophy of Necessity' &c. Crown 8vo. 3s. 6d.

BROWNE. — *AN EXPOSITION OF THE 39 ARTICLES,* Historical and Doctrinal. By E. H. BROWNE, D.D., Bishop of Winchester. 8vo. 16s.

BUCKLE. — *HISTORY OF CIVILISATION IN ENGLAND AND FRANCE, SPAIN AND SCOTLAND.* By HENRY THOMAS BUCKLE. 3 vols. crown 8vo. 24s.

BUCKTON. — *WORKS BY MRS. C. M. BUCKTON.*

FOOD AND HOME COOKERY; a Course of Instruction in Practical Cookery and Cleaning. With 11 Woodcuts. Crown 8vo. 2s. 6d.

HEALTH IN THE HOUSE: Twenty-five Lectures on Elementary Physiology. With 41 Woodcuts and Diagrams. Crown 8vo. 2s.

BULL. — *WORKS BY THOMAS BULL, M.D.*

HINTS TO MOTHERS ON THE MANAGEMENT OF THEIR HEALTH during the Period of Pregnancy and in the Lying-in Room. Fcp. 8vo. 1s. 6d.

THE MATERNAL MANAGEMENT OF CHILDREN IN HEALTH AND DISEASE. Fcp. 8vo. 1s. 6d.

CABINET LAWYER, The; a Popular Digest of the Laws of England, Civil, Criminal, and Constitutional. Fcp. 8vo. 9s.

CALVERT. — *THE WIFE'S MANUAL;* or Prayers, Thoughts, and Songs on Several Occasions of a Matron's Life. By the late W. CALVERT, Minor Canon of St. Paul's. Printed and ornamented in the style of *Queen Elizabeth's Prayer Book*. Crown 8vo. 6s.

CARLYLE. — *THOMAS AND JANE WELSH CARLYLE.*

THOMAS CARLYLE, a History of the first Forty Years of his Life, 1795–1835. By J. A. FROUDE, M.A. With 2 Portraits and 4 Illustrations, 2 vols. 8vo. 32s.

THOMAS CARLYLE, a History of his Life in London: from 1834 to his death in 1881. By JAMES A. FROUDE, M.A. with Portrait engraved on steel. 2 vols. 8vo. 32s.

REMINISCENCES. By THOMAS CARLYLE. Edited by J. A. FROUDE, M.A. 2 vols. crown 8vo. 18s.

LETTERS AND MEMORIALS OF JANE WELSH CARLYLE. Prepared for publication by THOMAS CARLYLE, and edited by J. A. FROUDE, M.A. 3 vols. 8vo. 36s.

CATES. — *A DICTIONARY OF GENERAL BIOGRAPHY.* Fourth Edition, with Supplement brought down to the end of 1884. By W. L. R. CATES. 8vo. 28s. cloth; 35s. half-bound russia. The Supplement, 1881-4, 2s. 6d.

CHESNEY. — *WATERLOO LECTURES;* a Study of the Campaign of 1815. By Col. C. C. CHESNEY, R.E. 8vo. 10s. 6d.

CICERO. — *THE CORRESPONDENCE OF CICERO:* a revised Text, with Notes and Prolegomena.—Vol. I., The Letters to the end of Cicero's Exile. By ROBERT Y. TYRRELL, M.A., Fellow of Trinity College, Dublin, 12s.

COATS. — *A MANUAL OF PATHOLOGY.* By JOSEPH COATS, M.D. Pathologist to the Western Infirmary and the Sick Children's Hospital, Glasgow; formerly Pathologist to the Royal Infirmary, and President of the Pathological and Clinical Society of Glasgow. With 339 Illustrations engraved on Wood. 8vo. 31s. 6d.

COLENSO. — *THE PENTATEUCH AND BOOK OF JOSHUA CRITICALLY EXAMINED.* By J. W. COLENSO, D.D., late Bishop of Natal. Crown 8vo. 6s.

CONDER. — *A HANDBOOK TO THE BIBLE,* or Guide to the Study of the Holy Scriptures derived from Ancient Monuments and Modern Exploration. By F. R. CONDER, and Lieut. C. R. CONDER, R.E. Post 8vo. 7s. 6d.

CONINGTON. — *Works by John Conington, M.A.*
The Æneid of Virgil. Translated into English Verse. Crown 8vo. 9s.
The Poems of Virgil. Translated into English Prose. Crown 8vo. 9s.

CONTANSEAU. — *Works by Professor Léon Contanseau.*
A Practical Dictionary of the French and English Languages. Post 8vo. 3s. 6d.
A Pocket Dictionary of the French and English Languages; being a careful Abridgment of the Author's 'Practical French and English Dictionary.' Square 18mo. 1s. 6d.

CONYBEARE & HOWSON. — *The Life and Epistles of St. Paul.* By the Rev. W. J. Conybeare, M.A., and the Very Rev. J. S. Howson, D.D. Dean of Chester.
Library Edition, with all the Original Illustrations, Maps, Landscapes on Steel, Woodcuts, &c. 2 vols. 4to. 42s.
Intermediate Edition, with a Selection of Maps, Plates, and Wood-cuts. 2 vols. square crown 8vo. 21s.
Student's Edition, revised and condensed, with 46 Illustrations and Maps. 1 vol. crown 8vo. 7s. 6d.

COOKE. — *Tablets of Anatomy and Physiology.* By Thomas Cooke, F.R.C.S. Being a Synopsis of Demonstrations given in the Westminster Hospital Medical School, A.D. 1871-1875. Anatomy, complete, Second Edition, 4to. 15s. Physiology, complete, Second Edition, 4to. 10s.
** These Tablets may still be had in separate Fasciculi as originally published.

COX. — *Works by the Rev. Sir G. W. Cox, Bart., M.A.*
A General History of Greece: from the Earliest Period to the Death of Alexander the Great; with a Sketch of the Subsequent History to the Present Time. With 11 Maps and Plans. Crown 8vo. 7s. 6d.
Lives of Greek Statesmen. Solon-Themistocles. Fcp. 8vo. 2s. 6d.

CRAWFORD. — *Across the Pampas and the Andes.* By Robert Crawford, M.A. With Map and 7 Illustrations. Crown 8vo. 7s. 6d.

CREIGHTON. — *History of the Papacy during the Reformation.* By the Rev. M. Creighton, M.A. Vols. I. and II. 8vo. 32s.

CRESY. — *Encyclopædia of Civil Engineering,* Historical, Theoretical, and Practical. By Edward Cresy. With above 3,000 Woodcuts, 8vo. 25s.

CULLEY. — *Handbook of Practical Telegraphy.* By R. S. Culley, M. Inst. C.E. Plates and Woodcuts. 8vo. 16s.

DANTE. — *The Divine Comedy of Dante Alighieri.* Translated verse for verse from the Original into Terza Rima. By James Innes Minchin. Crown 8vo. 15s.

DAVIDSON. — *An Introduction to the Study of the New Testament,* Critical, Exegetical, and Theological. By the Rev. S. Davidson, D.D. LL.D. Revised Edition. 2 vols. 8vo. 30s.

DEAD SHOT, The, *or Sportsman's Complete Guide*; a Treatise on the Use of the Gun, with Lessons in the Art of Shooting Game of all kinds, and Wild-Fowl, also Pigeon-Shooting, and Dog-Breaking. By Marksman. With 13 Illustrations. Crown 8vo. 10s. 6d.

DECAISNE & LE MAOUT. — *A General System of Botany.* Translated from the French of E. Le Maout, M.D., and J. Decaisne, by Lady Hooker; with Additions by Sir J. D. Hooker, C.B. F.R.S. Imp. 8vo. with 5,500 Woodcuts, 31s. 6d.

DENT. — *Above the Snow Line:* Mountaineering Sketches between 1870 and 1880. By Clinton Dent, Vice-President of the Alpine Club. With Two Engravings by Edward Whymper and an Illustration by Percy Macquoid. Crown 8vo. 7s. 6d.

D'EON DE BEAUMONT. — *The Strange Career of the Chevalier D'Eon de Beaumont,* Minister Plenipotentiary from France to Great Britain in 1763. By Captain J. Buchan Telfer, R.N. F.S.A. F.R.G.S. With 3 Portraits. 8vo. 12s.

DE TOCQUEVILLE. — *Democracy in America.* By Alexis de Tocqueville. Translated by H. Reeve. 2 vols. crown 8vo. 16s.

DE WITT. — *The Life of John de Witt, Grand Pensionary of Holland;* or, Twenty Years of a Parliamentary Republic in the 17th Century. By M. Antonin Lefèvre Pontalis. Translated from the French by S. E. and A. Stephenson. 2 vols. 8vo.

LONGMANS & CO.'S LIST OF GENERAL AND SCIENTIFIC BOOKS.   9

DEWES. —*THE LIFE AND LETTERS OF ST. PAUL.* By ALFRED DEWES, M.A. LL.D. D.D. Vicar of St. Augustine's, Pendlebury. With 4 Maps. 8vo. 7s. 6d.

DICKINSON. — *ON RENAL AND URINARY AFFECTIONS.* By W. HOWSHIP DICKINSON, M.D. Cantab. F.R.C.P. &c. With 12 Plates and 122 Woodcuts. 3 vols. 8vo. £3. 4s. 6d.

*** The Three Parts may be had separately: PART I.—*Diabetes*, 10s. 6d. sewed, 12s. cloth. PART II. *Albuminuria*, 20s. sewed, 21s. cloth. PART III.—*Miscellaneous Affections of the Kidneys and Urine*, 30s. sewed, 31s. 6d. cloth.

DIXON.—*RURAL BIRD LIFE;* Essays on Ornithology, with Instructions for Preserving Objects relating to that Science. By CHARLES DIXON. With 45 Woodcuts. Crown 8vo. 5s.

DOWELL. *A HISTORY OF TAXATION AND TAXES IN ENGLAND, FROM THE EARLIEST TIMES TO THE PRESENT DAY.* By STEPHEN DOWELL, Assistant Solicitor of Inland Revenue. 4 vols. 8vo. 48s.

DOYLE.—*THE ENGLISH IN AMERICA:* Virginia, Maryland, and the Carolinas. By J. A. DOYLE, Fellow of All Souls' College, Oxford. 8vo. Map, 18s.

DRESSER.—*JAPAN; ITS ARCHITECTURE, ART, AND ART MANUFACTURES.* By CHRISTOPHER DRESSER, Ph.D. F.L.S. &c. With 202 Graphic Illustrations engraved on Wood for the most part by Native Artists in Japan, the rest by G. Pearson, after Photographs and Drawings made on the spot. Square crown 8vo. 31s. 6d.

EASTLAKE.—*FIVE GREAT PAINTERS;* Essays on Leonardo da Vinci, Michael Angelo, Titian, Raphael, Albert Dürer. By LADY EASTLAKE. 2 vols. Crown 8vo. 16s.

EASTLAKE.—*WORKS BY C. L. EASTLAKE, F.R.S. B.A.*

HINTS ON HOUSEHOLD TASTE IN FURNITURE, UPHOLSTERY, &c. With 100 Illustrations. Square crown 8vo. 14s.

NOTES ON FOREIGN PICTURE GALLERIES. Crown 8vo.

The Louvre Gallery, *Paris*, with 114 Illustrations, 7s. 6d.

The Brera Gallery, *Milan*, with 55 Illustrations, 5s.

The Old Pinakothek, *Munich*, with 107 Illustrations, 7s. 6d.

EDERSHEIM.—*WORKS BY THE REV. ALFRED EDERSHEIM, D.D.*

THE LIFE AND TIMES OF JESUS THE MESSIAH. 2 vols. 8vo. 42s.

PROPHECY AND HISTORY IN RELATION TO THE MESSIAH: the Warburton Lectures, delivered at Lincoln's Inn Chapel, 1880-1884. 8vo. 12s.
[*Nearly ready.*

EDWARDS. *OUR SEAMARKS.* By E. PRICE EDWARDS. With numerous Illustrations of Lighthouses, &c. engraved on Wood by G. H. Ford. Crown 8vo. 8s. 6d.

ELLICOTT. — *WORKS BY C. J. ELLICOTT, D.D.*, Bishop of Gloucester and Bristol.

A CRITICAL AND GRAMMATICAL COMMENTARY ON ST. PAUL'S EPISTLES. 8vo. Galatians, 8s. 6d. Ephesians, 8s. 6d. Pastoral Epistles, 10s. 6d. Philippians, Colossians, and Philemon, 10s. 6d. Thessalonians, 7s. 6d. I. Corinthians
[*Nearly ready.*

HISTORICAL LECTURES ON THE LIFE OF OUR LORD JESUS CHRIST. 8vo. 12s.

EPOCHS OF ANCIENT HISTORY.
Edited by the Rev. Sir G. W. Cox, Bart. M.A. and C. SANKEY, M.A.

Beesly's Gracchi, Marius and Sulla, 2s. 6d.
Capes's Age of the Antonines, 2s. 6d.
—— Early Roman Empire, 2s. 6d.
Cox's Athenian Empire, 2s. 6d.
—— Greeks and Persians, 2s. 6d.
Curteis's Macedonian Empire, 2s. 6d.
Ihne's Rome to its Capture by the Gauls, 2s. 6d.
Merivale's Roman Triumvirates, 2s. 6d.
Sankey's Spartan and Theban Supremacies, 2s. 6d.
Smith's Rome and Carthage, 2s. 6d.

EPOCHS OF MODERN HISTORY.
Edited by C. COLBECK, M.A.

Church's Beginning of the Middle Ages, 2s. 6d.
Cox's Crusades, 2s. 6d.
Creighton's Age of Elizabeth, 2s. 6d.
Gairdner's Lancaster and York, 2s. 6d.
Gardiner's Puritan Revolution, 2s. 6d.
—————— Thirty Years' War, 2s. 6d.
—————— (Mrs.) French Revolution, 2s. 6d.
Hale's Fall of the Stuarts, 2s. 6d.
Johnson's Normans in Europe, 2s. 6d.
Longman's Frederick the Great, 2s. 6d.
Ludlow's War of American Independence, 2s. 6d.
M'Carthy's Epoch of Reform, 1830-1850, 2s. 6d.
Morris's Age of Anne, 2s. 6d.
Seebohm's Protestant Revolution, 2s. 6d.
Stubbs' Early Plantagenets, 2s. 6d.
Warburton's Edward III. 2s. 6d.

ERICHSEN.—*Works by John Eric Erichsen, F.R.S.*

THE SCIENCE AND ART OF SURGERY; Being a Treatise on Surgical Injuries, Diseases, and Operations. Illustrated by Engravings on Wood. 2 vols 8vo. 42s.; or bound in half-russia, 60s.

ON CONCUSSION OF THE SPINE, NERVOUS SHOCKS, and other Obscure Injuries of the Nervous System in their Clinical and Medico-Legal Aspects. Crown 8vo. 10s. 6d.

EVANS.—THE BRONZE IMPLEMENTS, ARMS, AND ORNAMENTS OF GREAT BRITAIN AND IRELAND. By JOHN EVANS, D.C.L. LL.D. F.R.S. With 540 Illustrations. 8vo. 25s.

EWALD.—*Works by Professor Heinrich Ewald, of Göttingen.*

THE ANTIQUITIES OF ISRAEL. Translated from the German by H. S. SOLLY, M.A. 8vo. 12s. 6d.

THE HISTORY OF ISRAEL. Translated from the German. Vols. I.–V. 8vo. 63s. Vol. VI. *Christ and his Times*, 8vo. 16s. Vol. VII. *The Apostolic Age*, 8vo. 21s.

FAIRBAIRN.—*Works by Sir W. Fairbairn, Bart, C.E.*

A TREATISE ON MILLS AND MILLWORK, with 18 Plates and 333 Woodcuts. 1 vol. 8vo. 25s.

USEFUL INFORMATION FOR ENGINEERS. With many Plates and Woodcuts. 3 vols. crown 8vo. 31s. 6d.

FARRAR.—LANGUAGE AND LANGUAGES. A Revised Edition of *Chapters on Language and Families of Speech*. By F. W FARRAR, D.D. Crown 8vo. 6s.

FITZWYGRAM. — HORSES AND STABLES. By Major-General Sir F. FITZWYGRAM, Bart. With 39 pages of Illustrations. 8vo. 10s. 6d.

FOX.—THE EARLY HISTORY OF CHARLES JAMES FOX. By the Right Hon. G. O. TREVELYAN, M.P. Library Edition, 8vo. 18s. Cabinet Edition, cr. 8vo. 6s.

FRANCIS.—A BOOK ON ANGLING; or, Treatise on the Art of Fishing in every branch; including full Illustrated Lists of Salmon Flies. By FRANCIS FRANCIS. Post 8vo. Portrait and Plates, 15s.

FREEMAN.—*Works by E. A. Freeman, D.C.L.*

THE HISTORICAL GEOGRAPHY OF EUROPE. With 65 Maps. 2 vols. 8vo. 31s. 6d.

SOME IMPRESSIONS OF THE UNITED STATES. Crown 8vo. 6s.

FRENCH. — NINETEEN CENTURIES OF DRINK IN ENGLAND, a History. By RICHARD VALPY FRENCH, D.C.L. LL.D. F.S.A.; Author of 'The History of Toasting' &c. Crown 8vo. 10s. 6d.

FROUDE.—*Works by James A. Froude, M.A.*

THE HISTORY OF ENGLAND, from the Fall of Wolsey to the Defeat of the Spanish Armada.
Cabinet Edition, 12 vols. cr. 8vo. £3. 12s.
Popular Edition, 12 vols. cr. 8vo. £2. 2s.

SHORT STUDIES ON GREAT SUBJECTS. 4 vols. crown 8vo. 24s.

THE ENGLISH IN IRELAND IN THE EIGHTEENTH CENTURY. 3 vols. crown 8vo. 18s.

THOMAS CARLYLE, a History of the first Forty Years of his Life, 1795 to 1835. 2 vols. 8vo. 32s.

THOMAS CARLYLE, a History of His Life in London from 1834 to his death in 1881. By JAMES A. FROUDE, M.A. with Portrait engraved on steel. 2 vols. 8vo. 32s.

GANOT.—*Works by Professor Ganot. Translated by E. ATKINSON, Ph.D. F.C.S.*

ELEMENTARY TREATISE ON PHYSICS, for the use of Colleges and Schools. With 5 Coloured Plates and 898 Woodcuts. Large crown 8vo. 15s.

NATURAL PHILOSOPHY FOR GENERAL READERS AND YOUNG PERSONS. With 2 Plates and 471 Woodcuts. Crown 8vo. 7s. 6d.

GARDINER.—*Works by Samuel Rawson Gardiner, LL.D.*

HISTORY OF ENGLAND, from the Accession of James I. to the Outbreak of the Civil War, 1603-1642. Cabinet Edition, thoroughly revised. 10 vols. crown 8vo. price 6s. each.

OUTLINE OF ENGLISH HISTORY, B.C. 55-A.D. 1880. With 96 Woodcuts, fcp. 8vo. 2s. 6d.

*** For Professor Gardiner's other Works, see 'Epochs of Modern History,' p. 9.

GARROD. — *Works by Alfred Baring Garrod, M.D. F.R.S.*

A Treatise on Gout and Rheumatic Gout (Rheumatoid Arthritis). With 6 Plates, comprising 21 Figures (14 Coloured), and 27 Illustrations engraved on Wood. 8vo. 21s.

The Essentials of Materia Medica and Therapeutics. Revised and edited, under the supervision of the Author, by E. B. Baxter, M.D, F.R.C.P. Professor of Materia Medica and Therapeutics in King's College, London. Crown 8vo. 12s. 6d.

GOETHE.—*Faust.* Translated by T. E. Webb, LL.D. Reg. Prof. of Laws and Public Orator in the Univ. of Dublin. 8vo. 12s. 6d.

Faust. A New Translation, chiefly in Blank Verse; with a complete Introduction and Copious Notes. By James Adey Birds, B.A. F.G.S. Large crown 8vo. 12s. 6d.

Faust. The German Text, with an English Introduction and Notes for Students. By Albert M. Selss, M.A. Ph.D. Crown 8vo. 5s.

GOODEVE. — *Works by T. M. Goodeve, M.A.*

Principles of Mechanics. With 253 Woodcuts. Crown 8vo. 6s.

The Elements of Mechanism. With 342 Woodcuts. Crown 8vo. 6s.

GRANT.— *Works by Sir Alexander Grant, Bart. LL.D. D.C.L. &c.*

The Story of the University of Edinburgh during its First Three Hundred Years. With numerous Illustrations. 2 vols. 8vo. 36s.

The Ethics of Aristotle. The Greek Text illustrated by Essays and Notes. 2 vols. 8vo. 32s.

GREVILLE. — Journal of the Reigns of King George IV. and King William IV. By the late C. C. F. Greville. Edited by H. Reeve, C.B. 3 vols. 8vo. 36s.

GRIMSTON.—*The Hon. Robert Grimston:* a Sketch of his Life. By Frederick Gale. With Portrait. Crown 8vo. 10s. 6d.

GRAY. — Anatomy, Descriptive and Surgical. By Henry Gray, F.R.S. late Lecturer on Anatomy at St. George's Hospital. With 557 large Woodcut Illustrations; those in the First Edition after Original Drawings by Dr. Carter, from Dissections made by the Author and Dr. Carter; the additional Drawings in the Second and subsequent Editions by Dr. Westmacott, and other Demonstrators of Anatomy. Re-edited by T. Pickering Pick, Surgeon to St. George's Hospital. Royal 8vo. 30s.

GWILT.—*An Encyclopædia of Architecture,* Historical, Theoretical, and Practical. By Joseph Gwilt, F.S.A. Illustrated with more than 1,100 Engravings on Wood. Revised, with Alterations and Considerable Additions, by Wyatt Papworth. Additionally illustrated with nearly 400 Wood Engravings by O. Jewitt, and nearly 200 other Woodcuts. 8vo. 52s. 6d.

GROVE.—*The Correlation of Physical Forces.* By the Hon. Sir W. R. Grove, F.R.S. &c. 8vo. 15s.

HALLIWELL-PHILLIPPS. — Outlines of the Life of Shakespeare. By J. O. Halliwell-Phillipps, F.R.S. 8vo. 7s. 6d.

HAMILTON.—*Life of Sir William R. Hamilton,* Kt. LL.D. D.C.L. M.R.I.A. &c. Including Selections from his Poems, Correspondence, and Miscellaneous Writings. By the Rev. R. P. Graves, M.A. Vol. I. 8vo. 15s.

HARTWIG. — *Works by Dr. G. Hartwig.*

The Sea and its Living Wonders. 8vo. with many Illustrations, 10s. 6d.

The Tropical World. With about 200 Illustrations. 8vo. 10s. 6d.

The Polar World; a Description of Man and Nature in the Arctic and Antarctic Regions of the Globe. Maps, Plates, and Woodcuts. 8vo. 10s. 6d.

The Arctic Regions (extracted from the 'Polar World'). 4to. 6d. sewed.

The Subterranean World. With Maps and Woodcuts. 8vo. 10s. 6d.

The Aerial World; a Popular Account of the Phenomena and Life of the Atmosphere. Map, Plates, Woodcuts. 8vo. 10s. 6d.

HARTE.—*ON THE FRONTIER.* Three Stories. By BRET HARTE. 16mo. 1s.

HASSALL. — *WORKS BY ARTHUR HILL HASSALL, M.D.*

FOOD; its Adulterations and the Methods for their Detection. Illustrated. Crown 8vo. 24s.

SAN REMO, climatically and medically considered. With 30 Illustrations. Crown 8vo. 5s.

HAUGHTON. — *SIX LECTURES ON PHYSICAL GEOGRAPHY,* delivered in 1876, with some Additions. By the Rev. SAMUEL HAUGHTON, F.R.S. M.D. D.C.L. With 23 Diagrams. 8vo. 15s.

HAVELOCK. — *MEMOIRS OF SIR HENRY HAVELOCK, K.C.B.* By JOHN CLARK MARSHMAN. Crown 8vo. 3s. 6d.

HAWARD.—*A TREATISE ON ORTHOPÆDIC SURGERY.* By J. WARRINGTON HAWARD, F.R.C.S. Surgeon to St. George's Hospital. With 30 Illustrations engraved on Wood. 8vo. 12s. 6d.

HELMHOLTZ.—*WORKS BY PROFESSOR HELMHOLTZ.*

POPULAR LECTURES ON SCIENTIFIC SUBJECTS. Translated and edited by EDMUND ATKINSON, Ph.D. F.C.S. With a Preface by Professor TYNDALL, F.R.S. and 68 Woodcuts. 2 vols. Crown 8vo. 15s. or separately, 7s. 6d. each.

ON THE SENSATIONS OF TONE AS A PHYSIOLOGICAL BASIS FOR THE THEORY OF MUSIC. Translated by A. J. ELLIS, F.R.S. Second English Edition. Royal 8vo. 21s.

HERSCHEL.—*OUTLINES OF ASTRONOMY.* By Sir J. F. W. HERSCHEL, Bart. M.A. With Plates and Diagrams. Square crown 8vo. 12s.

HEWITT. — *WORKS BY GRAILY HEWITT, M.D.*

THE DIAGNOSIS AND TREATMENT OF DISEASES OF WOMEN, INCLUDING THE DIAGNOSIS OF PREGNANCY. New Edition, in great part re-written and much enlarged, with 211 Engravings on Wood, of which 79 are new in this Edition. 8vo. 24s.

THE MECHANICAL SYSTEM OF UTERINE PATHOLOGY. With 31 Life-size Illustrations prepared expressly for this Work. Crown 4to. 7s. 6d.

HICKSON. — *IRELAND IN THE SEVENTEENTH CENTURY;* or, The Irish Massacres of 1641-2, their Causes and Results. Illustrated by Extracts from the unpublished State Papers, the unpublished MSS. in the Bodleian Library, Lambeth Library, &c.; a Selection from the unpublished Depositions relating to the Massacres, and the Reports of the Trials in the High Court of Justice, 1652-4, from the unpublished MSS. By MARY HICKSON. With a Preface by J. A. FROUDE, M.A. 2 vols. 8vo. 28s.

HOBART.—*THE MEDICAL LANGUAGE OF ST. LUKE:* a Proof from Internal Evidence that St. Luke's Gospel and the Acts were written by the same person, and that the writer was a Medical Man. By the Rev. W. K. HOBART, LL.D. 8vo. 16s.

HOLMES.—*A SYSTEM OF SURGERY,* Theoretical and Practical, in Treatises by various Authors. Edited by TIMOTHY HOLMES, M.A. Surgeon to St. George's Hospital; and J. W. HULKE, F.R.S. Surgeon to the Middlesex Hospital. In 3 Volumes, with Coloured Plates and Illustrations on Wood. 3 vols. royal 8vo. price Four Guineas.

HOMER.—*THE ILIAD OF HOMER,* Homometrically translated by C. B. CAYLEY. 8vo. 12s. 6d.

THE ILIAD OF HOMER. The Greek Text, with a Verse Translation, by W. C. GREEN, M.A. Vol. I. Books I.–XII. Crown 8vo. 6s.

HOPKINS.—*CHRIST THE CONSOLER;* a Book of Comfort for the Sick. By ELLICE HOPKINS. Fcp. 8vo. 2s. 6d.

HORSES AND ROADS; or How to Keep a Horse Sound on His Legs. By FREE-LANCE. Crown 8vo. 6s.

HORT.—*THE NEW PANTHEON,* or an Introduction to the Mythology of the Ancients. By W. J. HORT. 18mo. 2s. 6d.

HOWITT.—*VISITS TO REMARKABLE PLACES,* Old Halls, Battle-Fields, Scenes illustrative of Striking Passages in English History and Poetry. By WILLIAM HOWITT. With 80 Illustrations engraved on Wood. Crown 8vo. 7s. 6d.

HULLAH.—*WORKS BY JOHN HULLAH, LL.D.*

COURSE OF LECTURES ON THE HISTORY OF MODERN MUSIC. 8vo. 8s. 6d.

COURSE OF LECTURES ON THE TRANSITION PERIOD OF MUSICAL HISTORY. 8vo. 10s. 6d.

HUME.—*The Philosophical Works of David Hume.* Edited by T. H. Green, M.A. and the Rev. T. H. Grose, M.A. 4 vols. 8vo, 56s. Or separately, Essays, 2 vols. 28s. Treatise on Human Nature. 2 vols. 28s.

HUSBAND.—*Examination Questions in Anatomy, Physiology, Botany, Materia Medica, Surgery, Medicine, Midwifery, and State-Medicine.* Arranged by H. A. Husband, M.B. M.C. M.R.C.S. L.S.A. &c. 32mo. 4s. 6d.

INGELOW.—*Poetical Works of Jean Ingelow.* New Edition, reprinted, with Additional Matter, from the 23rd and 6th Editions of the two volumes respectively. With 2 Vignettes. 2 vols. Fcp. 8vo. 12s.

IN THE OLDEN TIME.—A Novel. By the Author of 'Mademoiselle Mori.' Crown 8vo. 6s.

JAMESON.—*Works by Mrs. Jameson.*
Legends of the Saints and Martyrs. With 19 Etchings and 187 Woodcuts. 2 vols. 31s. 6d.
Legends of the Madonna, the Virgin Mary as represented in Sacred and Legendary Art. With 27 Etchings and 165 Woodcuts. 1 vol. 21s.
Legends of the Monastic Orders. With 11 Etchings and 88 Woodcuts. 1 vol. 21s.
History of the Saviour, His Types and Precursors. Completed by Lady Eastlake. With 13 Etchings and 281 Woodcuts. 2 vols. 42s.

JEFFERIES.—*Works by Richard Jefferies.*
The Story of My Heart: My Autobiography. Crown 8vo. 5s.
Red Deer. Crown 8vo. 4s. 6d.

JOHNSON.—*The Patentee's Manual;* a Treatise on the Law and Practice of Letters Patent, for the use of Patentees and Inventors. By J. Johnson and J. H. Johnson. 8vo. 10s. 6d.

JOHNSTON.—*A General Dictionary of Geography,* Descriptive, Physical, Statistical, and Historical; a complete Gazetteer of the World. By Keith Johnston. Medium 8vo. 42s.

JONES.—*The Health of the Senses: Sight, Hearing, Voice, Smell and Taste, Skin;* with Hints on Health, Diet, Education, Health Resorts of Europe, &c. By H. Macnaughton Jones, M.D. Crown 8vo. 3s. 6d.

JUKES.—*Works by the Rev. Andrew Jukes.*
The New Man and the Eternal Life. Crown 8vo. 6s.
The Types of Genesis. Crown 8vo. 7s. 6d.
The Second Death and the Restitution of All Things. Crown 8vo. 3s. 6d.
The Mystery of the Kingdom. Crown 8vo. 2s. 6d.

JUSTINIAN.—*The Institutes of Justinian;* Latin Text, chiefly that of Huschke, with English Introduction, Translation, Notes, and Summary. By Thomas C. Sandars, M.A. Barrister-at-Law. 8vo. 18s.

KALISCH.—*Works by M. M. Kalisch, M.A.*
Bible Studies. Part I. The Prophecies of Balaam. 8vo. 10s. 6d. Part II. The Book of Jonah. 8vo. 10s. 6d.
Commentary on the Old Testament; with a New Translation. Vol. I. Genesis, 8vo. 18s. or adapted for the General Reader, 12s. Vol. II. Exodus, 15s. or adapted for the General Reader, 12s. Vol. III. Leviticus, Part I. 15s. or adapted for the General Reader, 8s. Vol. IV. Leviticus, Part II. 15s. or adapted for the General Reader, 8s.

KANT.—*Critique of Practical Reason,* and other Works on the Theory of Ethics. By Emmanuel Kant Translated by Thomas Kingsmill Abbott, B.D. With Memoir and Portrait. 8vo. 12s. 6d.

KELLER.—*The Lake Dwellings of Switzerland,* and other Parts of Europe. By Dr. F. Keller, President of the Antiquarian Association of Zürich. Translated and arranged by John E. Lee, F.S.A. F.G.S. 2 vols. royal 8vo. with 206 Illustrations, 42s.

KERL.—*A Practical Treatise on Metallurgy.* By Professor Kerl. Adapted from the last German Edition by W. Crookes, F.R.S. &c. and E. Röhrig, Ph.D. 3 vols. 8vo. with 625 Woodcuts, £4. 19s.

KILLICK.—*Handbook to Mill's System of Logic.* By the Rev. A. H. Killick, M.A. Crown 8vo. 3s. 6d.

KOLBE.—*A Short Text-book of Inorganic Chemistry.* By Dr. Hermann Kolbe. Translated from the German by T. S. Humpidge, Ph.D. With a Coloured Table of Spectra and 66 Illustrations. Crown 8vo. 7s. 6d.

LANG.—*WORKS BY ANDREW LANG, late Fellow of Merton College.*
CUSTOM AND MYTH; Studies of Early Usage and Belief. With 15 Illustrations. Crown 8vo. 7s. 6d.
THE PRINCESS NOBODY: a Tale of Fairyland. After the Drawings by Richard Doyle, printed in colours by Edmund Evans. Post 4to. 5s. boards.

LATHAM.—*WORKS BY ROBERT G. LATHAM, M.A. M.D.*
A DICTIONARY OF THE ENGLISH LANGUAGE. Founded on the Dictionary of Dr. JOHNSON. Four vols. 4to. £7.
A DICTIONARY OF THE ENGLISH LANGUAGE. Abridged from Dr. Latham's Edition of Johnson's Dictionary. One Volume. Medium 8vo. 14s.
HANDBOOK OF THE ENGLISH LANGUAGE. Crown 8vo. 6s.

LECKY.—*WORKS BY W. E. H. LECKY.*
HISTORY OF ENGLAND IN THE 18TH CENTURY. 4 vols. 8vo. 1700–1784, £3. 12s.
THE HISTORY OF EUROPEAN MORALS FROM AUGUSTUS TO CHARLEMAGNE. 2 vols. crown 8vo. 16s.
HISTORY OF THE RISE AND INFLUENCE OF THE SPIRIT OF RATIONALISM IN EUROPE. 2 vols. crown 8vo. 16s.
LEADERS OF PUBLIC OPINION IN IRELAND. — Swift, Flood, Grattan, O'Connell. Crown 8vo. 7s. 6d.

LEWES.—*THE HISTORY OF PHILOSOPHY, from Thales to Comte.* By GEORGE HENRY LEWES. 2 vols. 8vo. 32s.

LEWIS. — *ON THE INFLUENCE OF AUTHORITY IN MATTERS OF OPINION.* By Sir G. C. LEWIS, Bart. 8vo. 14s.

LINDLEY and MOORE. — *THE TREASURY OF BOTANY*, or Popular Dictionary of the Vegetable Kingdom. Edited by J. LINDLEY, F.R.S. and T. MOORE, F.L.S. With 274 Woodcuts and 20 Steel Plates. Two Parts, fcp. 8vo. 12s.

LIVEING.—*WORKS BY ROBERT LIVEING, M.A. and M.D. Cantab.*
HANDBOOK ON DISEASES OF THE SKIN. With especial reference to Diagnosis and Treatment. Fcp. 8vo. 5s.
NOTES ON THE TREATMENT OF SKIN DISEASES. 18mo. 3s.
ELEPHANTIASIS GRÆCORUM, OR TRUE LEPROSY. Crown 8vo. 4s. 6d.

LITTLE.—*ON IN-KNEE DISTORTION (Genu Valgum)*: Its Varieties and Treatment with and without Surgical Operation. By W. J. LITTLE, M.D. Assisted by MUIRHEAD LITTLE, M.R.C.S. With 40 Illustrations. 8vo. 7s. 6d.

LLOYD.—*A TREATISE ON MAGNETISM*, General and Terrestrial. By H. LLOYD, D.D. D.C.L. 8vo. 10s. 6d.

LLOYD.—*THE SCIENCE OF AGRICULTURE.* By F. J. LLOYD. 8vo. 12s.

LONGMAN.—*WORKS BY WILLIAM LONGMAN, F.S.A.*
LECTURES ON THE HISTORY OF ENGLAND from the Earliest Times to the Death of King Edward II. Maps and Illustrations. 8vo. 15s.
HISTORY OF THE LIFE AND TIMES OF EDWARD III. With 9 Maps, 8 Plates, and 16 Woodcuts. 2 vols. 8vo. 28s.

LONGMAN.—*WORKS BY FREDERICK W. LONGMAN, Balliol College, Oxon.*
CHESS OPENINGS. Fcp. 8vo. 2s. 6d.
FREDERICK THE GREAT AND THE SEVEN YEARS' WAR. With 2 Coloured Maps. 8vo. 2s. 6d.
A NEW POCKET DICTIONARY OF THE GERMAN AND ENGLISH LANGUAGES. Square 18mo. 2s. 6d.

LONGMAN'S MAGAZINE. Published Monthly. Price Sixpence.
Vols. 1–4, 8vo. price 5s. each.

LONGMORE.—*GUNSHOT INJURIES*; Their History, Characteristic Features, Complications, and General Treatment. By Surgeon-General T. LONGMORE, C.B. F.R.C.S. With 58 Illustrations. 8vo. price 31s. 6d.

LOUDON.—*WORKS BY J. C. LOUDON, F.L.S.*
ENCYCLOPÆDIA OF GARDENING; the Theory and Practice of Horticulture, Floriculture, Arboriculture, and Landscape Gardening. With 1,000 Woodcuts. 8vo. 21s.
ENCYCLOPÆDIA OF AGRICULTURE; the Laying-out, Improvement, and Management of Landed Property; the Cultivation and Economy of the Productions of Agriculture. With 1,100 Woodcuts. 8vo. 21s.
ENCYCLOPÆDIA OF PLANTS; the Specific Character, Description, Culture, History, &c. of all Plants found in Great Britain. With 12,000 Woodcuts. 8vo. 42s.

LUBBOCK.—THE ORIGIN OF CIVILIZATION AND THE PRIMITIVE CONDITION OF MAN. By Sir J. LUBBOCK, Bart. M.P. F.R.S. 8vo. Woodcuts, 18s.

LYRA GERMANICA; Hymns Translated from the German by Miss C. WINKWORTH. Fcp. 8vo. 5s.

MACALISTER.—AN INTRODUCTION TO THE SYSTEMATIC ZOOLOGY AND MORPHOLOGY OF VERTEBRATE ANIMALS. By A. MACALISTER, M.D. With 28 Diagrams. 8vo. 10s. 6d.

MACAULAY.—WORKS AND LIFE OF LORD MACAULAY.
HISTORY OF ENGLAND FROM THE ACCESSION OF JAMES THE SECOND:
Student's Edition, 2 vols. crown 8vo. 12s.
People's Edition, 4 vols. crown 8vo. 16s.
Cabinet Edition, 8 vols. post 8vo. 48s.
Library Edition, 5 vols. 8vo. £4.

CRITICAL AND HISTORICAL ESSAYS, with LAYS of ANCIENT ROME, in 1 volume:
Authorised Edition, crown 8vo. 2s. 6d. or 3s. 6d. gilt edges.
Popular Edition, crown 8vo. 2s. 6d.

CRITICAL AND HISTORICAL ESSAYS:
Student's Edition, 1 vol. crown 8vo. 6s.
People's Edition, 2 vols. crown 8vo. 8s.
Cabinet Edition, 4 vols. post 8vo. 24s.
Library Edition, 3 vols. 8vo. 36s.

ESSAYS which may be had separately price 6d. each sewed, 1s. each cloth:
Addison and Walpole.
Frederick the Great.
Croker's Boswell's Johnson.
Hallam's Constitutional History.
Warren Hastings.
The Earl of Chatham (Two Essays).
Ranke and Gladstone.
Milton and Machiavelli.
Lord Bacon.
Lord Clive.
Lord Byron, and The Comic Dramatists of the Restoration.
The Essay on Warren Hastings annotated by S. HALES, 1s. 6d.
The Essay on Lord Clive annotated by H. COURTHOPE-BOWEN, M.A. 2s. 6d.

SPEECHES:
People's Edition, crown 8vo. 3s. 6d.

MISCELLANEOUS WRITINGS
Library Edition, 2 vols. 8vo. Portrait, 21s.
People's Edition, 1 vol. crown 8vo. 4s. 6d.

[*Continued above.*

MACAULAY—WORKS AND LIFE OF LORD MACAULAY—continued.

LAYS OF ANCIENT ROME, &c.
Illustrated by G. Scharf, fcp. 4to. 10s. 6d.
——— Popular Edition, fcp. 4to. 6d. sewed, 1s. cloth.
Illustrated by J. R. Weguelin, crown 8vo. 3s. 6d. cloth extra, gilt edges.
Cabinet Edition, post 8vo. 3s. 6d.
Annotated Edition, fcp. 8vo. 1s. sewed, 1s. 6d. cloth, or 2s. 6d. cloth extra, gilt edges.

SELECTIONS FROM THE WRITINGS OF LORD MACAULAY. Edited, with Occasional Notes, by the Right Hon. G. O. TREVELYAN, M.P. Crown 8vo. 6s.

MISCELLANEOUS WRITINGS AND SPEECHES:
Student's Edition, in ONE VOLUME, crown 8vo. 6s.
Cabinet Edition, including Indian Penal Code, Lays of Ancient Rome, and Miscellaneous Poems, 4 vols. post 8vo. 24s.

THE COMPLETE WORKS OF LORD MACAULAY. Edited by his Sister, Lady TREVELYAN.
Library Edition, with Portrait, 8 vols. demy 8vo. £5. 5s.
Cabinet Edition, 16 vols. post 8vo. £4. 16s.

THE LIFE AND LETTERS OF LORD MACAULAY. By the Right Hon. G. O. TREVELYAN, M.P.
Popular Edition, 1 vol. crown 8vo. 6s.
Cabinet Edition, 2 vols. post 8vo. 12s.
Library Edition, 2 vols. 8vo. with Portrait, 36s.

MACDONALD,—WORKS BY GEORGE MACDONALD, LL.D.
UNSPOKEN SERMONS. Second Series. Crown 8vo. 7s. 6d.
A BOOK OF STRIFE, IN THE FORM OF THE DIARY OF AN OLD SOUL:
Poems. 12mo. 6s.
HAMLET. A Study with the Texts of the Folio of 1623. 8vo. 12s.

MACFARREN.—LECTURES ON HARMONY, delivered at the Royal Institution. By Sir G. A. MACFARREN. 8vo. 12s.

MACKENZIE.—ON THE USE OF THE LARYNGOSCOPE IN DISEASES OF THE THROAT; with an Appendix on Rhinoscopy. By MORELL MACKENZIE, M.D. Lond. With 47 Woodcut Illustrations. 8vo. 6s.

MACLEOD.—*Works by Henry D. Macleod, M.A.*

Principles of Economical Philosophy. In 2 vols. Vol. I. 8vo. 15s. Vol. II. Part I. 12s.

The Elements of Economics. In 2 vols. Vol. I. crown 8vo. 7s. 6d. Vol. II. crown 8vo.

The Elements of Banking. Crown 8vo. 5s.

The Theory and Practice of Banking. Vol. I. 8vo. 12s. Vol. II.

Elements of Political Economy. 8vo. 16s.

Economics for Beginners. 8vo. 2s. 6d.

Lectures on Credit and Banking. 8vo. 5s.

MACNAMARA.—*Himalayan and Sub-Himalayan Districts of British India*, their Climate, Medical Topography, and Disease Distribution. By F. N. Macnamara, M.D. With Map and Fever Chart. 8vo. 21s.

McCULLOCH.—*The Dictionary of Commerce and Commercial Navigation* of the late J. R. McCulloch, of H.M. Stationery Office. Latest Edition, containing the most recent Statistical Information by A. J. Wilson. 1 vol. medium 8vo. with 11 Maps and 30 Charts, price 63s. cloth, or 70s. strongly half-bound in russia.

MAHAFFY.—*A History of Classical Greek Literature.* By the Rev. J. P. Mahaffy, M.A. Crown 8vo. Vol. I. Poets, 7s. 6d. Vol. II. Prose Writers, 7s. 6d.

MALMESBURY.—*Memoirs of an Ex-Minister;* an Autobiography. By the Earl of Malmesbury, G.C.B. Cheap Edition, 1 vol. crown 8vo. 7s. 6d.

MANNING.—*The Temporal Mission of the Holy Ghost;* or, Reason and Revelation. By H. E. Manning, D.D. Cardinal-Archbishop. Crown 8vo. 8s. 6d.

THE MARITIME ALPS AND THEIR SEABOARD. By the Author of 'Vèra,' 'Blue Roses,' &c. With 14 Full-page Illustrations and 15 Woodcuts in the Text. 8vo. 21s.

MARTINEAU.—*Works by James Martineau, D.D.*

Hours of Thought on Sacred Things. Two Volumes of Sermons. 2 vols. crown 8vo. 7s. 6d. each.

Endeavours after the Christian Life. Discourses. Crown 8vo. 7s. 6d.

MAUNDER'S TREASURIES.

Biographical Treasury. Reconstructed, revised, and brought down to the year 1882, by W. L. R. Cates. Fcp. 8vo. 6s.

Treasury of Natural History; or, Popular Dictionary of Zoology. Fcp. 8vo. with 900 Woodcuts, 6s.

Treasury of Geography; Physical, Historical, Descriptive, and Political. With 7 Maps and 16 Plates. Fcp. 8vo. 6s.

Historical Treasury; Outlines of Universal History, Separate Histories of all Nations. Revised by the Rev. Sir G. W. Cox, Bart. M.A. Fcp. 8vo. 6s.

Treasury of Knowledge and Library of Reference. Comprising an English Dictionary and Grammar, Universal Gazetteer, Classical Dictionary, Chronology, Law Dictionary, &c. Fcp. 8vo. 6s.

Scientific and Literary Treasury: a Popular Encyclopædia of Science, Literature, and Art. Fcp. 8vo. 6s.

MAXWELL.—*Don John of Austria;* or, Passages from the History of the Sixteenth Century, 1547-1578. By the late Sir William Stirling Maxwell, Bart. K.T. With numerous Illustrations engraved on Wood taken from Authentic Contemporary Sources. Library Edition. 2 vols. royal 8vo. 42s.

MAY.—*Works by the Right Hon. Sir Thomas Erskine May, K.C.B.*

The Constitutional History of England since the Accession of George III. 1760-1870. 3 vols. crown 8vo. 18s.

Democracy in Europe; a History. 2 vols. 8vo. 32s.

MELVILLE.—*In the Lena Delta;* a Narrative of the Search for Lieut.-Commander De Long and his Companions, followed by an account of the Greely Relief Expedition, and a Proposed Method of reaching the North Pole. By George W. Melville, Chief Engineer, U.S.N. Edited by Melville Philips. With Maps and Illustrations. 8vo. 14s.

MENDELSSOHN.—*The Letters of Felix Mendelssohn.* Translated by Lady Wallace. 2 vols. crown 8vo. 10s.

MERIVALE.—*Works by the Very Rev. Charles Merivale, D.D. Dean of Ely.*
History of the Romans under the Empire. 8 vols. post 8vo. 48s.
The Fall of the Roman Republic: a Short History of the Last Century of the Commonwealth. 12mo. 7s. 6d.
General History of Rome from B.C. 753 to A.D. 476. Crown 8vo. 7s. 6d.
The Roman Triumvirates. With Maps. Fcp. 8vo. 2s. 6d.

MILES. — *Works by William Miles.*
The Horse's Foot, and How to keep it Sound. Imp. 8vo. 12s. 6d.
Stables and Stable Fittings. Imp. 8vo. with 13 Plates, 15s.
Remarks on Horses' Teeth, addressed to Purchasers. Post 8vo. 1s. 6d.
Plain Treatise on Horse-shoeing. Post 8vo. Woodcuts, 2s. 6d.

MILL.—*Analysis of the Phenomena of the Human Mind.* By James Mill. With Notes, Illustrative and Critical. 2 vols. 8vo. 28s.

MILL.—*Works by John Stuart Mill.*
Principles of Political Economy.
Library Edition, 2 vols. 8vo. 30s.
People's Edition, 1 vol. crown 8vo. 5s.
A System of Logic, Ratiocinative and Inductive.
Library Edition, 2 vols. 8vo. 25s.
People's Edition, crown 8vo. 5s.
On Liberty. Crown 8vo. 1s. 4d.
On Representative Government. Crown 8vo. 2s.
Autobiography, 8vo. 7s. 6d.
Essays on some Unsettled Questions of Political Economy. 8vo. 6s. 6d.
Utilitarianism. 8vo. 5s.
The Subjection of Women. Crown 8vo. 6s.
Examination of Sir William Hamilton's Philosophy. 8vo. 16s.
Dissertations and Discussions. 4 vols. £2. 6s. 6d.
Nature, the Utility of Religion, and Theism. Three Essays. 8vo. 10s. 6d.

MILLER.—*Works by W. Allen Miller, M.D. LL.D.*
The Elements of Chemistry, Theoretical and Practical Re-edited, with Additions, by H. Macleod, F.C.S. 3 vols. 8vo.
Part I. Chemical Physics, 16s.
Part II. Inorganic Chemistry, 24s.
Part III. Organic Chemistry, 31s. 6d.
An Introduction to the Study of Inorganic Chemistry. With 71 Woodcuts. Fcp. 8vo. 3s. 6d.

MILLER. — *Readings in Social Economy.* By Mrs. F. Fenwick Miller, Member of the London School Board. Library Edition, crown 8vo. 5s. Cheap Edition for Schools and Beginners, crown 8vo. 2s.

MILLER.—*Wintering in the Riviera:* with Notes of Travel in Italy and France, and Practical Hints to Travellers. By W. Miller. With 12 Illustrations. Post 8vo. 7s. 6d.

MITCHELL.—*A Manual of Practical Assaying.* By John Mitchell, F.C.S. Revised, with the Recent Discoveries incorporated. By W. Crookes, F.R.S. 8vo. Woodcuts, 31s. 6d.

MODERN NOVELIST'S LIBRARY (THE). Price 2s. each boards, or 2s. 6d. each cloth :—

By the Earl of Beaconsfield, K.G.
    Endymion.
  Lothair.   Henrietta Temple.
  Coningsby.   Contarini Fleming, &c.
  Sybil.   Alroy, Ixion, &c.
  Tancred.   The Young Duke, &c.
  Venetia.   Vivian Grey, &c.
By Mrs. Oliphant.
  In Trust.
By James Payn.
  Thicker than Water.
By Bret Harte.
  In the Carquinez Woods.
By Anthony Trollope.
  Barchester Towers.
  The Warden.
By Major Whyte-Melville.
  Digby Grand   Good for Nothing.
  General Bounce. Holmby House.
  Kate Coventry.   The Interpreter.
  The Gladiators.   Queen's Maries.
By Various Writers.
  The Atelier du Lys.
  Atherstone Priory.
  The Burgomaster's Family.
  Elsa and her Vulture.
  Mademoiselle Mori.
  The Six Sisters of the Valleys.
  Unawares.

MONCK. — *AN INTRODUCTION TO LOGIC.* By WILLIAM H. STANLEY MONCK, M.A. Prof. of Moral Philos. Univ. of Dublin. Crown 8vo. 5s.

MONSELL. — *SPIRITUAL SONGS FOR THE SUNDAYS AND HOLIDAYS THROUGH-OUT THE YEAR.* By J. S. B. MONSELL, LL.D. Fcp. 8vo. 5s. 18mo. 2s.

MOORE. — *THE WORKS OF THOMAS MOORE.*
LALLA ROOKH, TENNIEL'S Edition, with 68 Woodcut Illustrations. Crown 8vo. 10s. 6d.
IRISH MELODIES, MACLISE'S Edition, with 161 Steel Plates. Super-royal 8vo. 21s.

MOREHEAD. — *CLINICAL RESEARCHES ON DISEASE IN INDIA.* By CHARLES MOREHEAD, M.D. Surgeon to the Jamsetjee Jeejeebhoy Hospital. 8vo. 21s.

MORELL. — *HANDBOOK OF LOGIC*, adapted especially for the Use of Schools and Teachers. By J. D. MORELL, LL.D. Fcp. 8vo. 2s.

MOZLEY. — *WORKS BY THE REV. THOMAS MOZLEY, M.A.*
REMINISCENCES CHIEFLY OF ORIEL COLLEGE AND THE OXFORD MOVEMENT. 2 vols. crown 8vo. 18s.
REMINISCENCES CHIEFLY OF TOWNS, VILLAGES, AND SCHOOLS. 2 vols. crown 8vo. 18s.

MÜLLER. — *WORKS BY F. MAX MÜLLER, M.A.*
BIOGRAPHICAL ESSAYS. Crown 8vo. 7s. 6d.
SELECTED ESSAYS ON LANGUAGE, MYTHOLOGY AND RELIGION. 2 vols. crown 8vo. 16s.
LECTURES ON THE SCIENCE OF LANGUAGE. 2 vols. crown 8vo. 16s.
INDIA, WHAT CAN IT TEACH US? A Course of Lectures delivered before the University of Cambridge. 8vo. 12s. 6d.
HIBBERT LECTURES ON THE ORIGIN AND GROWTH OF RELIGION, as illustrated by the Religions of India. Crown 8vo. 7s. 6d.
INTRODUCTION TO THE SCIENCE OF RELIGION: Four Lectures delivered at the Royal Institution; with Notes and Illustrations on Vedic Literature, Polynesian Mythology, the Sacred Books of the East, &c. Crown 8vo. 7s. 6d.
A SANSKRIT GRAMMAR FOR BEGINNERS, in Devanagari and Roman Letters throughout. Royal 8vo. 7s. 6d.

MURCHISON. — *WORKS BY CHARLES MURCHISON, M.D. LL.D. F.R.C.S. &c.*
A TREATISE ON THE CONTINUED FEVERS OF GREAT BRITAIN. New Edition, revised by W. CAYLEY, M.D. Physician to the Middlesex Hospital. 8vo. with numerous Illustrations, 25s.
CLINICAL LECTURES ON DISEASES OF THE LIVER, JAUNDICE, AND ABDOMINAL DROPSY. New Edition, revised by T. LAUDER BRUNTON, M.D. 8vo. with numerous Illustrations. 24s.

NEISON. — *THE MOON*, and the Condition and Configurations of its Surface. By E. NEISON, F.R.A.S. With 26 Maps and 5 Plates. Medium 8vo. 31s. 6d.

NEVILE. — *WORKS BY GEORGE NEVILE, M.A.*
HORSES AND RIDING. With 31 Illustrations. Crown 8vo. 6s.
FARMS AND FARMING. With 13 Illustrations. Crown 8vo. 6s.

NEWMAN. — *APOLOGIA PRO VITA SUÂ*; being a History of his Religious Opinions by Cardinal NEWMAN. Crown 8vo. 6s.

NEW TESTAMENT (THE) of our Lord and Saviour Jesus Christ. Illustrated with Engravings on Wood after Paintings by the Early Masters chiefly of the Italian School. New and Cheaper Edition. 4to. 21s. cloth extra, or 42s. morocco.

NORTHCOTT. — *LATHES AND TURNING*, Simple, Mechanical, and Ornamental. By W. H. NORTHCOTT. With 338 Illustrations. 8vo. 18s.

OLIPHANT. — *MADAM.* A Novel. By Mrs. OLIPHANT. 3 vols. crown 8vo. 21s.

OWEN. — *THE COMPARATIVE ANATOMY AND PHYSIOLOGY OF THE VERTEBRATE ANIMALS.* By Sir RICHARD OWEN, K.C.B. &c. With 1,472 Woodcuts. 3 vols. 8vo. £3. 13s. 6d.

PAGET. — *WORKS BY SIR JAMES PAGET, BART. F.R.S. D.C.L. &c.*
CLINICAL LECTURES AND ESSAYS. Edited by F. HOWARD MARSH, Assistant-Surgeon to St. Bartholomew's Hospital. 8vo. 15s.
LECTURES ON SURGICAL PATHOLOGY. Delivered at the Royal College of Surgeons of England. Re-edited by the AUTHOR and W. TURNER, M.B. 8vo. with 131 Woodcuts, 21s.

PALEY.—*VIEW OF THE EVIDENCES OF CHRISTIANITY AND HORAE PAULINAE.* By Archdeacon PALEY. With Notes and an Analysis, and a Selection of Questions. By ROBERT POTTS, M.A. 8vo. 10s. 6d.

PASOLINI.—*MEMOIR OF COUNT GIUSEPPE PASOLINI, LATE PRESIDENT OF THE SENATE OF ITALY.* Compiled by his SON. Translated and Abridged by the DOWAGER-COUNTESS OF DALHOUSIE. With Portrait. 8vo. 16s.

PASTEUR.—*LOUIS PASTEUR, his Life and Labours.* By his SON-IN-LAW. Translated from the French by Lady CLAUD HAMILTON. Crown 8vo. 7s. 6d.

PAYEN.—*INDUSTRIAL CHEMISTRY;* a Manual for Manufacturers and for Colleges or Technical Schools; a Translation of PAYEN'S 'Précis de Chimie Industrielle.' Edited by B. H. PAUL. With 698 Woodcuts. Medium 8vo. 42s.

PEEL.—*A HIGHLAND GATHERING.* By E. LENNOX PEEL. With 31 Illustrations engraved on Wood by E. Whymper from original Drawings by Charles Whymper. Crown 8vo.

PENNELL.—*'FROM GRAVE TO GAY';* a Volume of Selections from the complete Poems of H. CHOLMONDELEY-PENNELL, Author of 'Puck on Pegasus' &c. Fcp. 8vo. 6s.

PEREIRA.—*MATERIA MEDICA AND THERAPEUTICS.* By Dr. PEREIRA. Abridged, and adapted for the use of Medical and Pharmaceutical Practitioners and Students. Edited by Professor R. BENTLEY, M.R.C.S. F.L.S. and by Professor T. REDWOOD, Ph.D. F.C.S. With 126 Woodcuts, 8vo. 25s.

PERRY.—*A POPULAR INTRODUCTION TO THE HISTORY OF GREEK AND ROMAN SCULPTURE,* designed to Promote the Knowledge and Appreciation of the Remains of Ancient Art. By WALTER C. PERRY. With 268 Illustrations. Square crown 8vo. 31s. 6d.

PIESSE.—*THE ART OF PERFUMERY,* and the Methods of Obtaining the Odours of Plants; with Instructions for the Manufacture of Perfumes, &c. By G. W. S. PIESSE, Ph.D. F.C.S. With 96 Woodcuts, square crown 8vo. 21s.

PLATO.—*THE PARMENIDES OF PLATO;* with Introduction, Analysis, and Notes. By THOMAS MAGUIRE, LL.D. D.Lit. Fellow and Tutor, Trinity College, Dublin. 8vo. 7s. 6d.

POLE.—*THE THEORY OF THE MODERN SCIENTIFIC GAME OF WHIST.* By W. POLE, F.R.S. Fcp. 8vo. 2s. 6d.

PROCTOR.—*WORKS BY R. A PROCTOR.*

THE SUN; Ruler, Light, Fire, and Life of the Planetary System. With Plates and Woodcuts. Crown 8vo. 14s.

THE ORBS AROUND US; a Series of Essays on the Moon and Planets, Meteors and Comets. With Chart and Diagrams, crown 8vo. 7s. 6d.

OTHER WORLDS THAN OURS; The Plurality of Worlds Studied under the Light of Recent Scientific Researches. With 14 Illustrations, crown 8vo. 10s. 6d.

THE MOON; her Motions, Aspects, Scenery, and Physical Condition. With Plates, Charts, Woodcuts, and Lunar Photographs, crown 8vo. 10s. 6d.

UNIVERSE OF STARS; Presenting Researches into and New Views respecting the Constitution of the Heavens. With 22 Charts and 22 Diagrams, 8vo. 10s. 6d.

NEW STAR ATLAS for the Library, the School, and the Observatory, in 12 Circular Maps (with 2 Index Plates). Crown 8vo. 5s.

LARGER STAR ATLAS for the Library, in 12 Circular Maps, with Introduction and 2 Index Pages. Folio, 15s. or Maps only, 12s. 6d.

LIGHT SCIENCE FOR LEISURE HOURS; Familiar Essays on Scientific Subjects, Natural Phenomena, &c. 3 vols. crown 8vo. 7s. 6d. each.

STUDIES OF VENUS-TRANSITS; an Investigation of the Circumstances of the Transits of Venus in 1874 and 1882. With 7 Diagrams and 10 Plates. 8vo. 5s.

TRANSITS OF VENUS. A Popular Account of Past and Coming Transits from the First Observed by Horrocks in 1639 to the Transit of 2012. With 20 Lithographic Plates (12 Coloured) and 38 Illustrations engraved on Wood, 8vo. 8s. 6d.

ESSAYS ON ASTRONOMY. A Series of Papers on Planets and Meteors, &c. With 10 Plates and 24 Woodcuts, 8vo. 12s.

A TREATISE ON THE CYCLOID AND ON ALL FORMS OF CYCLOIDAL CURVES, and on the use of Cycloidal Curves in dealing with the Motions of Planets, Comets, &c. &c. With 161 Diagrams. Crown 8vo. 10s. 6d.

PLEASANT WAYS IN SCIENCE, with numerous Illustrations. Crown 8vo. 6s.

MYTHS AND MARVELS OF ASTRONOMY, with numerous Illustrations. Crown 8vo. 6s. [*Continued on next page.*

PROCTOR—*Works by R. A. Proctor*—continued.

THE 'KNOWLEDGE' LIBRARY. Edited by RICHARD A. PROCTOR.

How to Play Whist: with the Laws and Etiquette of Whist; Whist Whittlings, and Forty fully-annotated Games. By 'FIVE OF CLUBS' (R. A. Proctor). Crown 8vo. 5s.

Science Byways. A Series of Familiar Dissertations on Life in Other Worlds. By RICHARD A. PROCTOR. Crown 8vo. 6s.

The Poetry of Astronomy. A Series of Familiar Essays on the Heavenly Bodies. By RICHARD A. PROCTOR. Crown 8vo. 6s.

Nature Studies. Reprinted from *Knowledge.* By GRANT ALLEN, ANDREW WILSON, THOMAS FOSTER, EDWARD CLODD, and RICHARD A. PROCTOR. Crown 8vo. 6s.

Leisure Readings. Reprinted from *Knowledge.* By EDWARD CLODD, ANDREW WILSON, THOMAS FOSTER, A. C. RUNYARD, and RICHARD A. PROCTOR. Crown 8vo. 6s.

The Stars in their Seasons. An Easy Guide to a Knowledge of the Star Groups, in Twelve Large Maps. By RICHARD A. PROCTOR. Imperial 8vo. 5s.

QUAIN'S ELEMENTS of ANATOMY. The Ninth Edition. Re-edited by ALLEN THOMSON, M.D. LL.D. F.R.S.S. L. & E. EDWARD ALBERT SCHÄFER, F.R.S. and GEORGE DANCER THANE. With upwards of 1,000 Illustrations engraved on Wood, of which many are Coloured. 2 vols. 8vo. 18s. each.

QUAIN.—*A Dictionary of Medicine.* Including General Pathology, General Therapeutics, Hygiene, and the Diseases peculiar to Women and Children. By Various Writers. Edited by R. QUAIN, M.D. F.R.S. &c. With 138 Woodcuts. Medium 8vo. 31s. 6d. cloth, or 40s. half-russia; to be had also in 2 vols. 34s. cloth.

RAWLINSON.—*The Seventh Great Oriental Monarchy;* or, a History of the Sassanians. By G. RAWLINSON, M.A. With Map and 95 Illustrations. 8vo. 28s.

READER.—*Voices from Flower-Land,* in Original Couplets. By EMILY E. READER. A Birthday-Book and Language of Flowers. 16mo. 2s. 6d. limp cloth; 3s. 6d. roan, gilt edges, or in vegetable vellum, gilt top.

REEVE.—*Cookery and Housekeeping;* a Manual of Domestic Economy for Large and Small Families. By Mrs. HENRY REEVE. With 8 Coloured Plates and 37 Woodcuts. Crown 8vo. 7s. 6d.

RICH.—*A Dictionary of Roman and Greek Antiquities.* With 2,000 Woodcuts. By A. RICH, B.A. Crown 8vo. 7s. 6d.

RICHARDSON. — *The Asclepiad:* a Book of Original Research and Observation in the Science, Art, and Literature of Medicine, Preventive and Curative. By BENJAMIN WARD RICHARDSON, M.D. F.R.S. Published Quarterly, price 2s. 6d. Vol. I. 1884. 8vo. 12s. 6d.

RIVERS. — *Works by Thomas Rivers.*

The Orchard-House; or, the Cultivation of Fruit Trees under Glass. Crown 8vo. with 25 Woodcuts, 5s.

The Rose Amateur's Guide. Fcp. 8vo. 4s. 6d.

ROGERS. — *Works by Henry Rogers.*

The Eclipse of Faith; or, a Visit to a Religious Sceptic. Fcp. 8vo. 5s.

Defence of the Eclipse of Faith. Fcp. 8vo. 3s. 6d.

ROGET.—*Thesaurus of English Words and Phrases,* classified and arranged so as to facilitate the expression of Ideas, and assist in Literary Composition. By PETER M. ROGET, M.D. Crown 8vo. 10s. 6d.

RONALDS. — *The Fly-Fisher's Entomology.* By ALFRED RONALDS. With 20 Coloured Plates. 8vo. 14s.

SALTER.—*Dental Pathology and Surgery.* By S. J. A. SALTER, M.B. F.R.S. With 133 Illustrations. 8vo. 18s.

SCOTT.—*The Farm-Valuer.* By JOHN SCOTT. Crown 8vo. 5s.

SEEBOHM.—*Works by Frederick Seebohm.*

The Oxford Reformers—John Colet, Erasmus, and Thomas More; a History of their Fellow-Work. 8vo. 14s.

The English Village Community Examined in its Relations to the Manorial and Tribal Systems, and to the Common or Openfield System of Husbandry. 13 Maps and Plates. 8vo. 16s.

The Era of the Protestant Revolution. With Map. Fcp. 8vo. 2s. 6d.

SENNETT.—*THE MARINE STEAM ENGINE*; a Treatise for the use of Engineering Students and Officers of the Royal Navy. By RICHARD SENNETT, Chief Engineer, Royal Navy. With 244 Illustrations. 8vo. 21s.

SEWELL.—*WORKS BY ELIZABETH M. SEWELL.*
STORIES AND TALES. Cabinet Edition, in Eleven Volumes, crown 8vo. 3s. 6d. each, in cloth extra, with gilt edges:—
 Amy Herbert. Gertrude.
 The Earl's Daughter.
 The Experience of Life.
 A Glimpse of the World.
 Cleve Hall. Ivors.
 Katharine Ashton.
 Margaret Percival.
 Laneton Parsonage. Ursula.
PASSING THOUGHTS ON RELIGION. Fcp. 8vo. 3s. 6d.
PREPARATION FOR THE HOLY COMMUNION; the Devotions chiefly from the works of JEREMY TAYLOR. 32mo. 3s.
NIGHT LESSONS FROM SCRIPTURE. 32mo. 3s. 6d.

SEYMOUR.—*THE PSALMS OF DAVID;* a new Metrical English Translation of the Hebrew Psalter or Book of Praises. By WILLIAM DIGBY SEYMOUR, Q.C. LL.D. Crown 8vo. 2s. 6d.

SHORT.—*SKETCH OF THE HISTORY OF THE CHURCH OF ENGLAND TO THE REVOLUTION OF 1688.* By T. V. SHORT, D.D. Crown 8vo. 7s. 6d.

SHAKESPEARE.—*BOWDLER'S FAMILY SHAKESPEARE.* Genuine Edition, in 1 vol. medium 8vo. large type, with 36 Woodcuts, 14s. or in 6 vols. fcp. 8vo. 21s.
OUTLINES OF THE LIFE OF SHAKESPEARE. By J. O. HALLIWELL-PHILLIPPS, F.R.S. 8vo. 7s. 6d.

SIMCOX.—*A HISTORY OF LATIN LITERATURE.* By G. A. SIMCOX, M.A. Fellow of Queen's College, Oxford. 2 vols. 8vo. 32s.

SMITH, Rev. SYDNEY.—*THE WIT AND WISDOM OF THE REV. SYDNEY SMITH.* Crown 8vo. 3s. 6d.

SMITH, R. BOSWORTH.—*CARTHAGE AND THE CARTHAGINIANS.* By R. BOSWORTH SMITH, M.A. Maps, Plans, &c. Crown 8vo. 10s. 6d.

SMITH, R. A.—*AIR AND RAIN;* the Beginnings of a Chemical Climatology. By R. A. SMITH, F.R.S. 8vo. 24s.

SMITH, JAMES.—*THE VOYAGE AND SHIPWRECK OF ST. PAUL.* By JAMES SMITH, of Jordanhill. With Dissertations on the Life and Writings of St. Luke, and the Ships and Navigation of the Ancients. With numerous Illustrations. Crown 8vo. 7s. 6d.

SMITH, T.—*A MANUAL OF OPERATIVE SURGERY ON THE DEAD BODY.* By THOMAS SMITH, Surgeon to St. Bartholomew's Hospital. A New Edition, re-edited by W. J. WALSHAM. With 46 Illustrations. 8vo. 12s.

SMITH, H. F.—*THE HANDBOOK FOR MIDWIVES.* By HENRY FLY SMITH, M.B. Oxon. M.R.C.S. late Assistant-Surgeon at the Hospital for Sick Women, Soho Square. With 41 Woodcuts. Crown 8vo. 5s.

SOPHOCLES.—*SOPHOCLIS TRAGŒDIÆ* superstites; recensuit et brevi Annotatione instruxit GULIELMUS LINWOOD, M.A. Ædis Christi apud Oxonienses nuper Alumnus. Editio Quarta, auctior et emendatior. 8vo. 16s.

SOUTHEY.—*THE POETICAL WORKS OF ROBERT SOUTHEY*, with the Author's last Corrections and Additions. Medium 8vo. with Portrait, 14s.
THE CORRESPONDENCE OF ROBERT SOUTHEY WITH CAROLINE BOWLES. Edited by EDWARD DOWDEN, LL.D. 8vo. Portrait, 14s.

STANLEY.—*A FAMILIAR HISTORY OF BIRDS.* By E. STANLEY, D.D. Revised and enlarged, with 160 Woodcuts. Crown 8vo. 6s.

STEEL.—*A TREATISE ON THE DISEASES OF THE OX;* being a Manual of Bovine Pathology specially adapted for the use of Veterinary Practitioners and Students. By J. H. STEEL, M.R.C.V.S. F.Z.S. With 2 Plates and 116 Woodcuts. 8vo. 15s.

STEPHEN.—*ESSAYS IN ECCLESIASTICAL BIOGRAPHY.* By the Right Hon. Sir J. STEPHEN, LL.D. Crown 8vo. 7s. 6d.

STEVENSON.—*THE CHILD'S GARDEN OF POEMS.* By ROBERT LOUIS STEVENSON. 1 vol. small fcp. 8vo. printed on hand-made paper, 5s.

'STONEHENGE.'—*THE DOG IN HEALTH AND DISEASE.* By 'STONEHENGE.' With 78 Wood Engravings. Square crown 8vo. 7s. 6d.
THE GREYHOUND. By 'STONEHENGE.' With 25 Portraits of Greyhounds, &c. Square crown 8vo. 15s.

STURGIS.—*My Friends and I.* By Julian Sturgis. With Frontispiece. Crown 8vo. 5s.

SULLY.—*Outlines of Psychology*, with Special Reference to the Theory of Education. By James Sully, M.A. 8vo. 12s. 6d.

SUPERNATURAL RELIGION; an Inquiry into the Reality of Divine Revelation. Complete Edition, thoroughly revised. 3 vols. 8vo. 36s.

SWINBURNE.—*Picture Logic;* an Attempt to Popularise the Science of Reasoning. By A. J. Swinburne, B.A. Post 8vo. 5s.

SWINTON.—*The Principles and Practice of Electric Lighting.* By Alan A. Campbell Swinton. With 54 Illustrations engraved on Wood. Crown 8vo. 5s.

TAYLOR.—*Student's Manual of the History of India,* from the Earliest Period to the Present Time. By Colonel Meadows Taylor, C.S.I. Crown 8vo. 7s. 6d.

TEXT-BOOKS OF SCIENCE: a Series of Elementary Works on Science, Mechanical and Physical, forming a Series of Text-books of Science, adapted for the use of Students in Public and Science Schools. Fcp. 8vo. fully illustrated with Woodcuts.

Abney's Photography, 3s. 6d.
Anderson's Strength of Materials, 3s. 6d.
Armstrong's Organic Chemistry, 3s. 6d.
Ball's Elements of Astronomy, 6s.
Barry's Railway Appliances, 3s. 6d.
Bauerman's Systematic Mineralogy, 6s.
—— Descriptive Mineralogy, 6s.
Bloxam and Huntington's Metals, 5s.
Glazebrook's Physical Optics, 6s.
Glazebrook and Shaw's Practical Physics, 6s.
Gore's Electro-Metallurgy, 6s.
Griffin's Algebra and Trigonometry, 3s. 6d.
Jenkin's Electricity and Magnetism, 3s. 6d.
Maxwell's Theory of Heat, 3s. 6d.
Merrifield's Technical Arithmetic, 3s. 6d.
Miller's Inorganic Chemistry, 3s. 6d.
Preece and Sivewright's Telegraphy, 5s.
Rutley's Petrology, or Study of Rocks, 4s. 6d.
Shelley's Workshop Appliances, 4s. 6d.
Thomé's Structural and Physiological Botany, 6s.
Thorpe's Quantitative Analysis, 4s. 6d.
Thorpe and Muir's Qualitative Analysis, 3s. 6d.
Tilden's Chemical Philosophy, 3s. 6d. With Answers to Problems, 4s. 6d.
Unwin's Machine Design, 6s.
Watson's Plane and Solid Geometry, 3s. 6d.

TAYLOR.—*The Complete Works of Bishop Jeremy Taylor.* With Life by Bishop Heber. Revised and corrected by the Rev. C. P. Eden. 10 vols. £5. 5s.

THOMSON.—*An Outline of the Necessary Laws of Thought;* a Treatise on Pure and Applied Logic. By W. Thomson, D.D. Archbishop of York. Crown 8vo. 6s.

THOMSON'S CONSPECTUS *Adapted to the British Pharmacopœia.* By Edmund Lloyd Birkett, M.D. &c. Latest Edition. 18mo. 6s.

THOMPSON.—*A System of Psychology.* By Daniel Greenleaf Thompson. 2 vols. 8vo. 36s.

THREE IN NORWAY. By Two of Them. With a Map and 59 Illustrations on Wood from Sketches by the Authors. Crown 8vo. 6s.

TREVELYAN. — *Works by the Right Hon. G. O. Trevelyan, M.P.*

The Life and Letters of Lord Macaulay. By the Right Hon. G. O. Trevelyan, M.P.
  Library Edition, 2 vols. 8vo. 36s.
  Cabinet Edition, 2 vols. crown 8vo. 12s.
  Popular Edition, 1 vol. crown 8vo. 6s.

The Early History of Charles James Fox. Library Edition, 8vo. 18s. Cabinet Edition, crown 8vo. 6s.

TWISS.—*Works by Sir Travers Twiss.*

The Rights and Duties of Nations, considered as Independent Communities in Time of War. 8vo. 21s.

On the Rights and Duties of Nations in Time of Peace. 8vo. 15s.

TYNDALL.—*Works by John Tyndall, F.R.S. &c.*

Fragments of Science. 2 vols. crown 8vo. 16s.

Heat a Mode of Motion. Crown 8vo. 12s.

Sound. With 204 Woodcuts. Crown 8vo. 10s. 6d.

Essays on the Floating-Matter of the Air in relation to Putrefaction and Infection. With 24 Woodcuts. Crown 8vo. 7s. 6d.

[*Continued on next page.*

TYNDALL.—*Works by John Tyndall, F.R.S. &c.*—continued.

Lectures on Light, delivered in America in 1872 and 1873. With Portrait, Plate, and Diagrams. Crown 8vo. 7s. 6d.

Lessons in Electricity at the Royal Institution, 1875-76. With 58 Woodcuts. Crown 8vo. 2s. 6d.

Notes of a Course of Seven Lectures on Electrical Phenomena and Theories, delivered at the Royal Institution. Crown 8vo. 1s. sewed, 1s. 6d. cloth.

Notes of a Course of Nine Lectures on Light, delivered at the Royal Institution. Crown 8vo. 1s. sewed, 1s. 6d. cloth.

Faraday as a Discoverer. Fcp. 8vo. 3s. 6d.

URE.—*A Dictionary of Arts, Manufactures, and Mines.* By Dr. Ure. Seventh Edition, re-written and enlarged by R. Hunt, F.R.S. With 2,064 Woodcuts. 4 vols. medium 8vo. £7. 7s.

VERNEY.—*Chess Eccentricities.* Including Four-handed Chess, Chess for Three, Six, or Eight Players, Round Chess for Two, Three, or Four Players, and several different ways of Playing Chess for Two Players. By Major George Hope Verney. Crown 8vo. 10s. 6d.

VILLE.—*On Artificial Manures*, their Chemical Selection and Scientific Application to Agriculture. By Georges Ville. Translated and edited by W. Crookes, F.R.S. With 31 Plates. 8vo. 21s.

VIRGIL. *Publi Vergili Maronis Bucolica, Georgica, Æneis:* the Works of Virgil, Latin Text, with English Commentary and Index. By B. H. Kennedy, D.D. Crown 8vo. 10s. 6d.

The Æneid of Virgil. Translated into English Verse. By J. Conington, M.A. Crown 8vo. 9s.

The Poems of Virgil. Translated into English Prose. By John Conington, M.A. Crown 8vo. 9s.

WALKER.—*The Correct Card;* or, How to Play at Whist: a Whist Catechism. By Major A. Campbell-Walker, F.R.G.S. Fcp. 8vo. 2s. 6d.

WALPOLE.—*History of England from the Conclusion of the Great War in 1815 to the Year 1841.* By Spencer Walpole. 3 vols. 8vo. £2. 14s.

WATSON.—*Lectures on the Principles and Practice of Physic*, delivered at King's College, London, by Sir Thomas Watson, Bart. M.D. With Two Plates. 2 vols. 8vo. 36s.

WATTS.—*A Dictionary of Chemistry and the Allied Branches of other Sciences.* Edited by Henry Watts, F.R.S. 9 vols. medium 8vo. £15. 2s. 6d.

WEBB.—*Celestial Objects for Common Telescopes.* By the Rev. T. W. Webb, M.A. Map, Plate, Woodcuts. Crown 8vo. 9s.

WEBB.—*The Veil of Isis:* a Series of Essays on Idealism. By Thomas W. Webb, LL.D. 8vo. 10s. 6d.

WELLINGTON.—*Life of the Duke of Wellington.* By the Rev. G. R. Gleig, M.A. Crown 8vo. Portrait, 6s.

WEST.—*Lectures on the Diseases of Infancy and Childhood.* By Charles West, M.D. &c. Founder of, and formerly Physician to, the Hospital for Sick Children. 8vo. 18s.

WHATELY. — *English Synonyms.* By E. Jane Whately. Edited by her Father, R. Whately, D.D. Fcp. 8vo. 3s.

WHATELY.—*Works by R. Whately, D.D.*

Elements of Logic. 8vo. 10s. 6d. Crown 8vo. 4s. 6d.

Elements of Rhetoric. 8vo. 10s. 6d. Crown 8vo. 4s. 6d.

Lessons on Reasoning. Fcp. 8vo. 1s. 6d.

Bacon's Essays, with Annotations. 8vo. 10s. 6d.

WHITE.—*A Concise Latin-English Dictionary*, for the Use of Advanced Scholars and University Students. By the Rev. J. T. White, D.D. Royal 8vo. 12s.

WHITE & RIDDLE.—*A Latin-English Dictionary.* By J. T. White, D.D. Oxon, and J. J. E. Riddle, M.A. Oxon. Founded on the larger Dictionary of Freund. Royal 8vo. 21s.

WILCOCKS.—THE SEA FISHERMAN. Comprising the Chief Methods of Hook and Line Fishing in the British and other Seas, and Remarks on Nets, Boats, and Boating. By J. C. WILCOCKS. Profusely Illustrated. New and Cheaper Edition, much enlarged, crown 8vo. 6s.

WILLICH.—POPULAR TABLES for giving Information for ascertaining the value of Lifehold, Leasehold, and Church Property, the Public Funds, &c. By CHARLES M. WILLICH. Edited by MONTAGU MARRIOTT. Crown 8vo. 10s.

WITT.—WORKS BY PROF. WITT, Head Master of the Alstadt Gymnasium, Königsberg. Translated from the German by FRANCES YOUNGHUSBAND.

THE TROJAN WAR. With a Preface by the Rev. W. G. RUTHERFORD, M.A. Head-Master of Westminster School. Crown 8vo. 2s.

MYTHS OF HELLAS; or, Greek Tales. Crown 8vo. 3s. 6d.

THE WANDERINGS OF ULYSSES. Crown 8vo. 3s. 6d.

WOOD.—WORKS BY REV. J. G. WOOD.

HOMES WITHOUT HANDS; a Description of the Habitations of Animals, classed according to the Principle of Construction. With about 140 Vignettes on Wood. 8vo. 10s. 6d.

INSECTS AT HOME: a Popular Account of British Insects, their Structure, Habits, and Transformations. 8vo. Woodcuts, 10s. 6d.

INSECTS ABROAD: a Popular Account of Foreign Insects, their Structure, Habits, and Transformations. 8vo. Woodcuts, 10s. 6d.

BIBLE ANIMALS; a Description of every Living Creature mentioned in the Scriptures. With 112 Vignettes. 8vo. 10s. 6d.

STRANGE DWELLINGS; a Description of the Habitations of Animals, abridged from 'Homes without Hands.' With Frontispiece and 60 Woodcuts. Crown 8vo. 5s. Popular Edition, 4to. 6d.

OUT OF DOORS: a Selection of Original Articles on Practical Natural History. With 6 Illustrations. Crown 8vo. 5s.

[Continued above.

WOOD.—WORKS BY REV. J. G. WOOD—continued.

COMMON BRITISH INSECTS: BEETLES, MOTHS, AND BUTTERFLIES. Crown 8vo. with 130 Woodcuts, 3s. 6d.

PETLAND REVISITED. With numerous Illustrations, drawn specially by Miss Margery May, engraved on Wood by G. Pearson. Crown 8vo. 7s. 6d.

WYLIE.—HISTORY OF ENGLAND UNDER HENRY THE FOURTH. By JAMES HAMILTON WYLIE, M.A. one of Her Majesty's Inspectors of Schools. Vol. 1, crown 8vo. 10s. 6d.

WYLIE.—LABOUR, LEISURE, AND LUXURY; a Contribution to Present Practical Political Economy. By ALEXANDER WYLIE, of Glasgow. Crown 8vo. 6s.

YONGE.—THE NEW ENGLISH-GREEK LEXICON, containing all the Greek words used by Writers of good authority. By CHARLES DUKE YONGE, M.A. 4to. 21s.

YOUATT. — WORKS BY WILLIAM YOUATT.

THE HORSE. Revised and enlarged by W. WATSON, M.R.C.V.S. 8vo. Woodcuts, 7s. 6d.

THE DOG. Revised and enlarged. 8vo. Woodcuts. 6s.

ZELLER. — WORKS BY DR. E. ZELLER.

HISTORY OF ECLECTICISM IN GREEK PHILOSOPHY. Translated by SARAH F. ALLEYNE. Crown 8vo. 10s. 6d.

THE STOICS, EPICUREANS, AND SCEPTICS. Translated by the Rev. O. J. REICHEL, M.A. Crown 8vo. 15s.

SOCRATES AND THE SOCRATIC SCHOOLS. Translated by the Rev. O. J. REICHEL, M.A. Crown 8vo. 10s. 6d.

PLATO AND THE OLDER ACADEMY. Translated by S. FRANCES ALLEYNE and ALFRED GOODWIN, B.A. Crown 8vo. 18s.

THE PRE-SOCRATIC SCHOOLS; a History of Greek Philosophy from the Earliest Period to the time of Socrates. Translated by SARAH F. ALLEYNE. 2 vols. crown 8vo. 30s.

www.ingramcontent.com/pod-product-compliance
Lightning Source LLC
Chambersburg PA
CBHW022114290426
44112CB00008B/670